D1564752

written and drawn by

SHANNON WHEELER

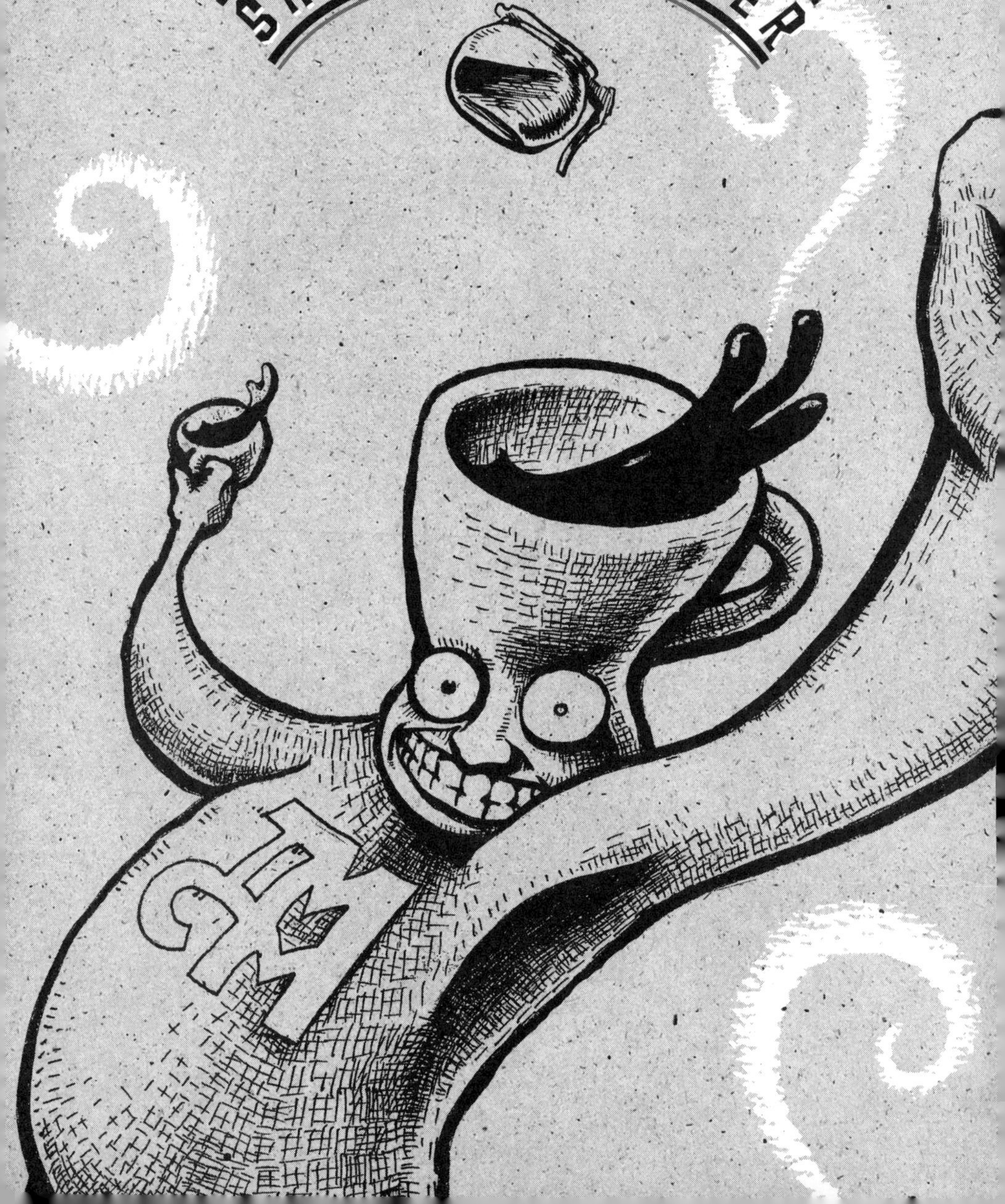

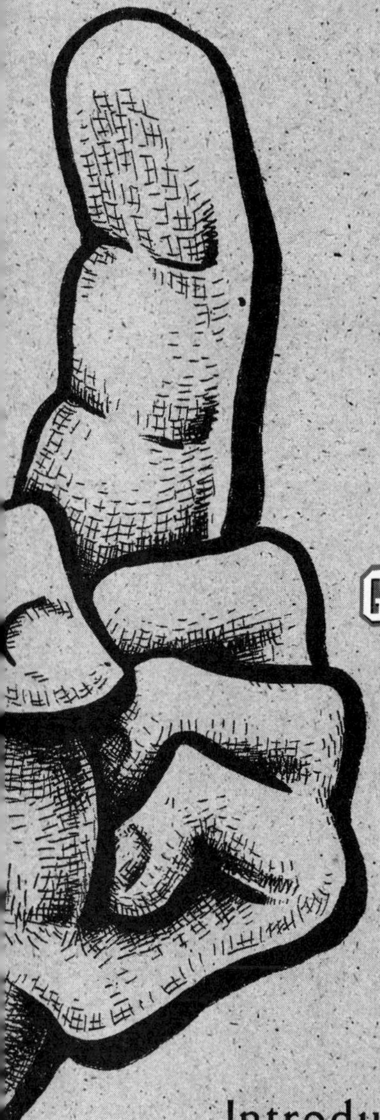

TOO MUCH COFFEE MAN'S™

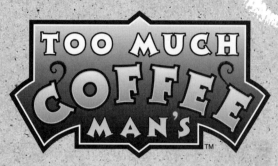

GUIDE FOR THE PERPLEXED

cover drawn by
SHANNON WHEELER

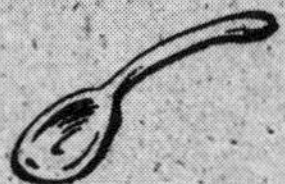

painted on computer by
MARTIN THOMAS

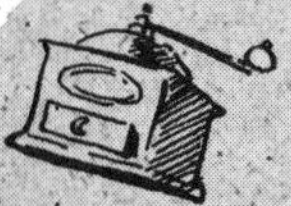

Introduction by
MIKE JUDGE

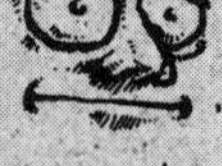

publisher
MIKE RICHARDSON

DARK HORSE COMICS®

FOREWORD

I first met Shannon Wheeler a few years back in East Austin in a restaurant called Nuevo Leon, one of the finest Mexican food restaurants on Earth. I had just been reading a **Too Much Coffee Man** comic book, and someone told me that Shannon lived in Austin.

I was thinking about trying to do some still cartoons at the time (I had only done animation at that point), so Shannon invited me to the headquarters of the Too Much Coffee Empire — a nineteenth-century farmhouse in Austin — where he showed me how to use a crow-quill pen and loaded me up with Too Much Coffee Man merchandise. (I still have my **TMCM** sponge, coffee mug, and unlicensed Japanese T-shirt.) He had done an impressive job making TMCM appear to be a much, much huger franchise than it really was, and today — partially due to that, I imagine —it has actually become almost as huge as he once made it appear!

At first glance, **Too Much Coffee Man** might look to some like a one-joke comic. However, if you read it, you realize it's actually many jokes — all about the same thing! Just kidding. It's not at all a one-joke comic. It's actually very funny, makes for good bathroom reading, is very well drawn, has occasional political commentary and satire, and I think it's even a little bit autobiographical at times . . . except for the part about space aliens and stuff.

COFFEE IS COOL! HUH-HUH HUH

LM BR YA WHEELER S

Check it out.

Mike Judge

creator, **Beavis and Butt-head** and **King of the Hill**

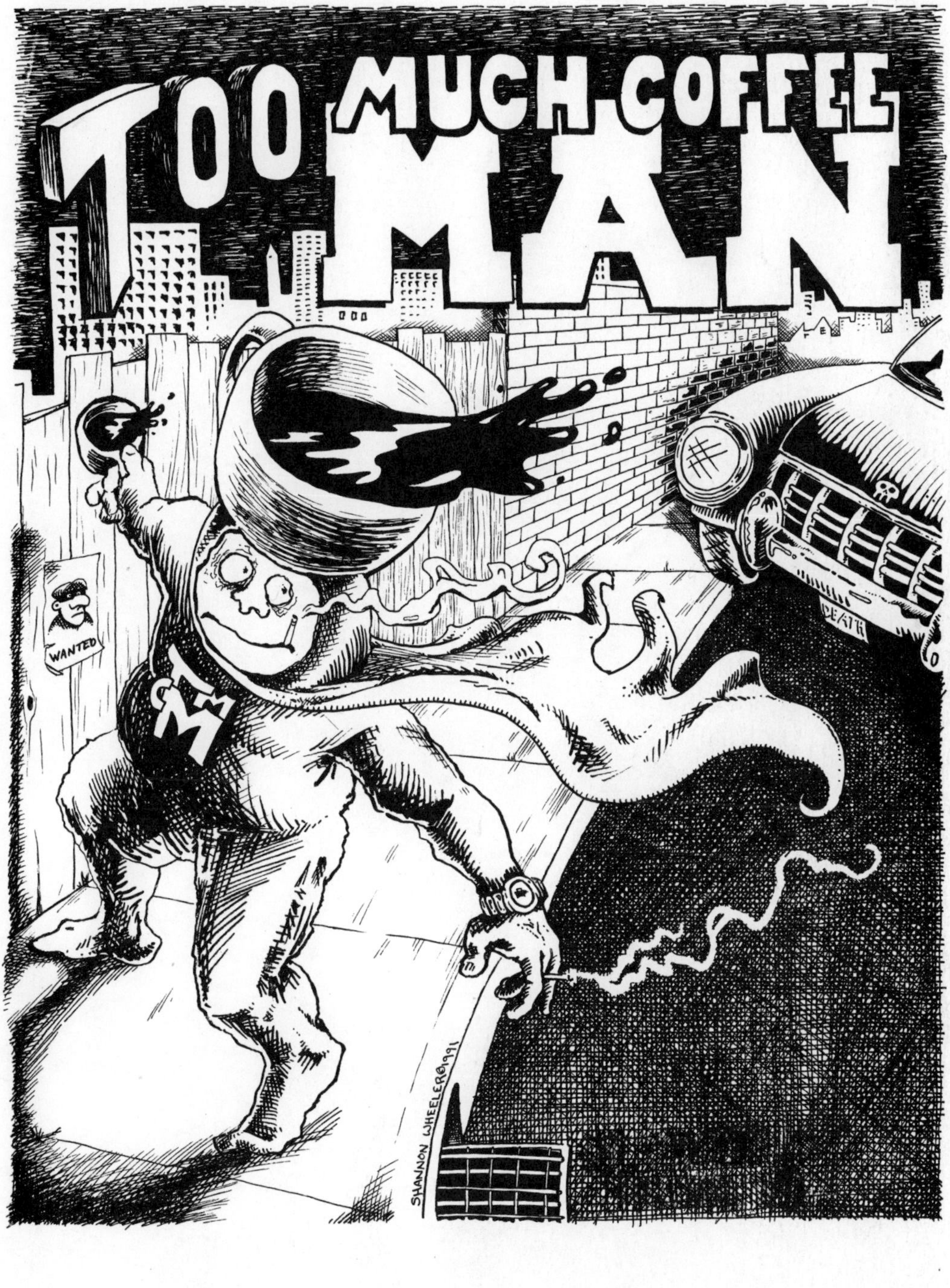
TOO MUCH COFFEE MAN
WANTED
DEATH
SHANNON WHEELER©1991

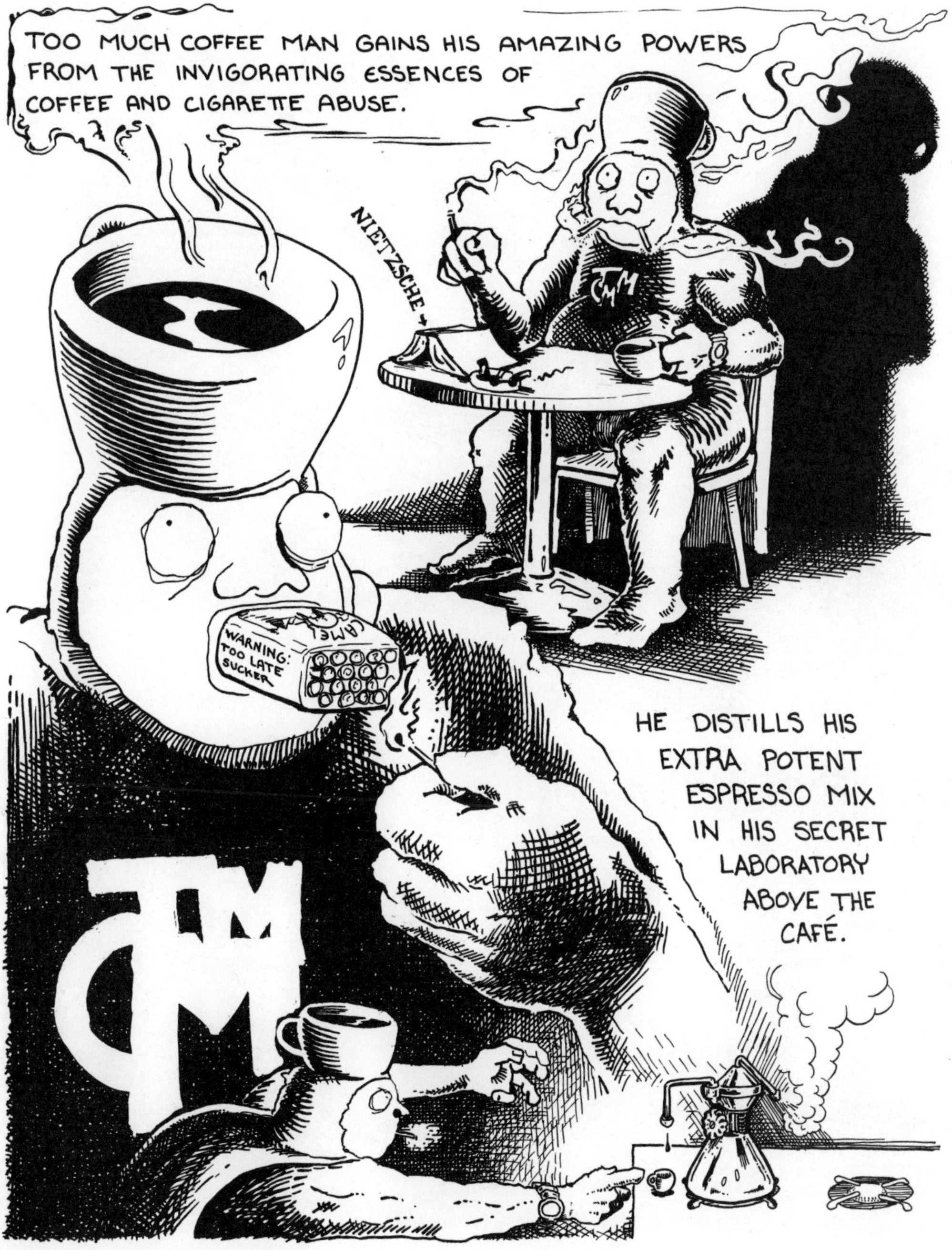
TOO MUCH COFFEE MAN GAINS HIS AMAZING POWERS FROM THE INVIGORATING ESSENCES OF COFFEE AND CIGARETTE ABUSE.
NIETZSCHE
CAMEL
WARNING: TOO LATE SUCKER
HE DISTILLS HIS EXTRA POTENT ESPRESSO MIX IN HIS SECRET LABORATORY ABOVE THE CAFÉ.

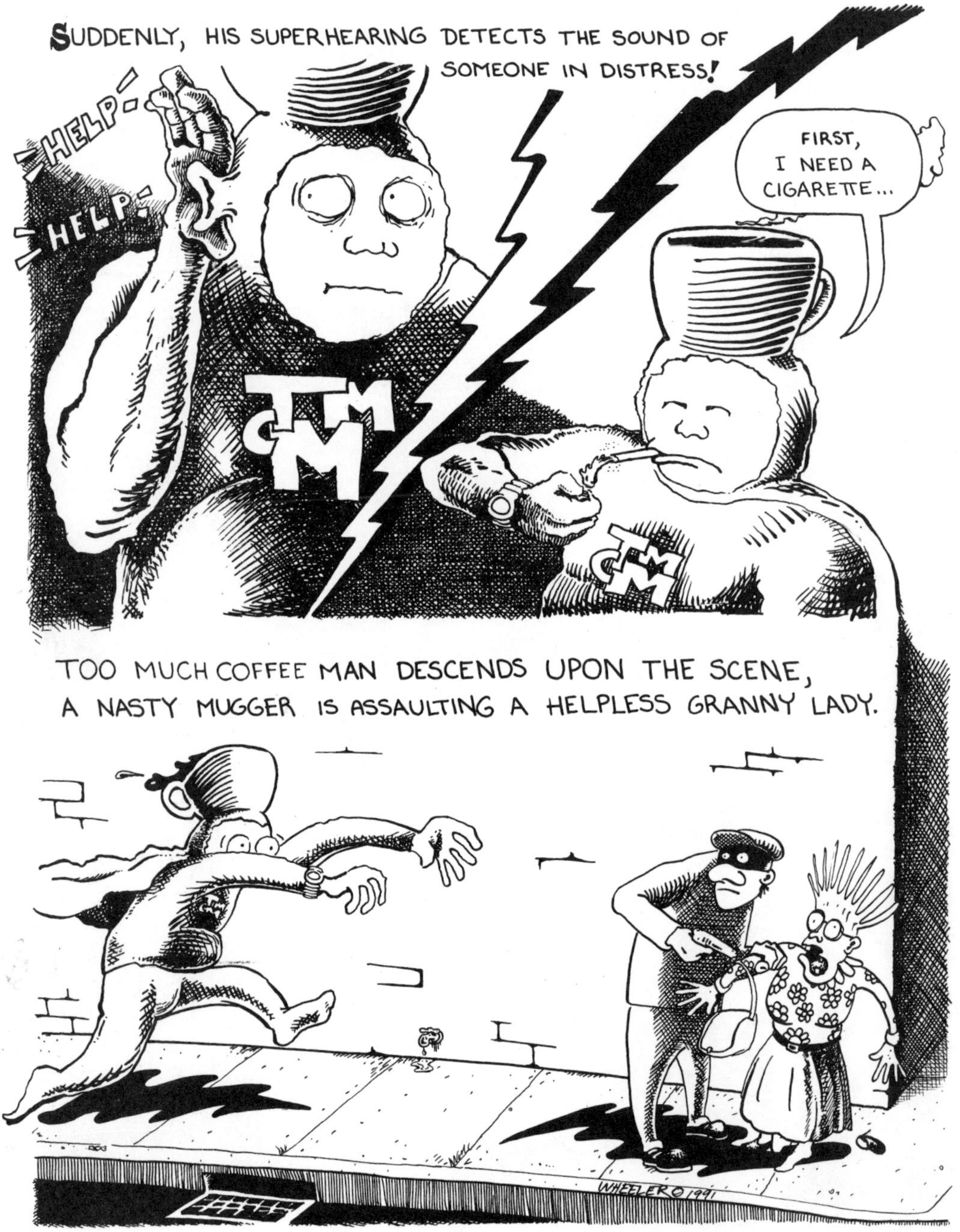
SUDDENLY, HIS SUPERHEARING DETECTS THE SOUND OF SOMEONE IN DISTRESS!
HELP!
HELP!
FIRST, I NEED A CIGARETTE...
TCM
TCM
TOO MUCH COFFEE MAN DESCENDS UPON THE SCENE, A NASTY MUGGER IS ASSAULTING A HELPLESS GRANNY LADY.
WHEELER © 1991

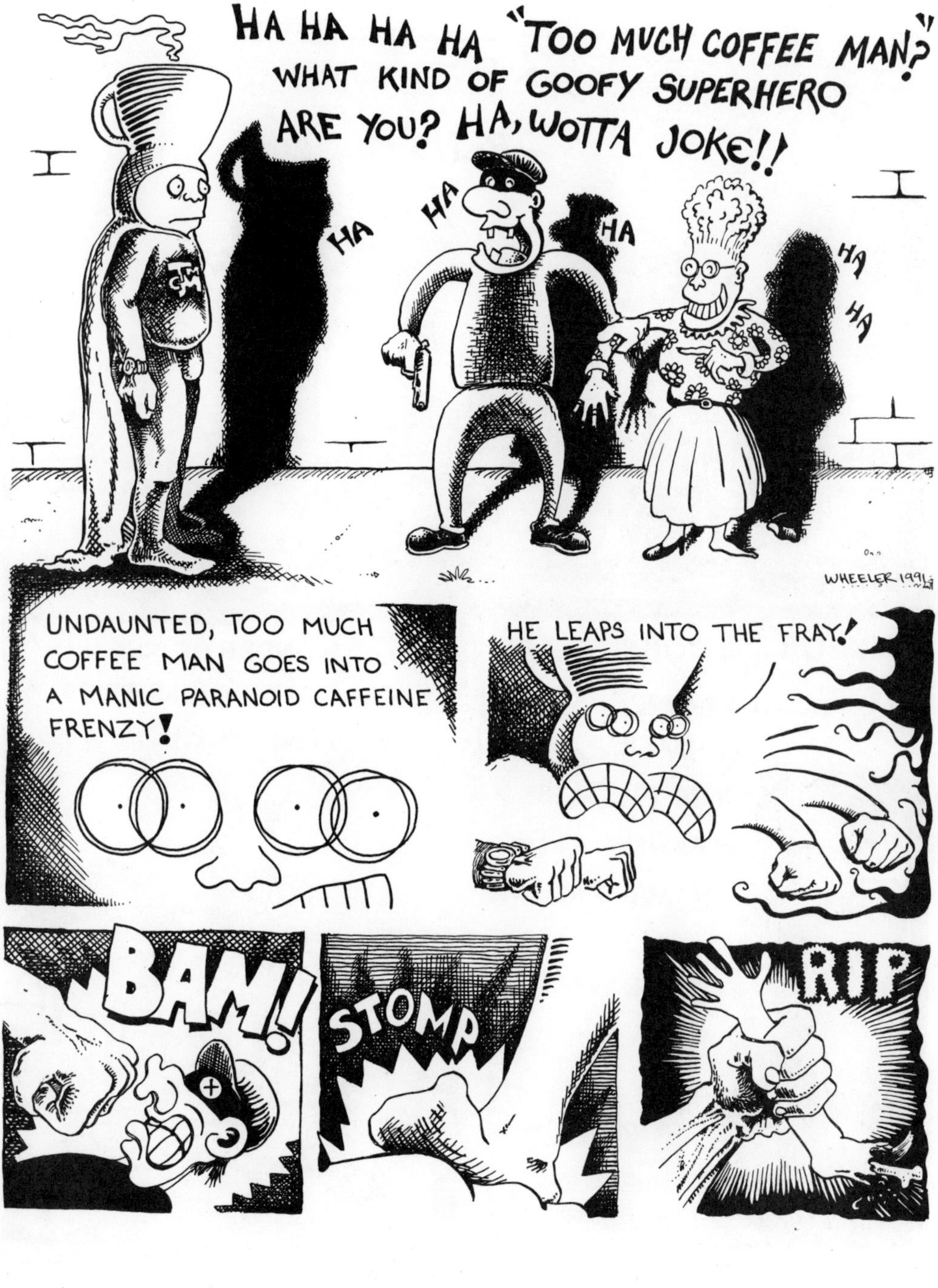
HA HA HA HA "TOO MUCH COFFEE MAN?" WHAT KIND OF GOOFY SUPERHERO ARE YOU? HA, WOTTA JOKE!!
HA
HA
HA
HA
HA
WHEELER 1991
UNDAUNTED, TOO MUCH COFFEE MAN GOES INTO A MANIC PARANOID CAFFEINE FRENZY!
HE LEAPS INTO THE FRAY!
BAM!
STOMP
RIP

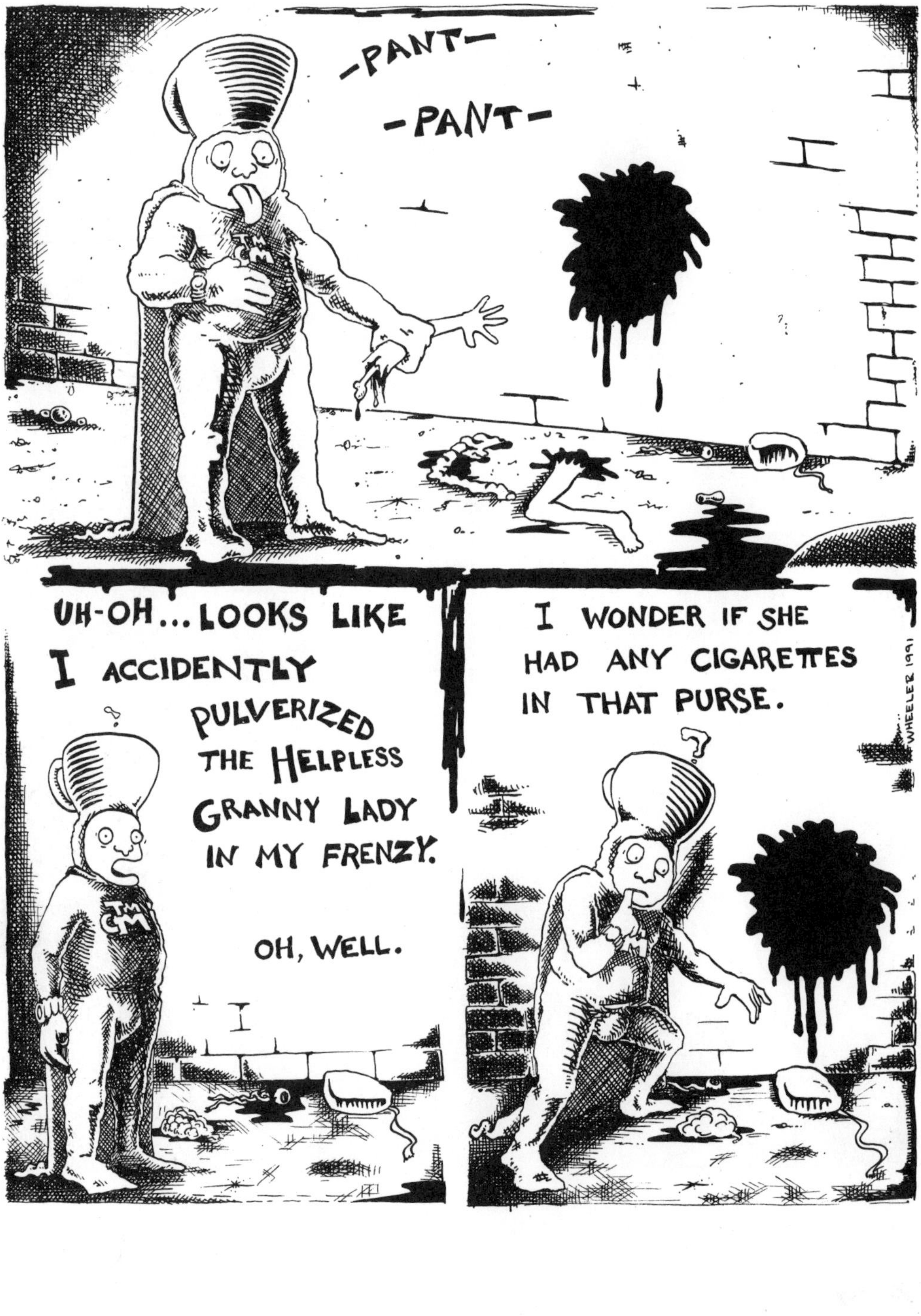
-PANT-
-PANT-
UH-OH... LOOKS LIKE I ACCIDENTLY PULVERIZED THE HELPLESS GRANNY LADY IN MY FRENZY.
OH, WELL.
I WONDER IF SHE HAD ANY CIGARETTES IN THAT PURSE.
WHEELER 1991

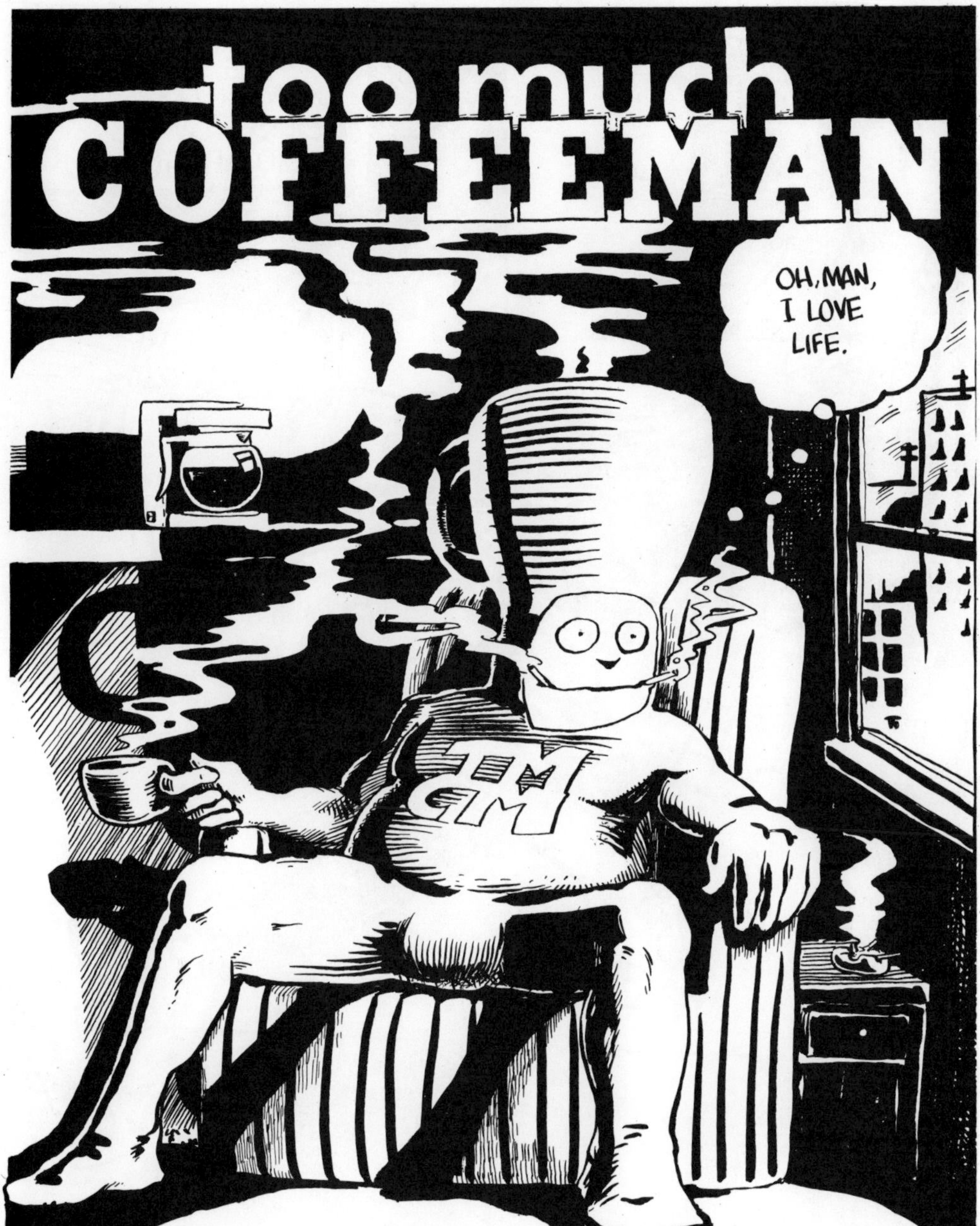
too much
COFFEEMAN
OH, MAN, I LOVE LIFE.
TM CM

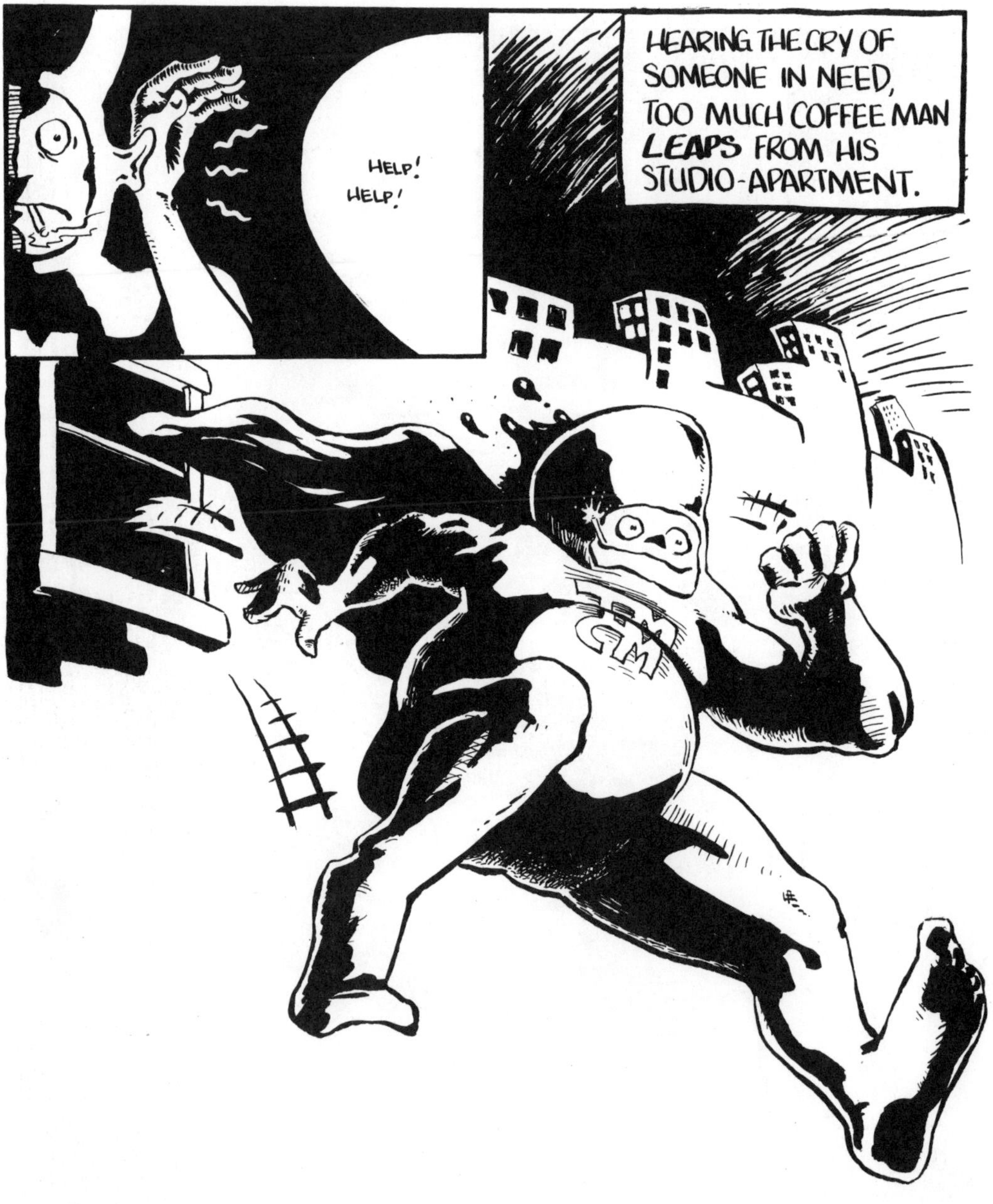
HELP!
HELP!
HEARING THE CRY OF SOMEONE IN NEED, TOO MUCH COFFEE MAN LEAPS FROM HIS STUDIO-APARTMENT.
TCM

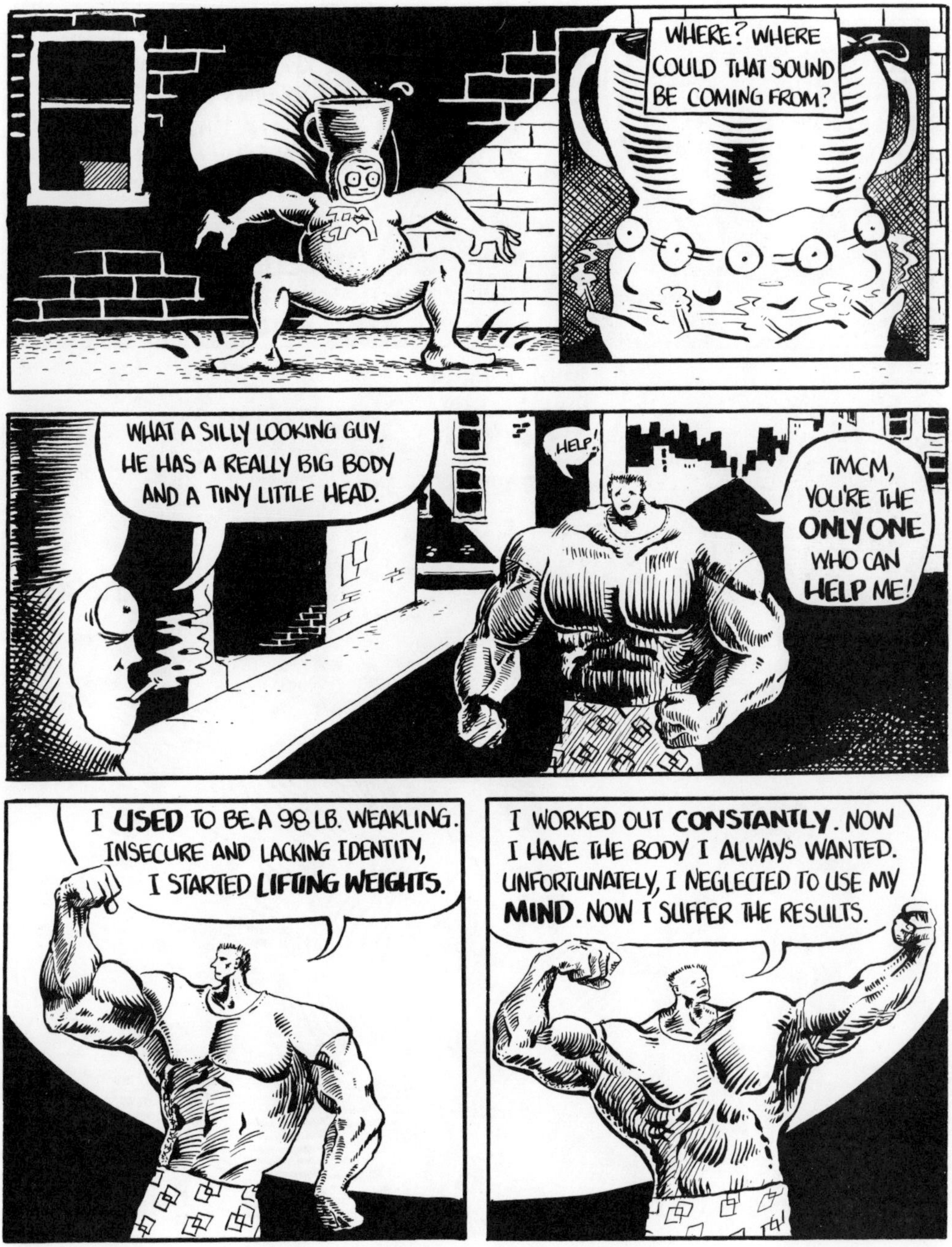
WHERE? WHERE COULD THAT SOUND BE COMING FROM?
WHAT A SILLY LOOKING GUY. HE HAS A REALLY BIG BODY AND A TINY LITTLE HEAD.
HELP!
TMCM, YOU'RE THE ONLY ONE WHO CAN HELP ME!
I USED TO BE A 98 LB. WEAKLING. INSECURE AND LACKING IDENTITY, I STARTED LIFTING WEIGHTS.
I WORKED OUT CONSTANTLY. NOW I HAVE THE BODY I ALWAYS WANTED. UNFORTUNATELY, I NEGLECTED TO USE MY MIND. NOW I SUFFER THE RESULTS.

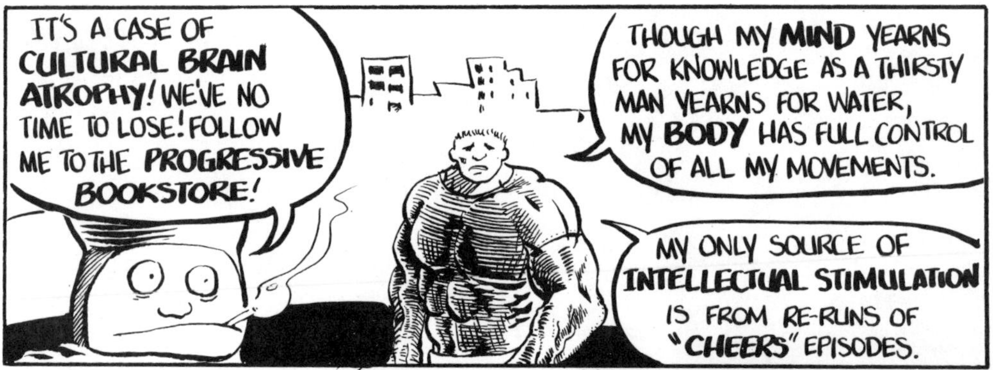
IT'S A CASE OF CULTURAL BRAIN ATROPHY! WE'VE NO TIME TO LOSE! FOLLOW ME TO THE PROGRESSIVE BOOKSTORE!
THOUGH MY MIND YEARNS FOR KNOWLEDGE AS A THIRSTY MAN YEARNS FOR WATER, MY BODY HAS FULL CONTROL OF ALL MY MOVEMENTS.
MY ONLY SOURCE OF INTELLECTUAL STIMULATION IS FROM RE-RUNS OF "CHEERS" EPISODES.

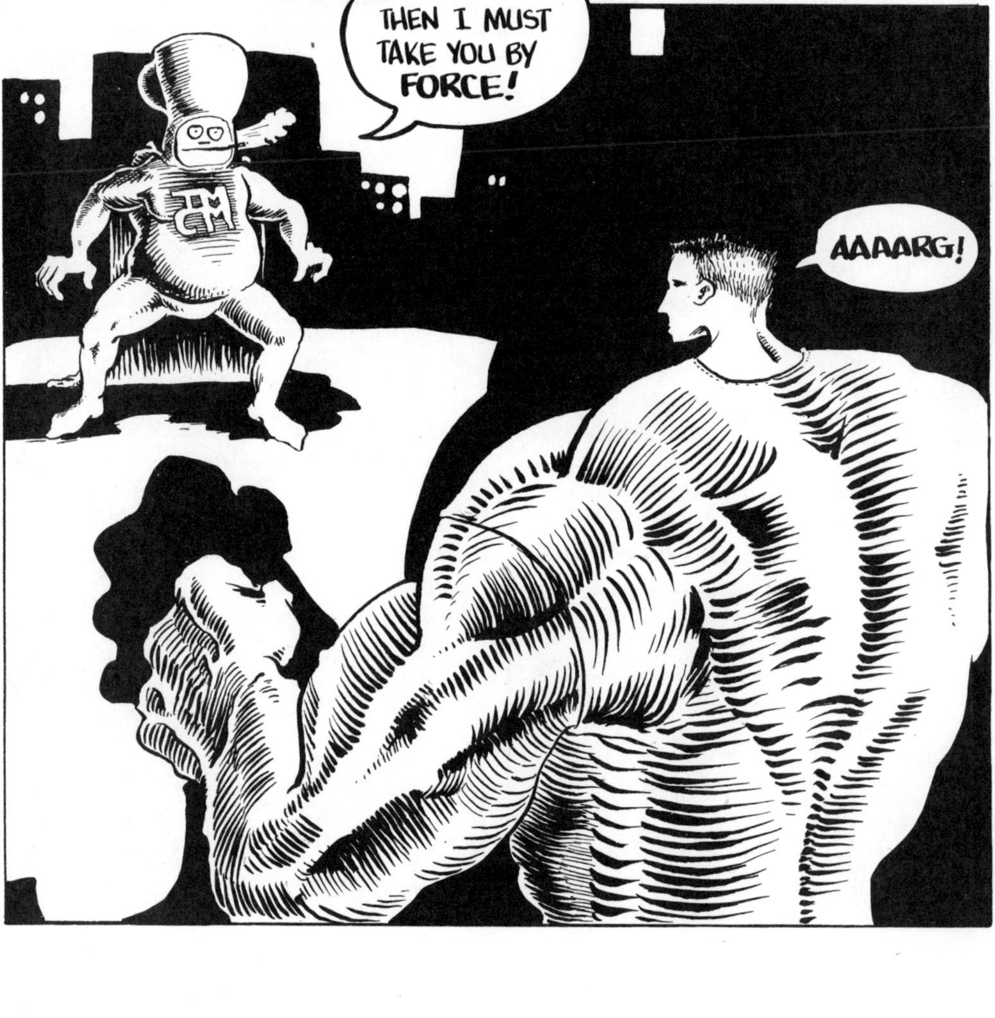
THEN I MUST TAKE YOU BY FORCE!
AAAARG!

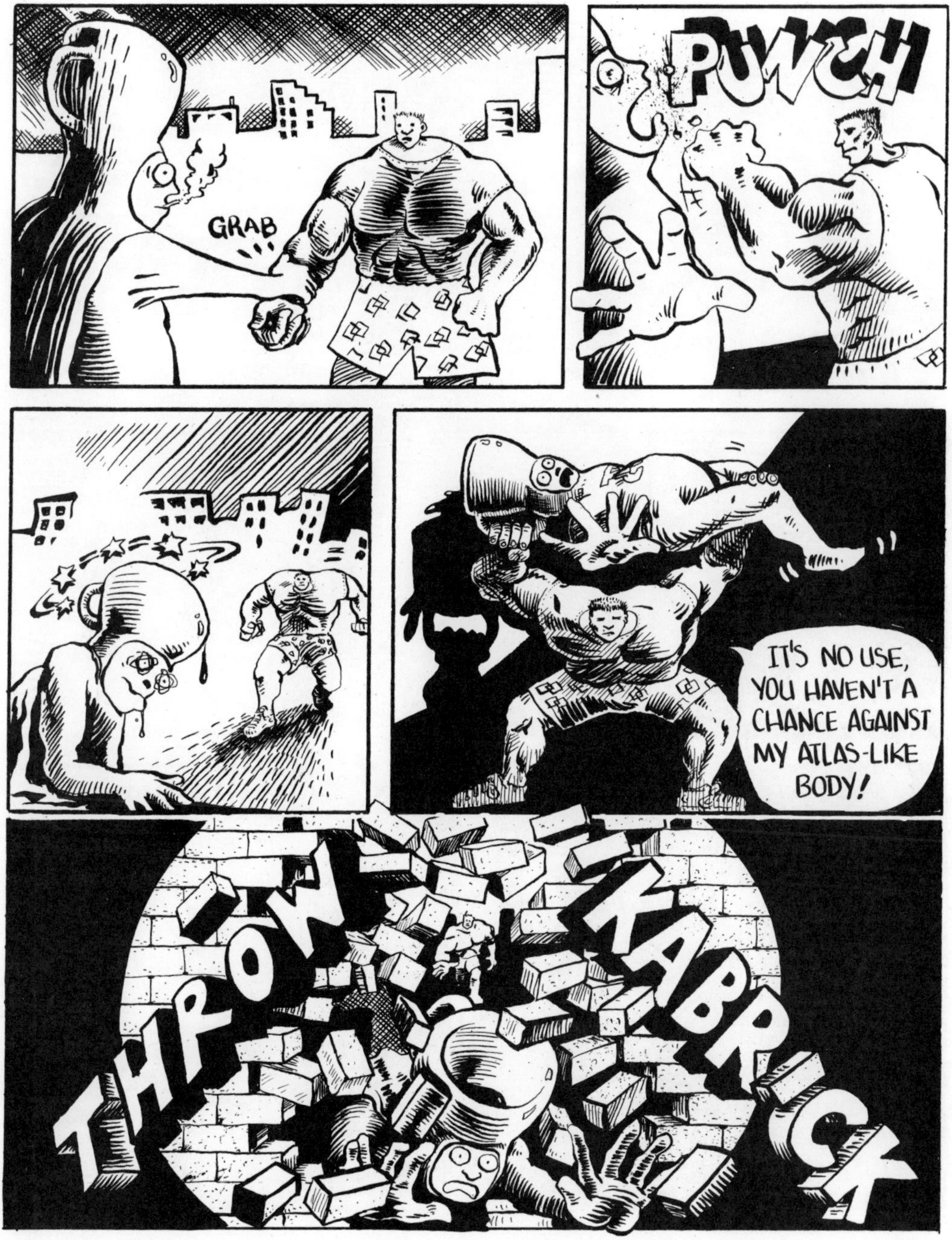
GRAB
PUNCH
IT'S NO USE, YOU HAVEN'T A CHANCE AGAINST MY ATLAS-LIKE BODY!
THROW
KABRICK

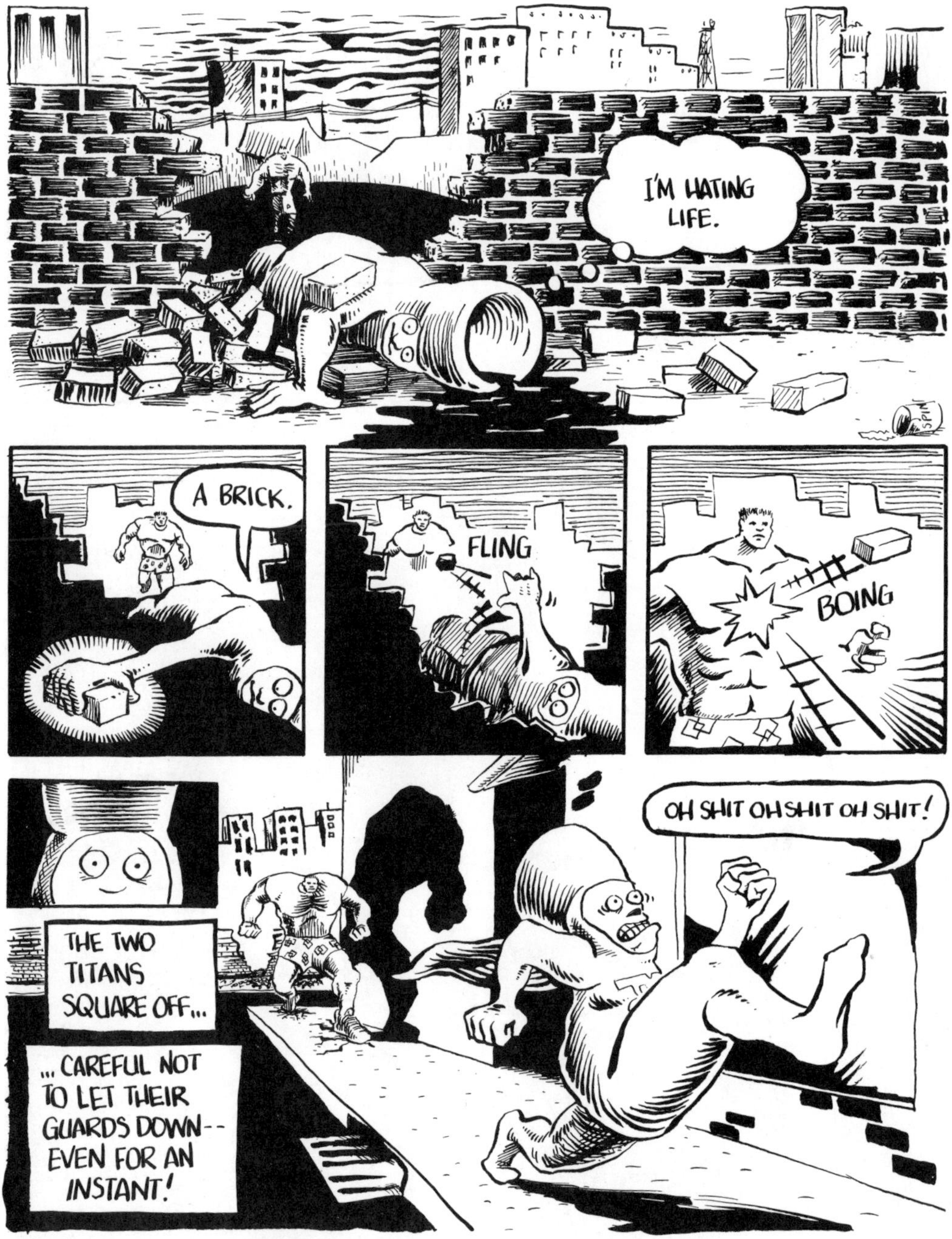
I'M HATING LIFE.
SPIN
A BRICK.
FLING
BOING
OH SHIT OH SHIT OH SHIT!
THE TWO TITANS SQUARE OFF...
...CAREFUL NOT TO LET THEIR GUARDS DOWN-- EVEN FOR AN INSTANT!

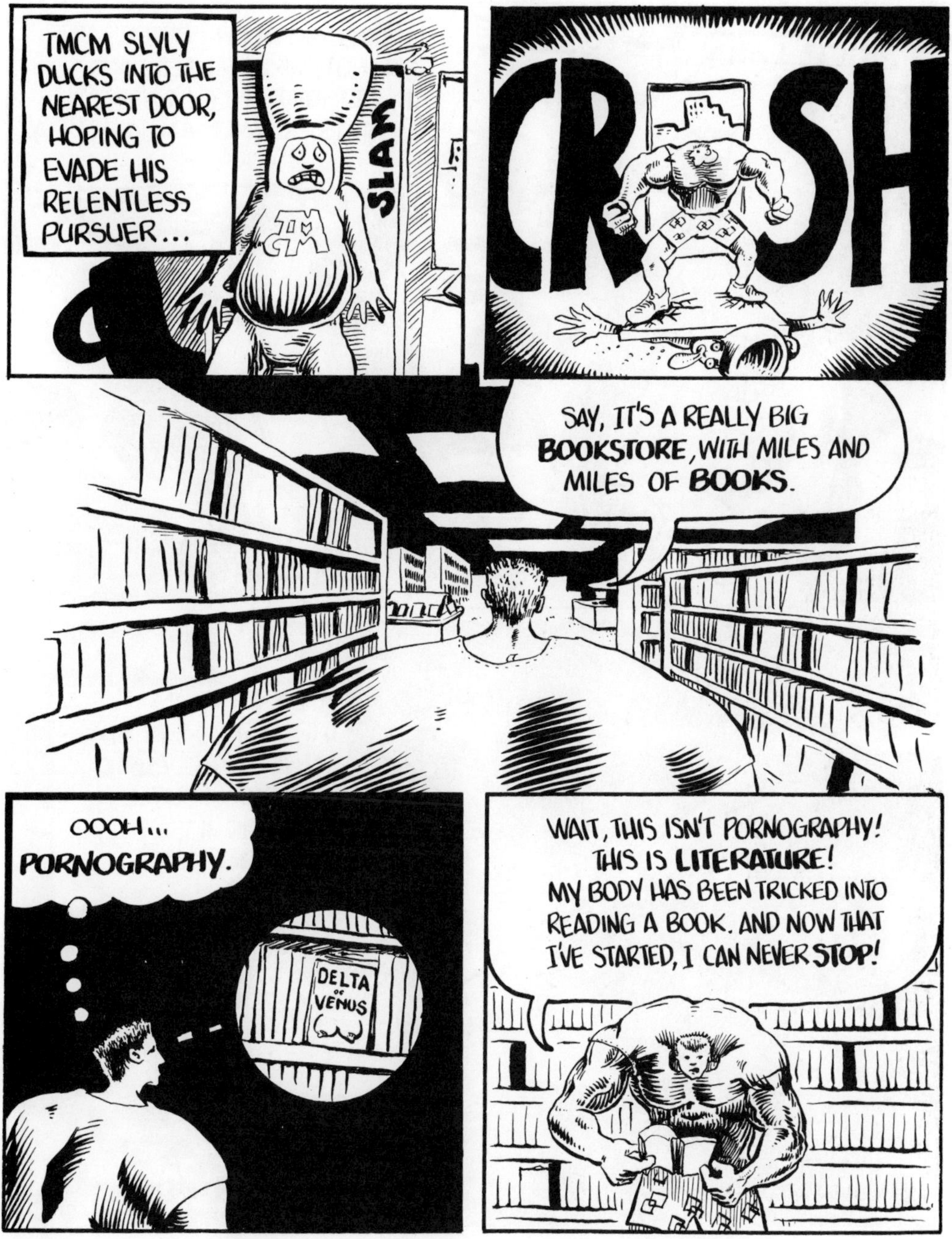
TMCM SLYLY DUCKS INTO THE NEAREST DOOR, HOPING TO EVADE HIS RELENTLESS PURSUER...
SLAM
CRASH
SAY, IT'S A REALLY BIG BOOKSTORE, WITH MILES AND MILES OF BOOKS.
OOOH... PORNOGRAPHY.
DELTA OF VENUS
WAIT, THIS ISN'T PORNOGRAPHY! THIS IS LITERATURE! MY BODY HAS BEEN TRICKED INTO READING A BOOK. AND NOW THAT I'VE STARTED, I CAN NEVER STOP!

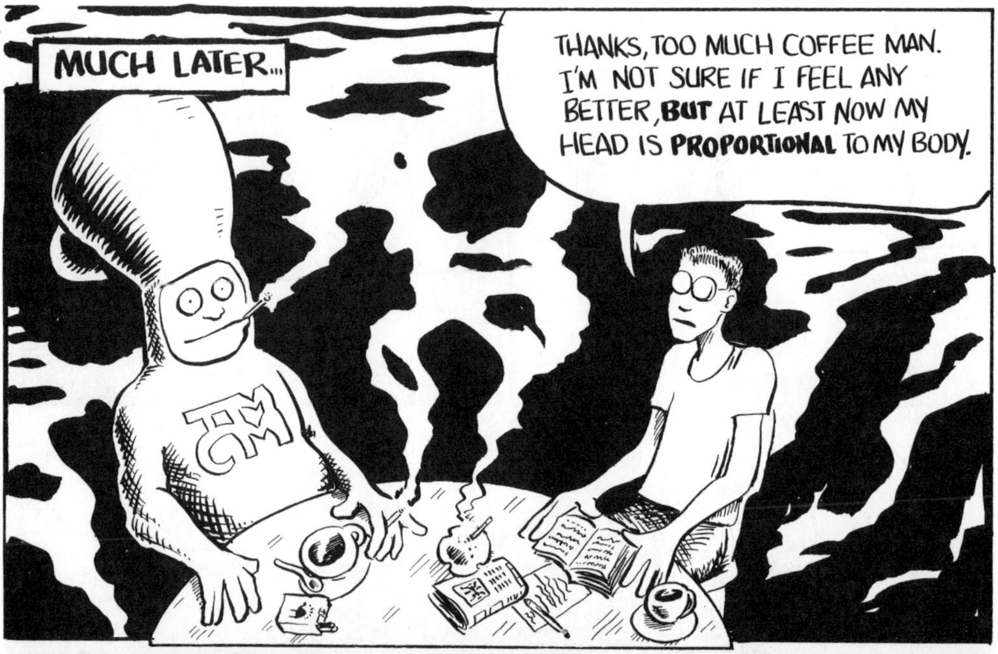
MUCH LATER...
THANKS, TOO MUCH COFFEE MAN. I'M NOT SURE IF I FEEL ANY BETTER, BUT AT LEAST NOW MY HEAD IS PROPORTIONAL TO MY BODY.

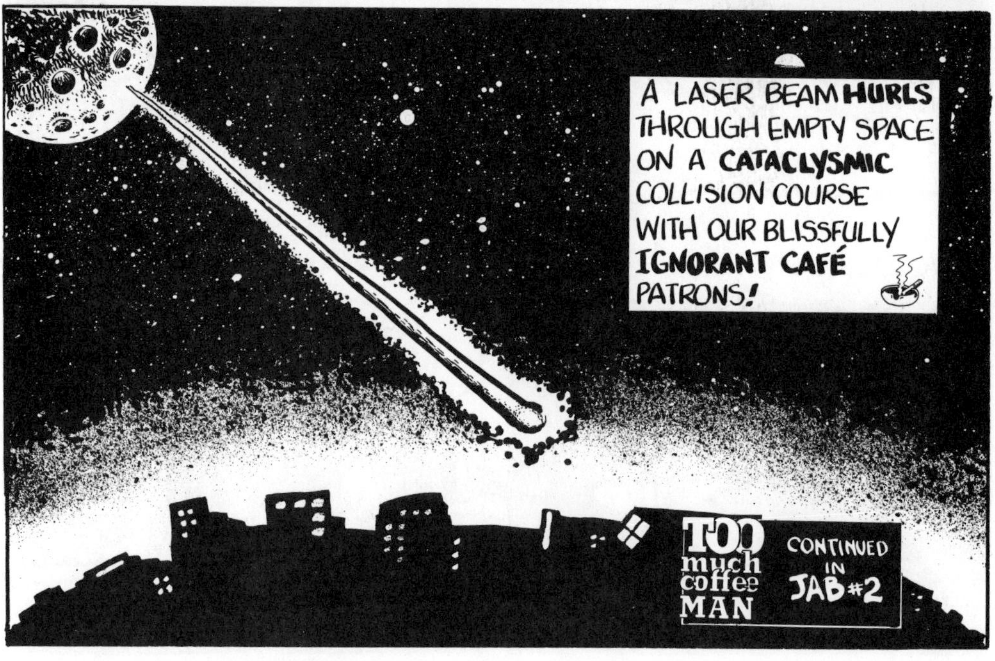
A LASER BEAM HURLS THROUGH EMPTY SPACE ON A CATACLYSMIC COLLISION COURSE WITH OUR BLISSFULLY IGNORANT CAFÉ PATRONS!
TOO much coffee MAN
CONTINUED IN JAB #2

TELL ME, TMCM*, WHY DO YOU SMOKE SO MANY CIGARETTES AND DRINK SO MUCH COFFEE?
* TOO MUCH COFFEE MAN
ESPRESSO EXPRESS
ABIERTO
BECAUSE LIFE IS SHORT...
...AND GETTING SHORTER BY THE MINUTE...
OH, HOW TRUE THAT IS, AS A LASER BEAM IS DUE TO MEET TMCM VERY, VERY SOON!

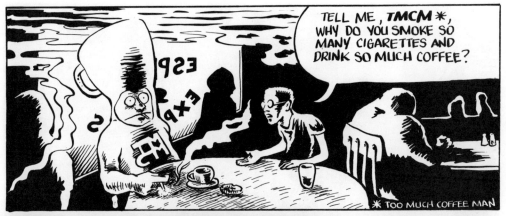

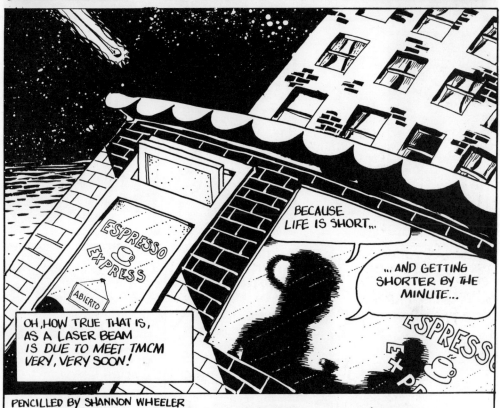

PENCILLED BY SHANNON WHEELER
LETTERED BY TOM KING. EVERYTHING ELSE BY AND ©1991 SHANNON WHEELER

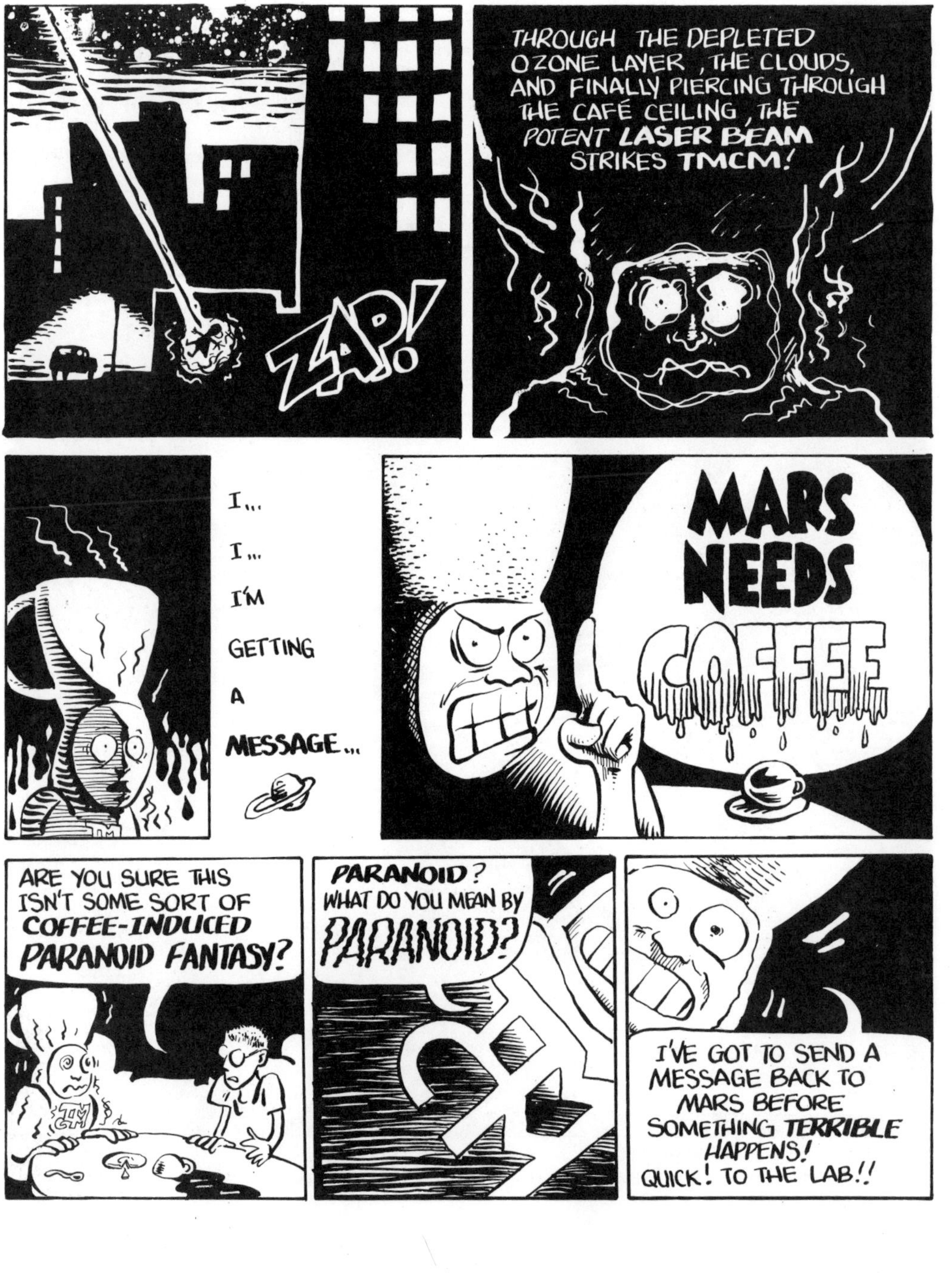

ZAP!
THROUGH THE DEPLETED OZONE LAYER, THE CLOUDS, AND FINALLY PIERCING THROUGH THE CAFÉ CEILING, THE POTENT LASER BEAM STRIKES TMCM!
I...
I...
I'M
GETTING
A
MESSAGE...
MARS NEEDS COFFEE
ARE YOU SURE THIS ISN'T SOME SORT OF COFFEE-INDUCED PARANOID FANTASY?
PARANOID? WHAT DO YOU MEAN BY PARANOID?
I'VE GOT TO SEND A MESSAGE BACK TO MARS BEFORE SOMETHING TERRIBLE HAPPENS! QUICK! TO THE LAB!!

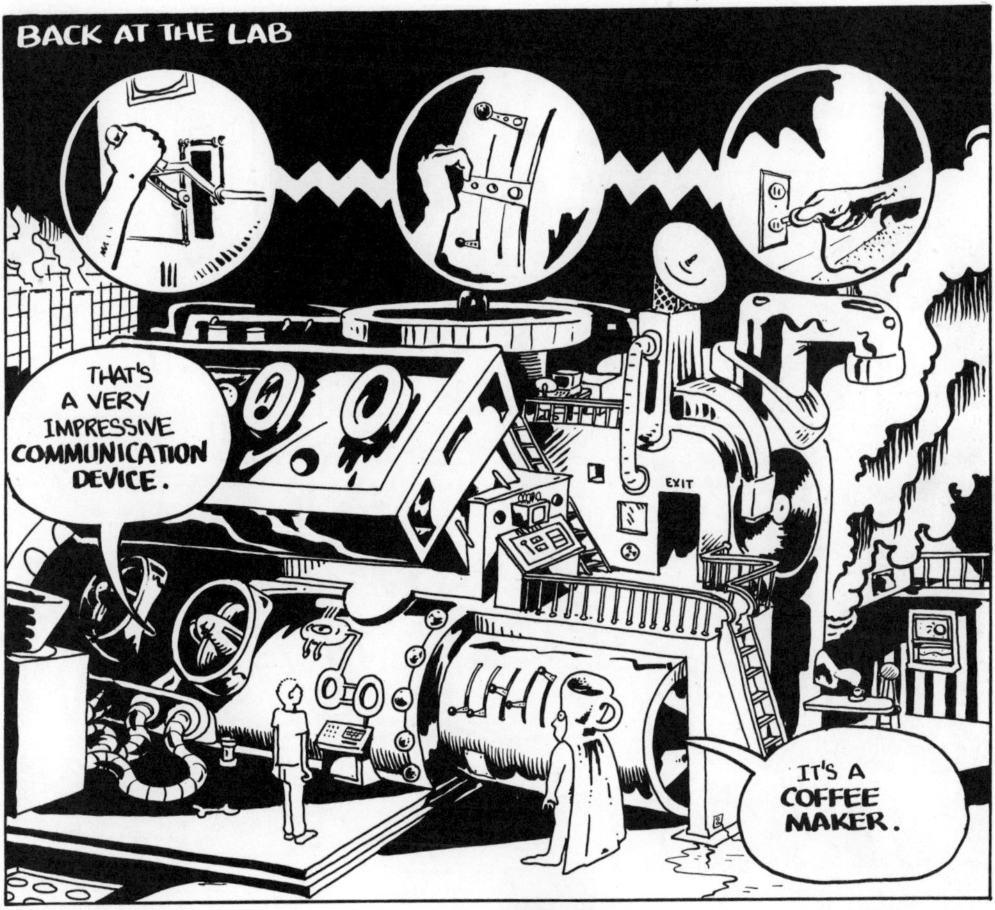
BACK AT THE LAB
THAT'S A VERY IMPRESSIVE COMMUNICATION DEVICE.
EXIT
IT'S A COFFEE MAKER.

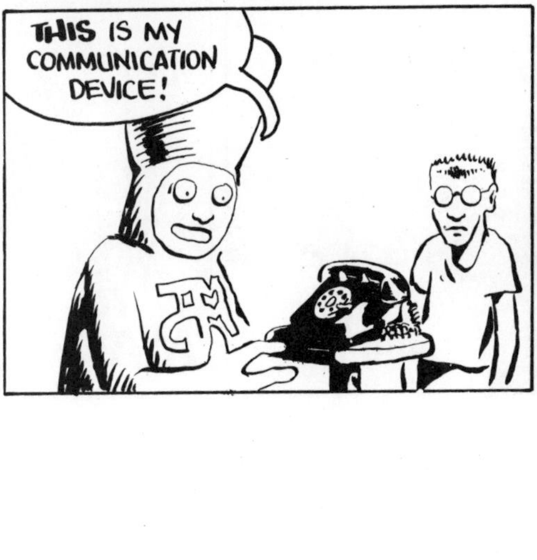
THIS IS MY COMMUNICATION DEVICE!

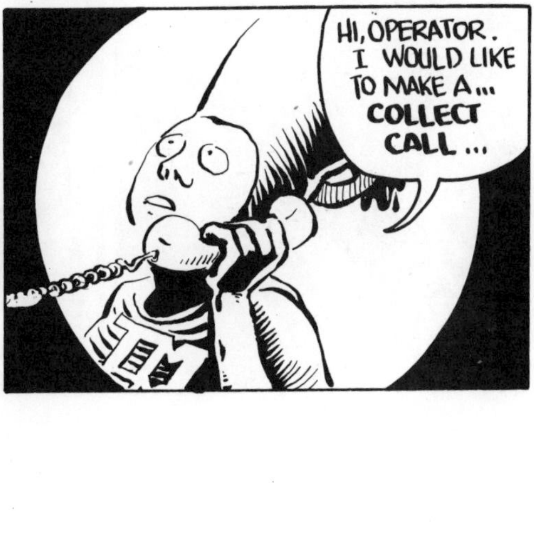
HI, OPERATOR. I WOULD LIKE TO MAKE A... COLLECT CALL...

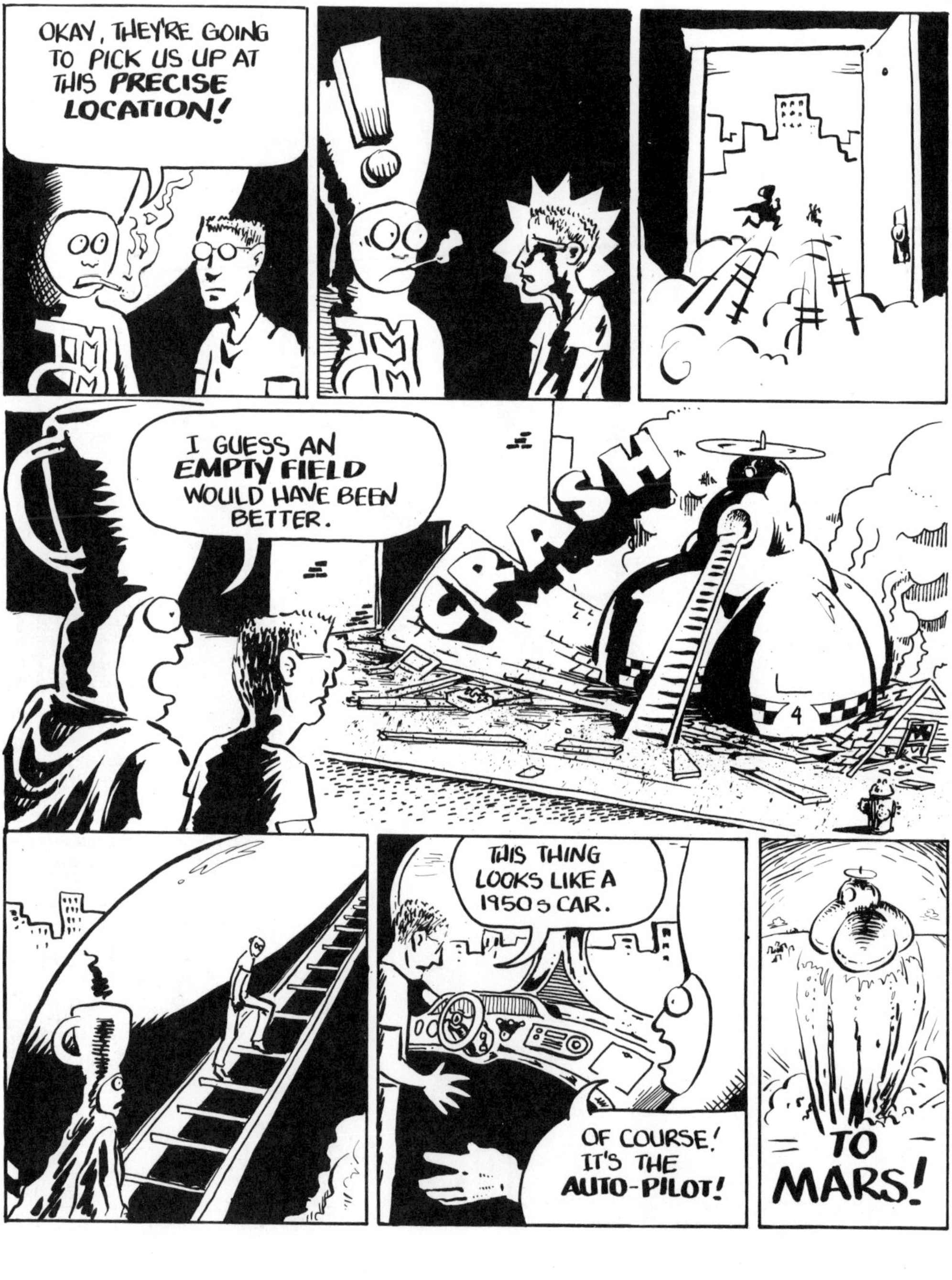
OKAY, THEY'RE GOING TO PICK US UP AT THIS PRECISE LOCATION!
I GUESS AN EMPTY FIELD WOULD HAVE BEEN BETTER.
CRASH
4
THIS THING LOOKS LIKE A 1950s CAR.
OF COURSE! IT'S THE AUTO-PILOT!
TO MARS!

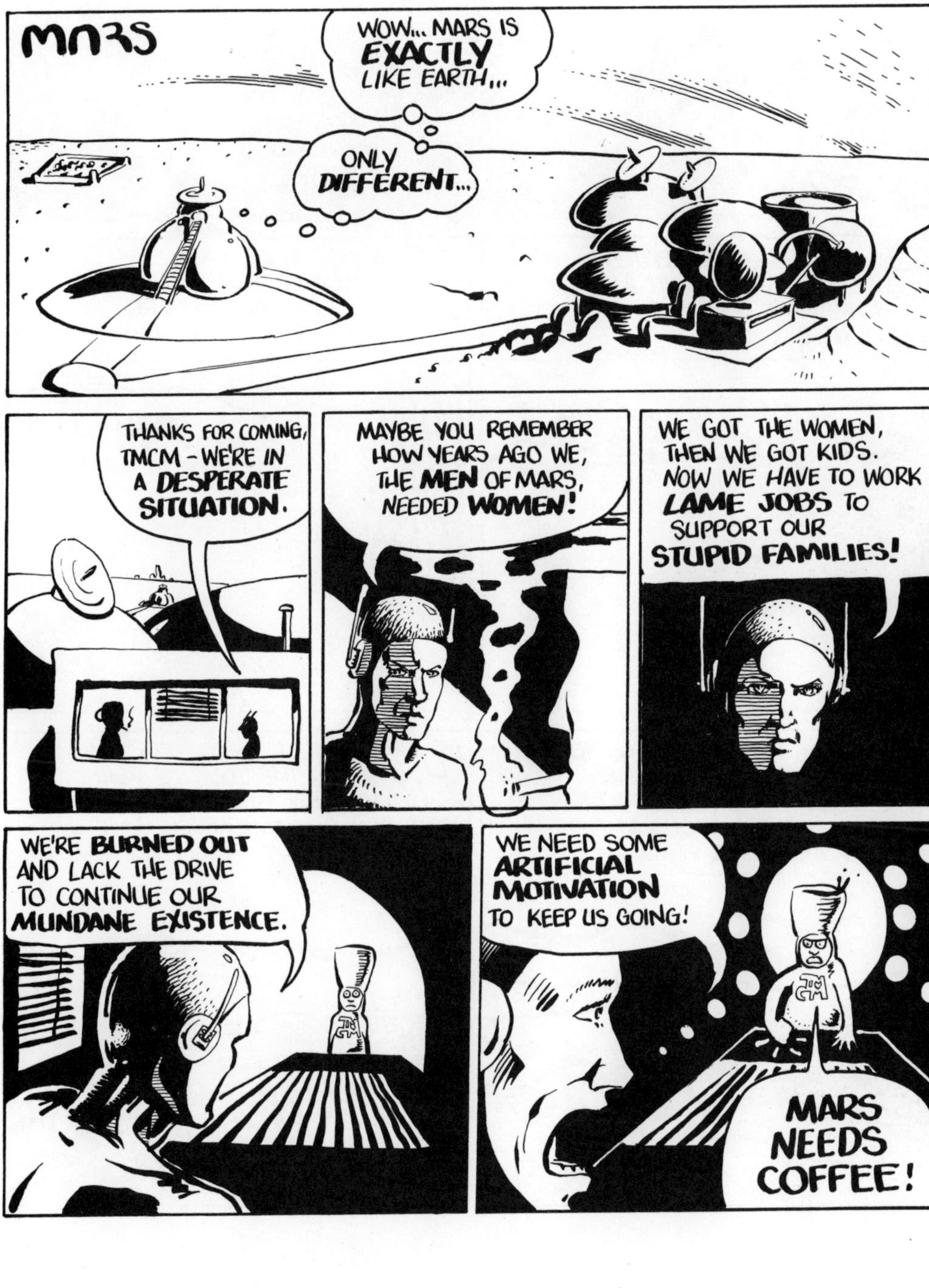
MARS
WOW... MARS IS EXACTLY LIKE EARTH...
ONLY DIFFERENT...
THANKS FOR COMING, TMCM - WE'RE IN A DESPERATE SITUATION.
MAYBE YOU REMEMBER HOW YEARS AGO WE, THE MEN OF MARS, NEEDED WOMEN!
WE GOT THE WOMEN, THEN WE GOT KIDS. NOW WE HAVE TO WORK LAME JOBS TO SUPPORT OUR STUPID FAMILIES!
WE'RE BURNED OUT AND LACK THE DRIVE TO CONTINUE OUR MUNDANE EXISTENCE.
WE NEED SOME ARTIFICIAL MOTIVATION TO KEEP US GOING!
MARS NEEDS COFFEE!

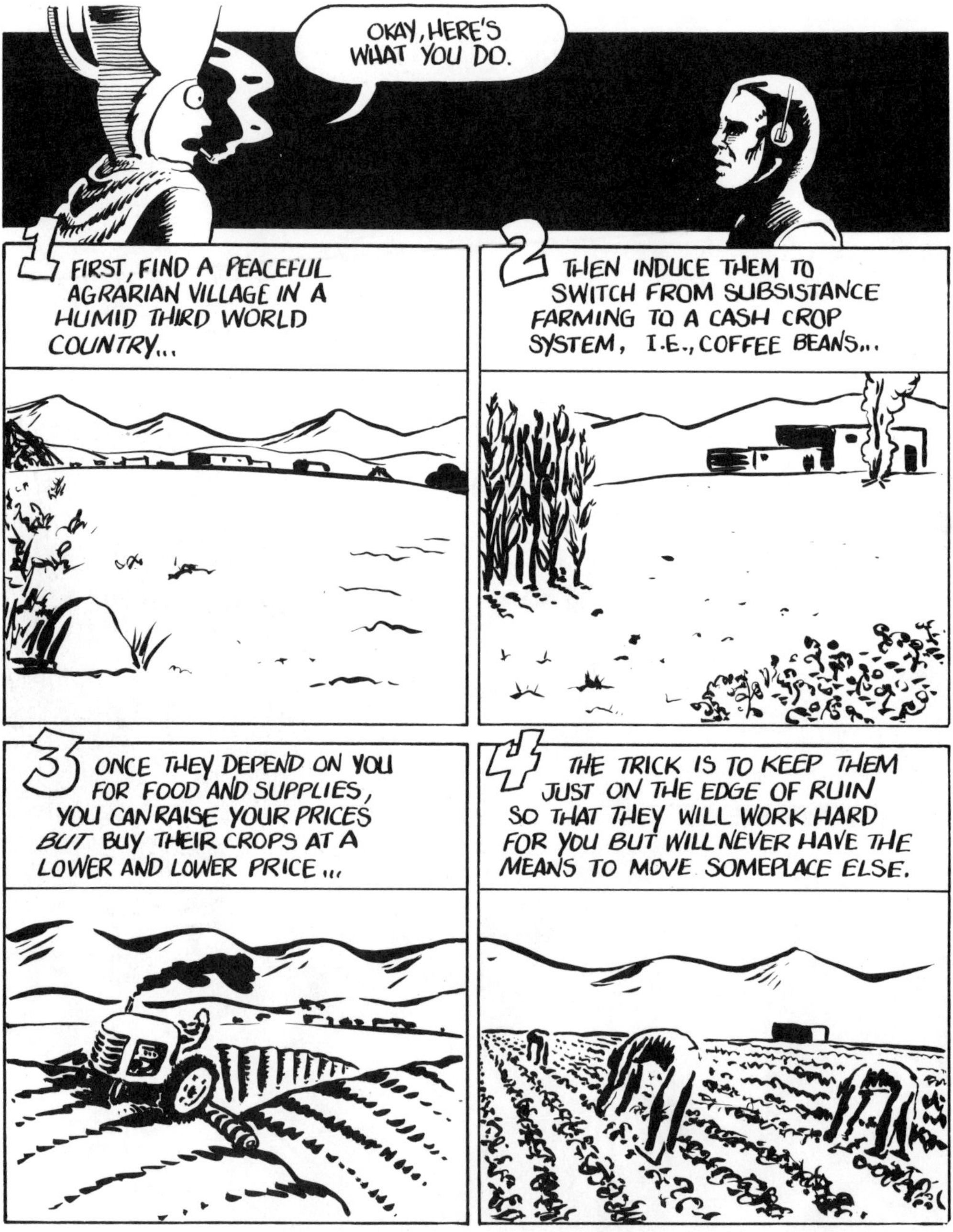
OKAY, HERE'S WHAT YOU DO.
1 FIRST, FIND A PEACEFUL AGRARIAN VILLAGE IN A HUMID THIRD WORLD COUNTRY...
2 THEN INDUCE THEM TO SWITCH FROM SUBSISTANCE FARMING TO A CASH CROP SYSTEM, I.E., COFFEE BEANS...
3 ONCE THEY DEPEND ON YOU FOR FOOD AND SUPPLIES, YOU CAN RAISE YOUR PRICES BUT BUY THEIR CROPS AT A LOWER AND LOWER PRICE...
4 THE TRICK IS TO KEEP THEM JUST ON THE EDGE OF RUIN SO THAT THEY WILL WORK HARD FOR YOU BUT WILL NEVER HAVE THE MEANS TO MOVE SOMEPLACE ELSE.

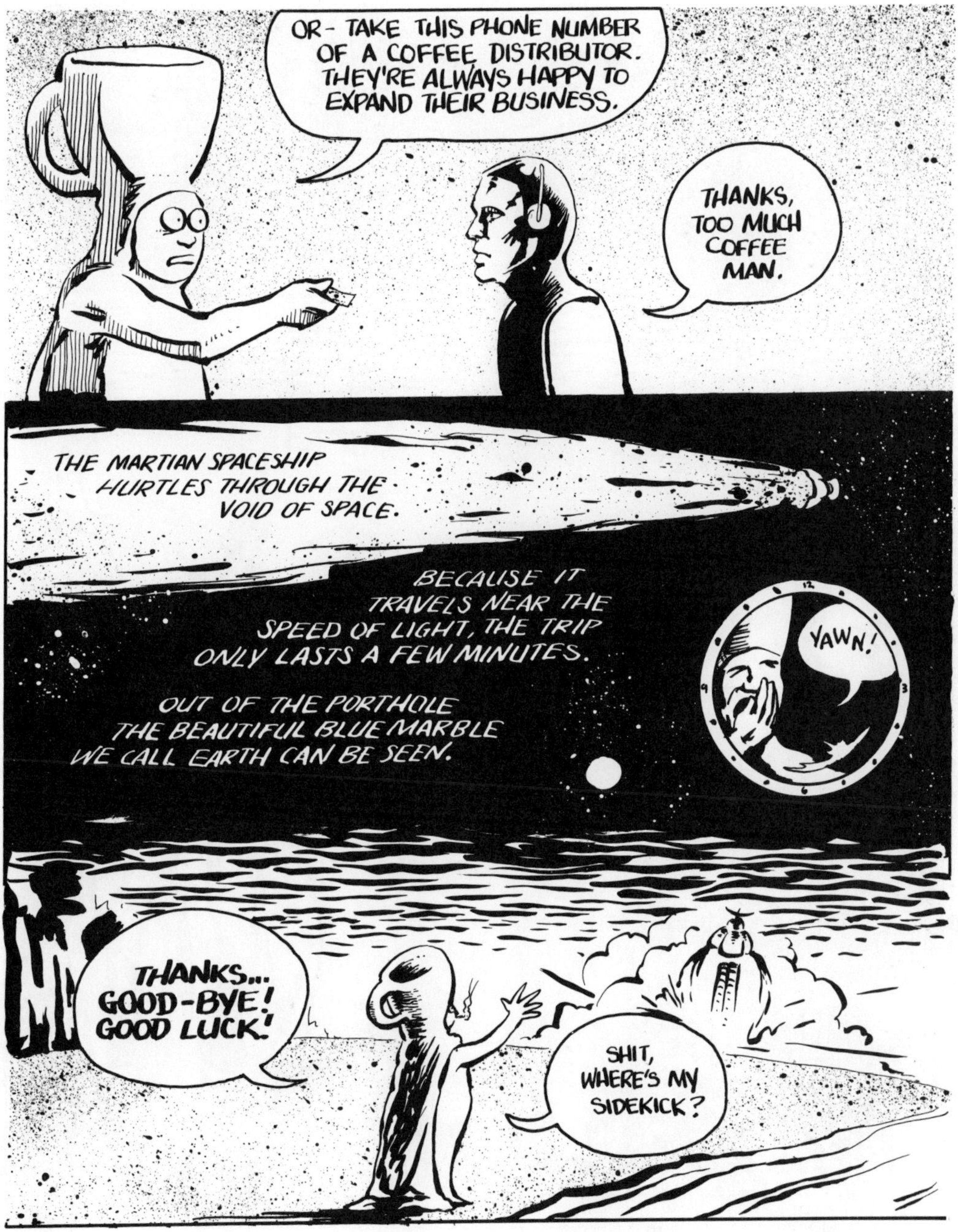

OR- TAKE THIS PHONE NUMBER OF A COFFEE DISTRIBUTOR. THEY'RE ALWAYS HAPPY TO EXPAND THEIR BUSINESS.
THANKS, TOO MUCH COFFEE MAN.
THE MARTIAN SPACESHIP HURTLES THROUGH THE VOID OF SPACE.
BECAUSE IT TRAVELS NEAR THE SPEED OF LIGHT, THE TRIP ONLY LASTS A FEW MINUTES.
OUT OF THE PORTHOLE THE BEAUTIFUL BLUE MARBLE WE CALL EARTH CAN BE SEEN.
YAWN!
THANKS... GOOD-BYE! GOOD LUCK!
SHIT, WHERE'S MY SIDEKICK?

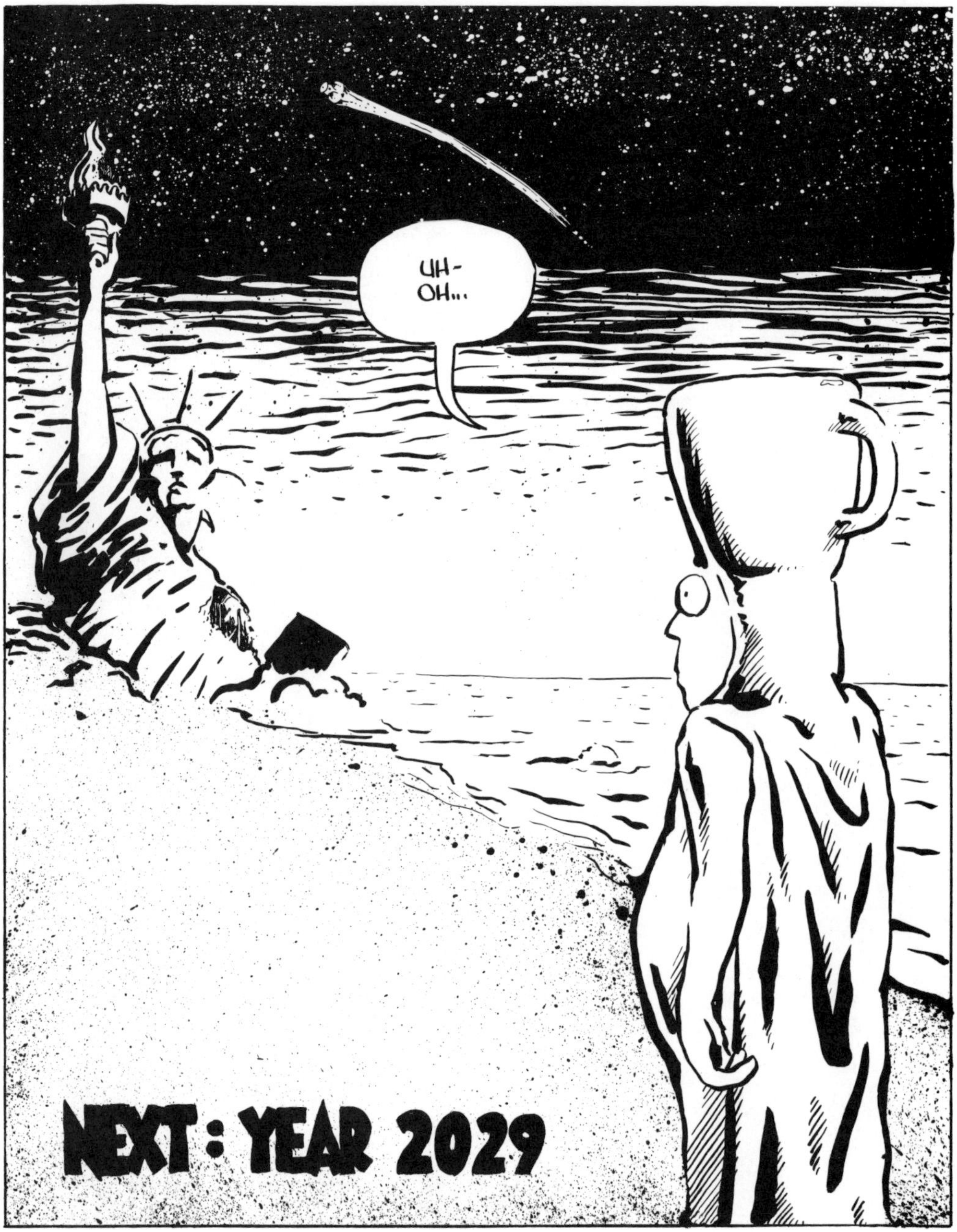
UH-
OH...
NEXT: YEAR 2029

TOO MUCH COFFEE MAN

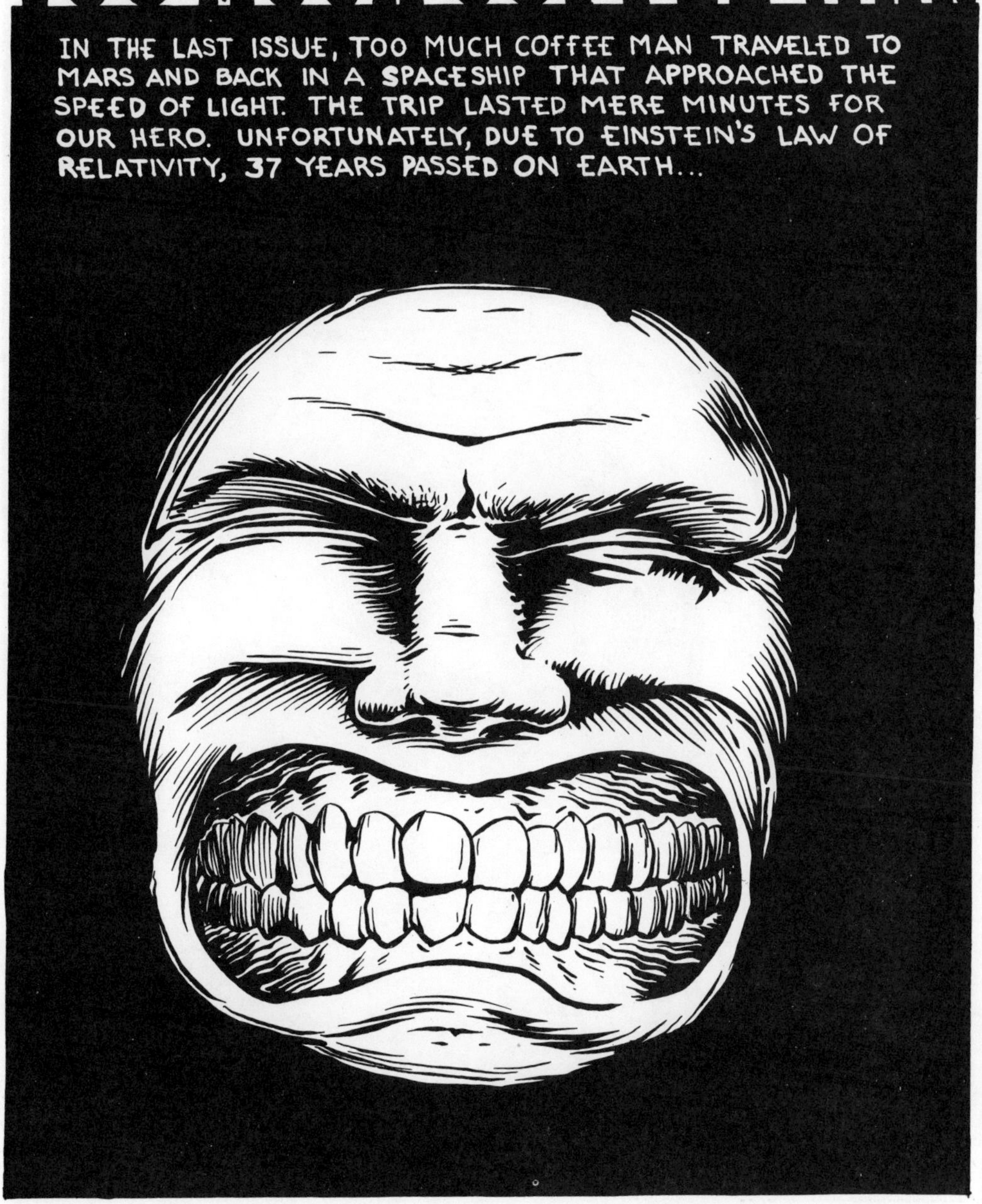
IN THE LAST ISSUE, TOO MUCH COFFEE MAN TRAVELED TO MARS AND BACK IN A SPACESHIP THAT APPROACHED THE SPEED OF LIGHT. THE TRIP LASTED MERE MINUTES FOR OUR HERO. UNFORTUNATELY, DUE TO EINSTEIN'S LAW OF RELATIVITY, 37 YEARS PASSED ON EARTH...

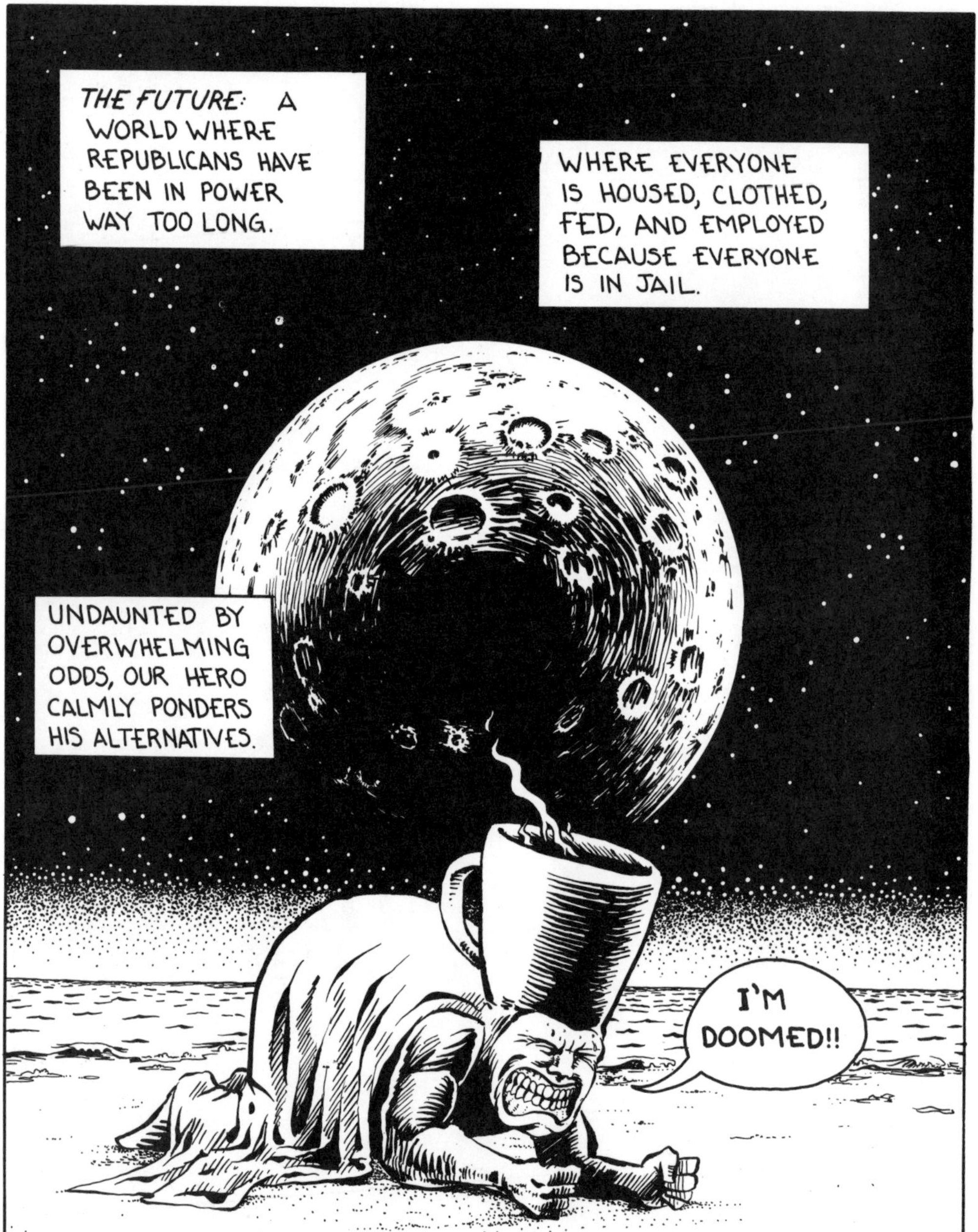
THE FUTURE: A WORLD WHERE REPUBLICANS HAVE BEEN IN POWER WAY TOO LONG.
WHERE EVERYONE IS HOUSED, CLOTHED, FED, AND EMPLOYED BECAUSE EVERYONE IS IN JAIL.
UNDAUNTED BY OVERWHELMING ODDS, OUR HERO CALMLY PONDERS HIS ALTERNATIVES.
I'M DOOMED!!

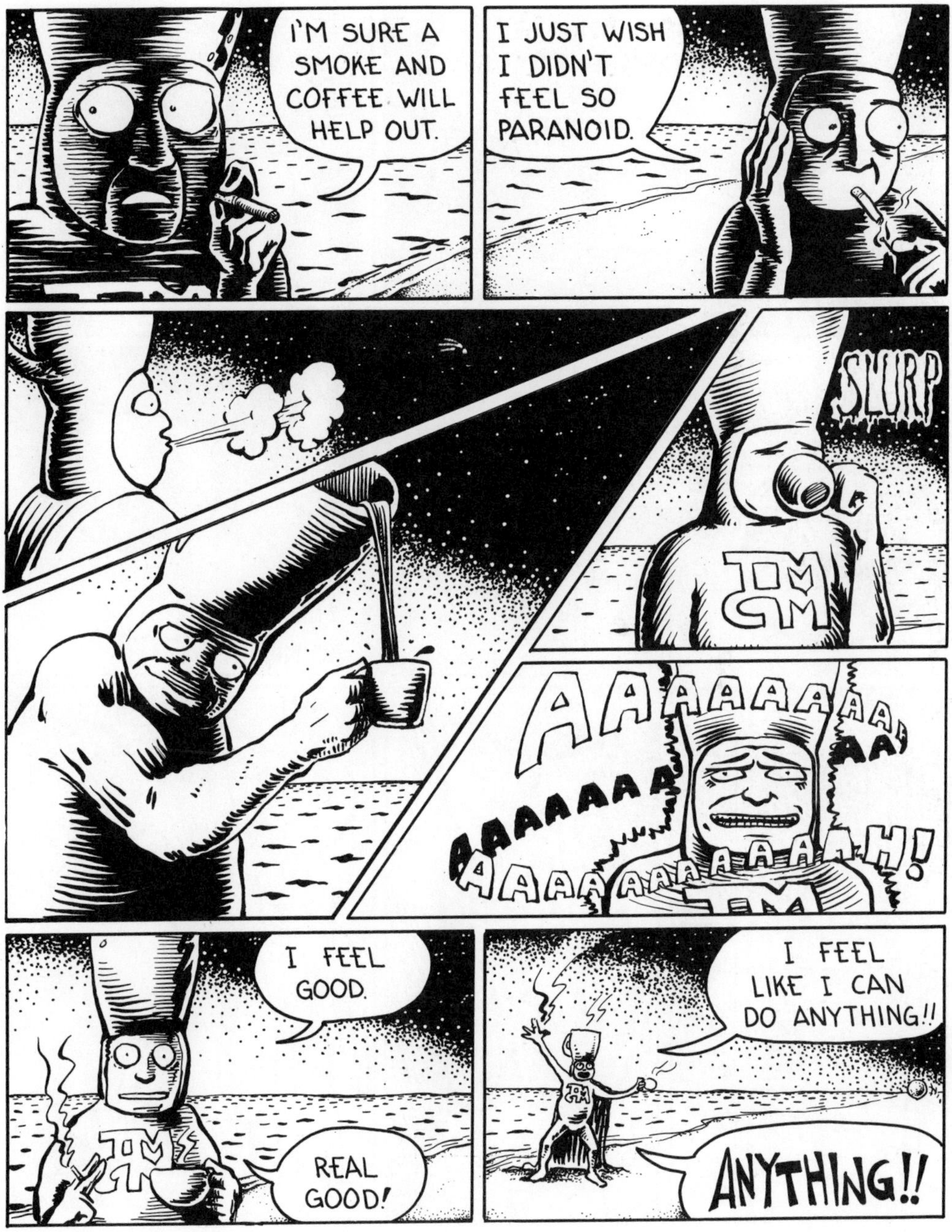
I'M SURE A SMOKE AND COFFEE WILL HELP OUT.
I JUST WISH I DIDN'T FEEL SO PARANOID.
SLURP
AAAAAAAAAAAAAAAAAAAAAAAAAAAAH!
I FEEL GOOD.
REAL GOOD!
I FEEL LIKE I CAN DO ANYTHING!!
ANYTHING!!

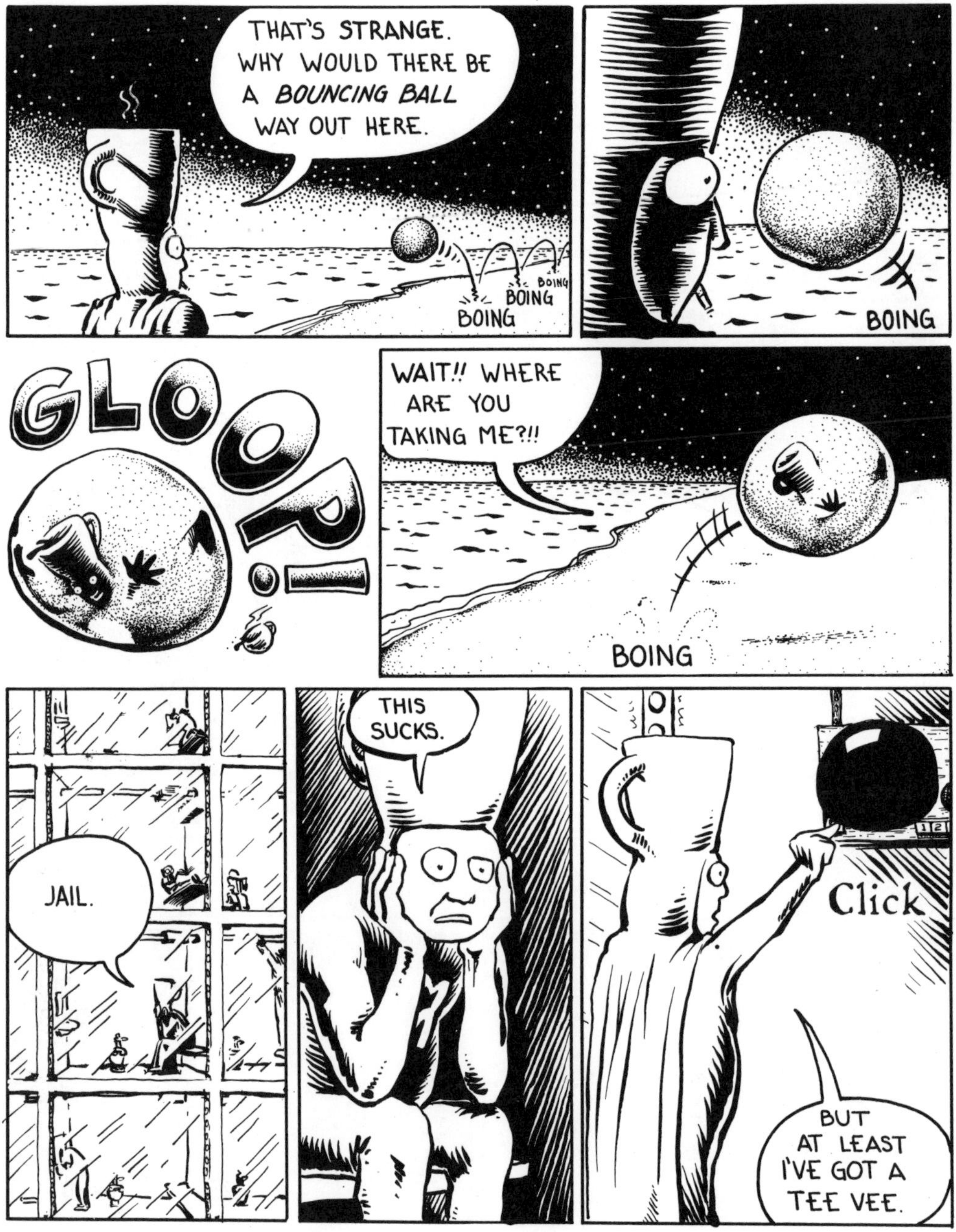
THAT'S STRANGE. WHY WOULD THERE BE A *BOUNCING BALL* WAY OUT HERE.
BOING BOING BOING
BOING
GLOOP!
WAIT!! WHERE ARE YOU TAKING ME?!!
BOING
JAIL.
THIS SUCKS.
Click
BUT AT LEAST I'VE GOT A TEE VEE.

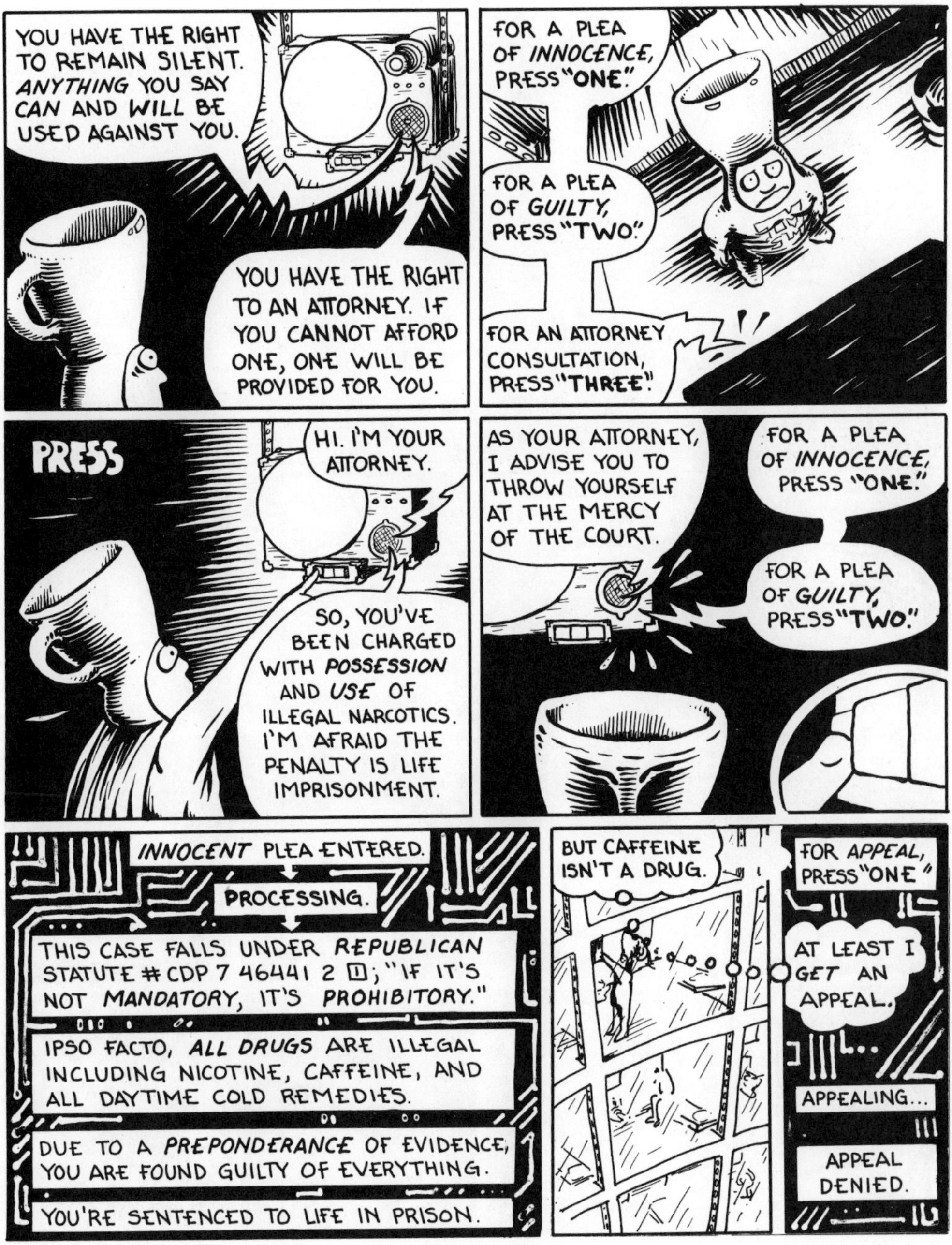
YOU HAVE THE RIGHT TO REMAIN SILENT. ANYTHING YOU SAY CAN AND WILL BE USED AGAINST YOU.
YOU HAVE THE RIGHT TO AN ATTORNEY. IF YOU CANNOT AFFORD ONE, ONE WILL BE PROVIDED FOR YOU.
FOR A PLEA OF INNOCENCE, PRESS "ONE."
FOR A PLEA OF GUILTY, PRESS "TWO."
FOR AN ATTORNEY CONSULTATION, PRESS "THREE."
PRESS
HI. I'M YOUR ATTORNEY.
SO, YOU'VE BEEN CHARGED WITH POSSESSION AND USE OF ILLEGAL NARCOTICS. I'M AFRAID THE PENALTY IS LIFE IMPRISONMENT.
AS YOUR ATTORNEY, I ADVISE YOU TO THROW YOURSELF AT THE MERCY OF THE COURT.
FOR A PLEA OF INNOCENCE, PRESS "ONE."
FOR A PLEA OF GUILTY, PRESS "TWO."
INNOCENT PLEA ENTERED.
PROCESSING.
THIS CASE FALLS UNDER REPUBLICAN STATUTE # CDP 7 46441 2 ①; "IF IT'S NOT MANDATORY, IT'S PROHIBITORY."
IPSO FACTO, ALL DRUGS ARE ILLEGAL INCLUDING NICOTINE, CAFFEINE, AND ALL DAYTIME COLD REMEDIES.
DUE TO A PREPONDERANCE OF EVIDENCE, YOU ARE FOUND GUILTY OF EVERYTHING.
YOU'RE SENTENCED TO LIFE IN PRISON.
BUT CAFFEINE ISN'T A DRUG.
FOR APPEAL, PRESS "ONE"
AT LEAST I GET AN APPEAL.
APPEALING...
APPEAL DENIED.

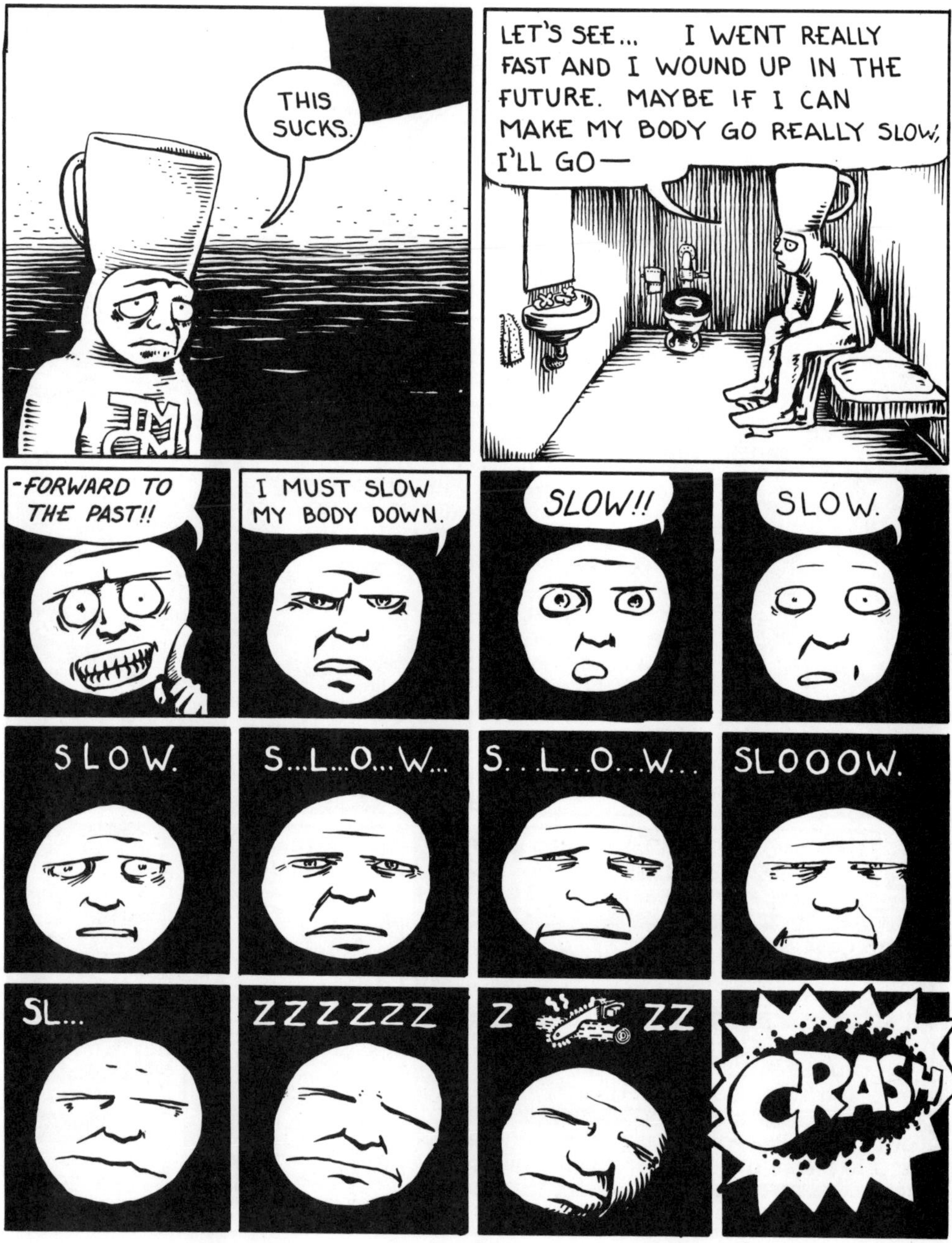
THIS SUCKS.
LET'S SEE... I WENT REALLY FAST AND I WOUND UP IN THE FUTURE. MAYBE IF I CAN MAKE MY BODY GO REALLY SLOW, I'LL GO—
-FORWARD TO THE PAST!!
I MUST SLOW MY BODY DOWN.
SLOW!!
SLOW.
SLOW.
S...L...O...W...
S. . L. . O. . W. . .
SLOOOW.
SL...
ZZZZZZ
Z ZZ
CRASH

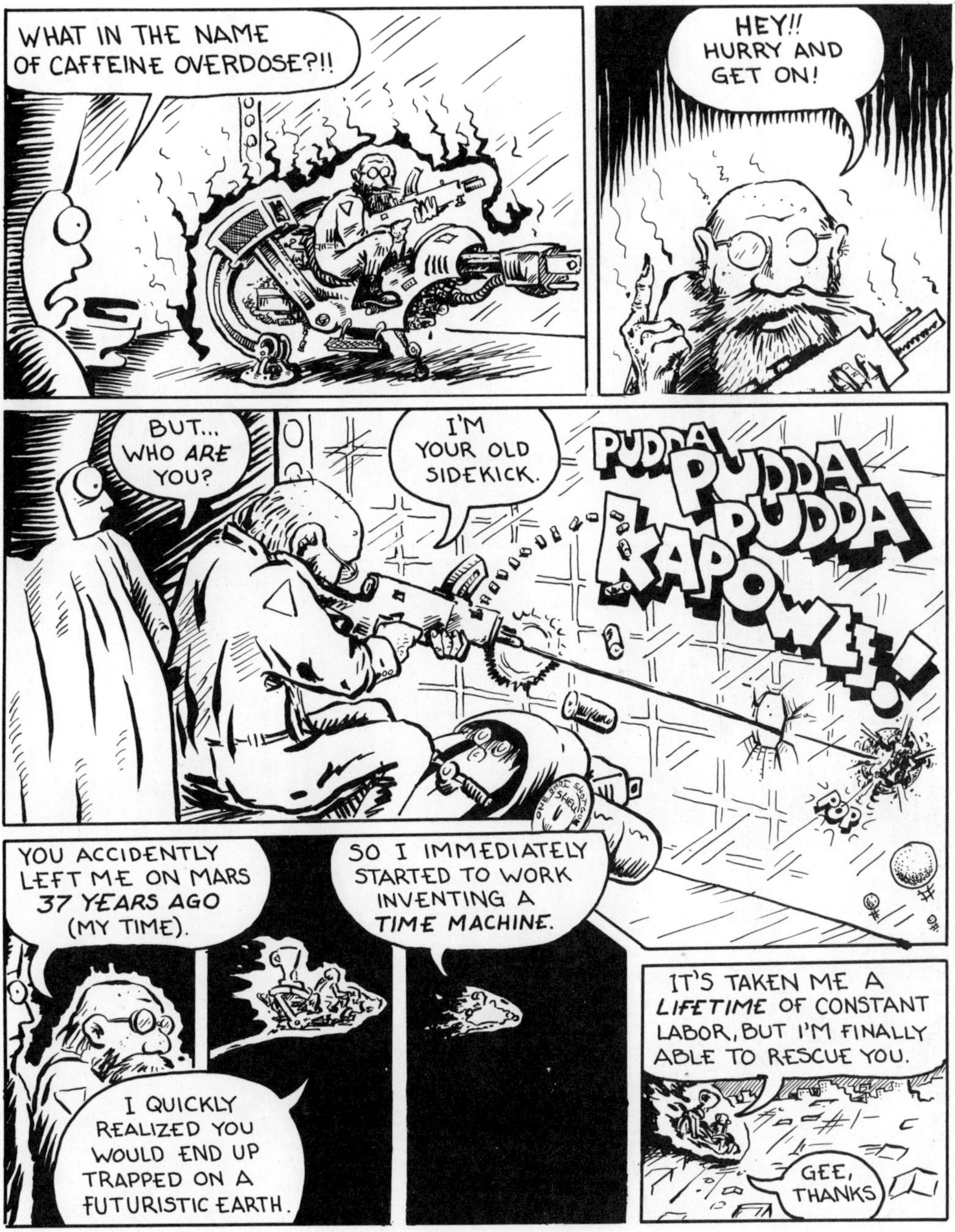
WHAT IN THE NAME OF CAFFEINE OVERDOSE?!!
HEY!! HURRY AND GET ON!
BUT... WHO *ARE* YOU?
I'M YOUR OLD SIDEKICK.
PUDDA PUDDA PUDDA KAPOWEE!
ONE SHOT SHOTGUN SHELL
POP
YOU ACCIDENTLY LEFT ME ON MARS *37 YEARS AGO* (MY TIME).
I QUICKLY REALIZED YOU WOULD END UP TRAPPED ON A FUTURISTIC EARTH.
SO I IMMEDIATELY STARTED TO WORK INVENTING A *TIME MACHINE*.
IT'S TAKEN ME A *LIFETIME* OF CONSTANT LABOR, BUT I'M FINALLY ABLE TO RESCUE YOU.
GEE, THANKS

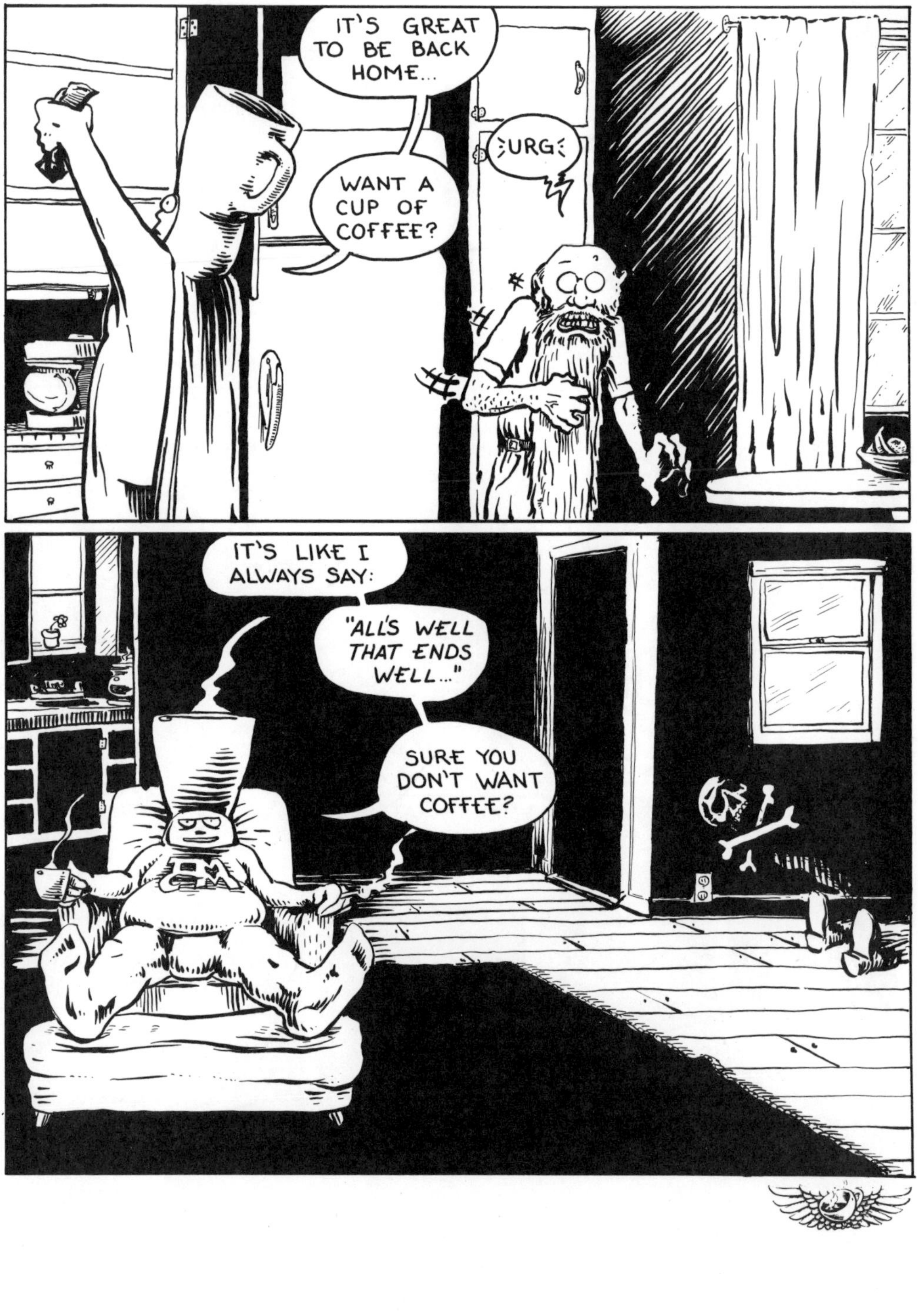
IT'S GREAT TO BE BACK HOME...
WANT A CUP OF COFFEE?
URG
IT'S LIKE I ALWAYS SAY:
"ALL'S WELL THAT ENDS WELL..."
SURE YOU DON'T WANT COFFEE?

TOO MUCH COFFEE MAN™

meets his
COFFEE MAKER

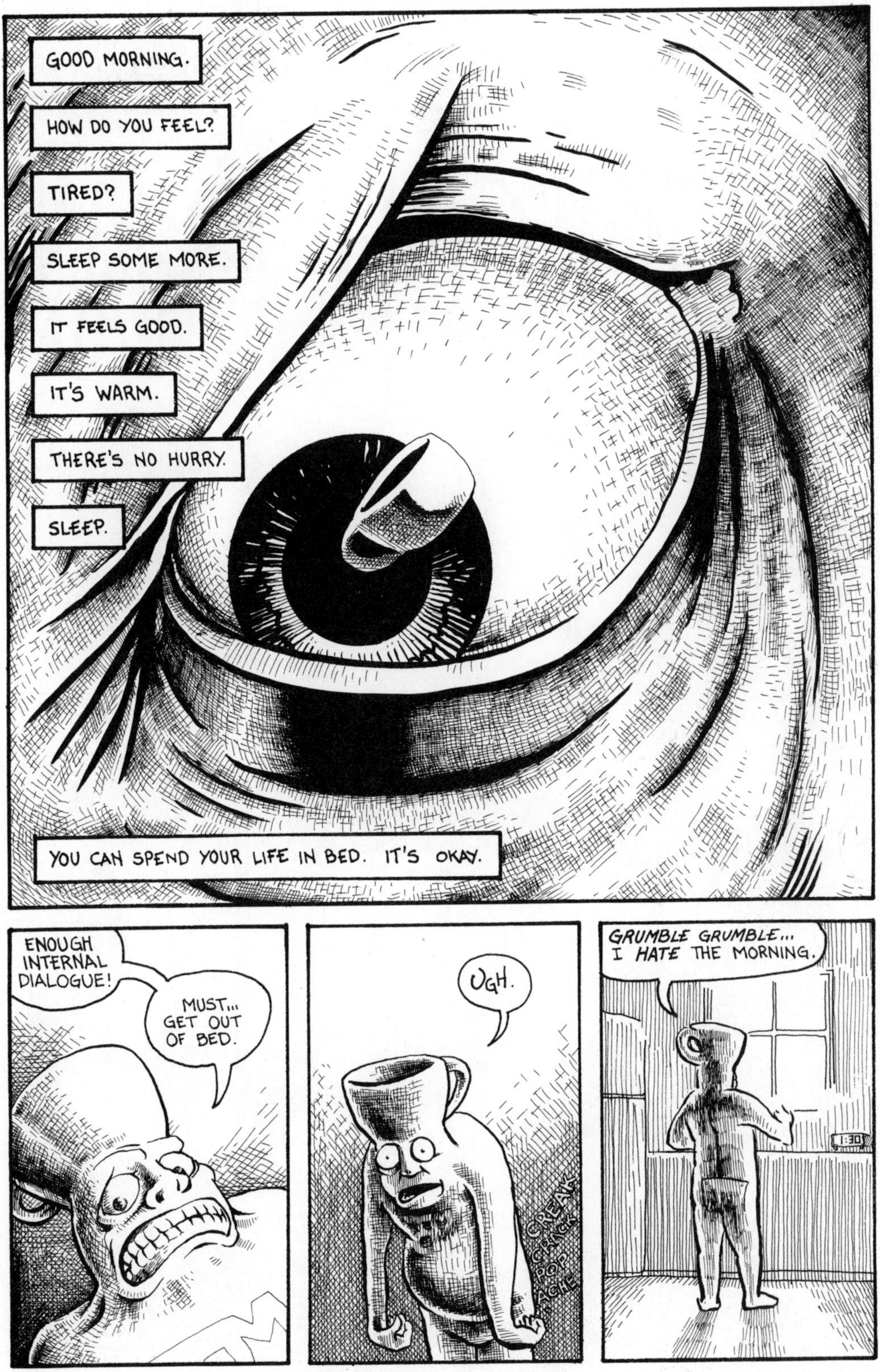
GOOD MORNING.
HOW DO YOU FEEL?
TIRED?
SLEEP SOME MORE.
IT FEELS GOOD.
IT'S WARM.
THERE'S NO HURRY.
SLEEP.
YOU CAN SPEND YOUR LIFE IN BED. IT'S OKAY.
ENOUGH INTERNAL DIALOGUE!
MUST... GET OUT OF BED.
UGH.
CREAK
CRACK
POP
ACHE
GRUMBLE GRUMBLE... I *HATE* THE MORNING.
1:30

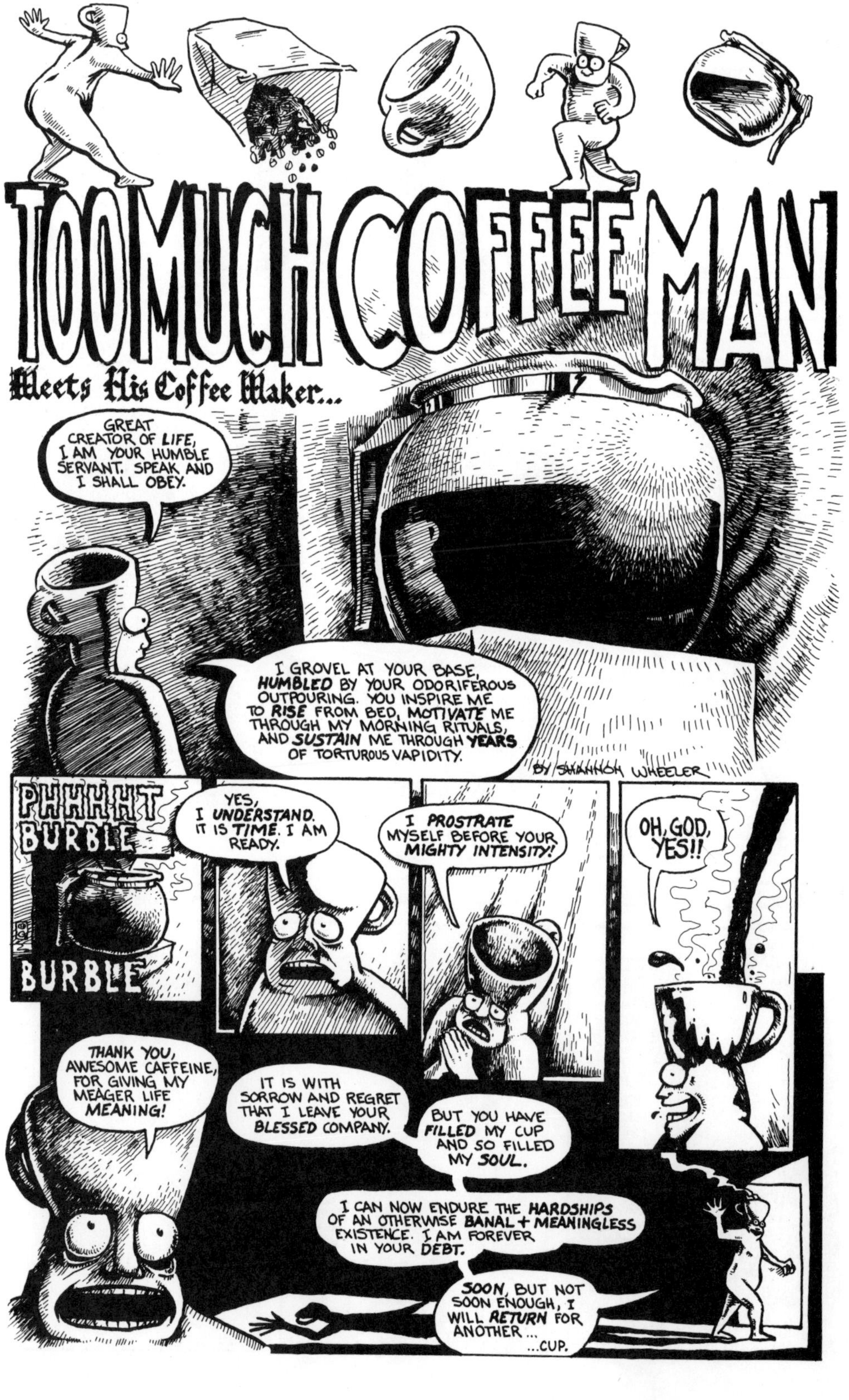
TOO MUCH COFFEE MAN
Meets His Coffee Maker...
GREAT CREATOR OF LIFE, I AM YOUR HUMBLE SERVANT. SPEAK AND I SHALL OBEY.
I GROVEL AT YOUR BASE, HUMBLED BY YOUR ODORIFEROUS OUTPOURING. YOU INSPIRE ME TO RISE FROM BED, MOTIVATE ME THROUGH MY MORNING RITUALS, AND SUSTAIN ME THROUGH YEARS OF TORTUROUS VAPIDITY.
BY SHANNON WHEELER
PHHHHT BURBLE
BURBLE
YES, I UNDERSTAND. IT IS TIME. I AM READY.
I PROSTRATE MYSELF BEFORE YOUR MIGHTY INTENSITY!
OH, GOD, YES!!
THANK YOU, AWESOME CAFFEINE, FOR GIVING MY MEAGER LIFE MEANING!
IT IS WITH SORROW AND REGRET THAT I LEAVE YOUR BLESSED COMPANY.
BUT YOU HAVE FILLED MY CUP AND SO FILLED MY SOUL.
I CAN NOW ENDURE THE HARDSHIPS OF AN OTHERWISE BANAL + MEANINGLESS EXISTENCE. I AM FOREVER IN YOUR DEBT.
SOON, BUT NOT SOON ENOUGH, I WILL RETURN FOR ANOTHER ...
...CUP.

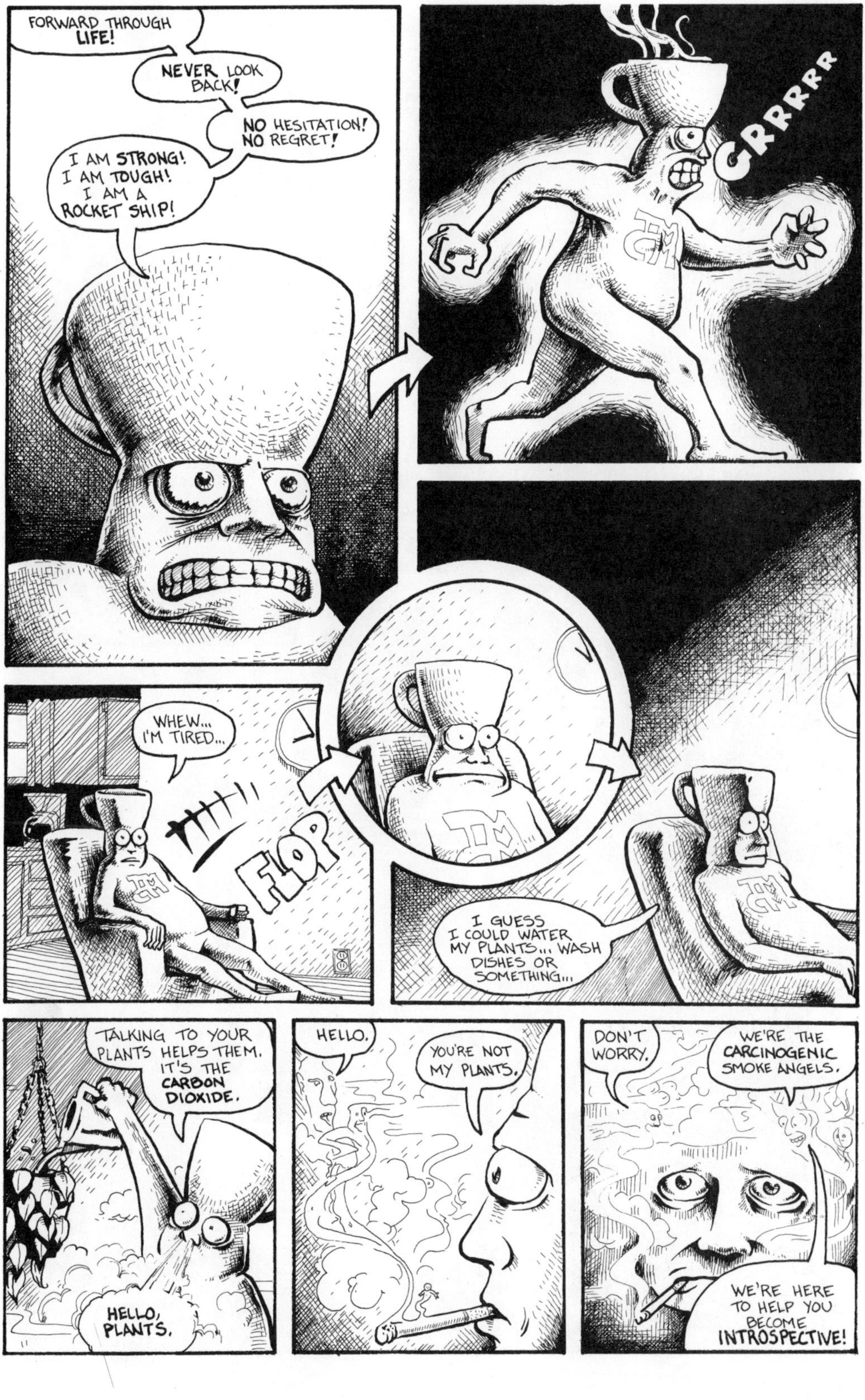
FORWARD THROUGH LIFE!
NEVER LOOK BACK!
NO HESITATION! NO REGRET!
I AM STRONG! I AM TOUGH! I AM A ROCKET SHIP!
GRRRRR
WHEW... I'M TIRED...
FLOP
I GUESS I COULD WATER MY PLANTS... WASH DISHES OR SOMETHING...
TALKING TO YOUR PLANTS HELPS THEM. IT'S THE CARBON DIOXIDE.
HELLO, PLANTS.
HELLO.
YOU'RE NOT MY PLANTS.
DON'T WORRY.
WE'RE THE CARCINOGENIC SMOKE ANGELS.
WE'RE HERE TO HELP YOU BECOME INTROSPECTIVE!

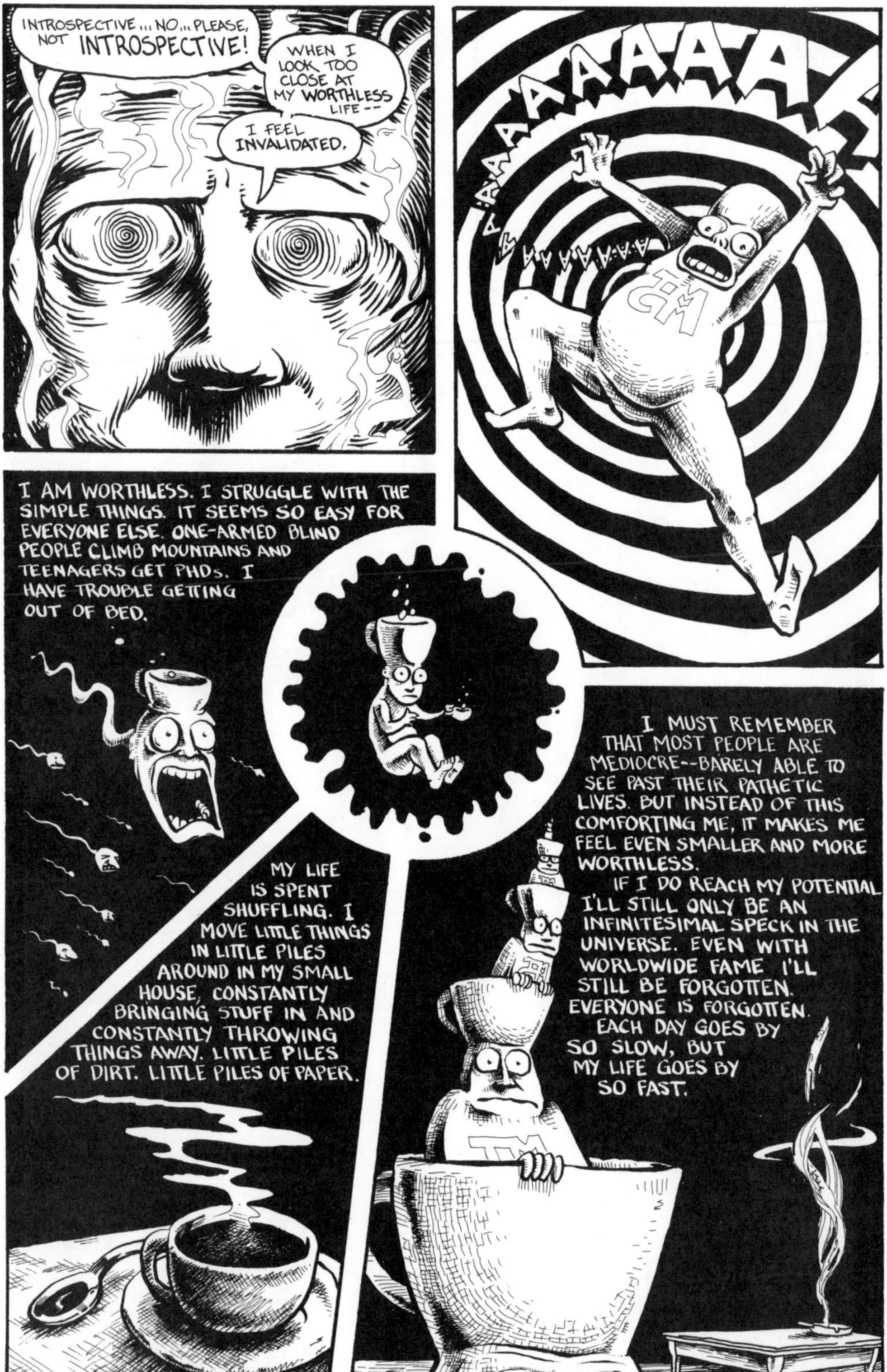
INTROSPECTIVE... NO... PLEASE, NOT INTROSPECTIVE!
WHEN I LOOK TOO CLOSE AT MY WORTHLESS LIFE --
I FEEL INVALIDATED.
AAAAAAAAAAAH
AAAAAAAAA
I AM WORTHLESS. I STRUGGLE WITH THE SIMPLE THINGS. IT SEEMS SO EASY FOR EVERYONE ELSE. ONE-ARMED BLIND PEOPLE CLIMB MOUNTAINS AND TEENAGERS GET PHDs. I HAVE TROUBLE GETTING OUT OF BED.
MY LIFE IS SPENT SHUFFLING. I MOVE LITTLE THINGS IN LITTLE PILES AROUND IN MY SMALL HOUSE, CONSTANTLY BRINGING STUFF IN AND CONSTANTLY THROWING THINGS AWAY. LITTLE PILES OF DIRT. LITTLE PILES OF PAPER.
I MUST REMEMBER THAT MOST PEOPLE ARE MEDIOCRE--BARELY ABLE TO SEE PAST THEIR PATHETIC LIVES. BUT INSTEAD OF THIS COMFORTING ME, IT MAKES ME FEEL EVEN SMALLER AND MORE WORTHLESS.
IF I DO REACH MY POTENTIAL I'LL STILL ONLY BE AN INFINITESIMAL SPECK IN THE UNIVERSE. EVEN WITH WORLDWIDE FAME I'LL STILL BE FORGOTTEN. EVERYONE IS FORGOTTEN.
EACH DAY GOES BY SO SLOW, BUT MY LIFE GOES BY SO FAST.

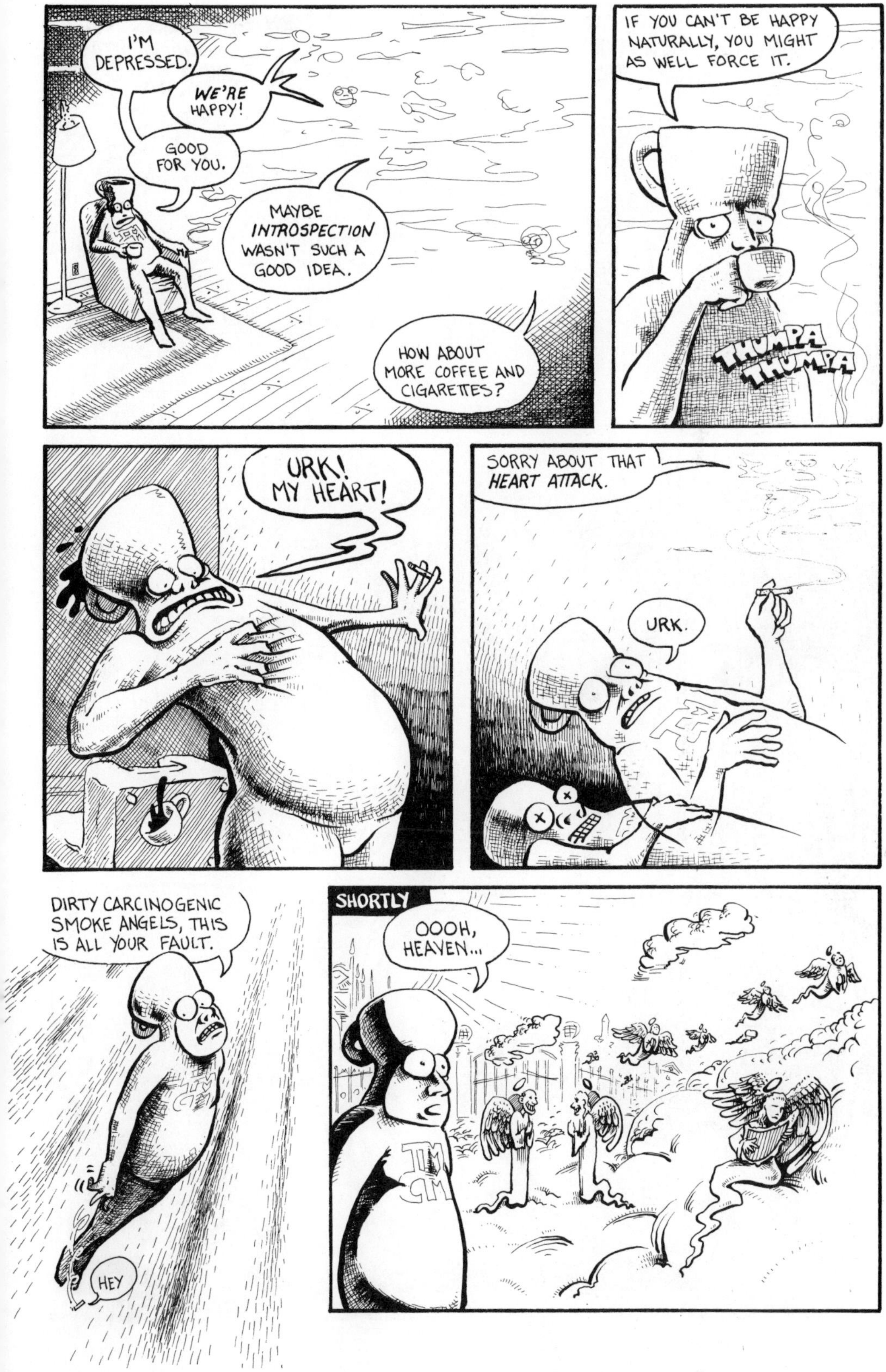
I'M DEPRESSED.
WE'RE HAPPY!
GOOD FOR YOU.
MAYBE INTROSPECTION WASN'T SUCH A GOOD IDEA.
HOW ABOUT MORE COFFEE AND CIGARETTES?
IF YOU CAN'T BE HAPPY NATURALLY, YOU MIGHT AS WELL FORCE IT.
THUMPA THUMPA
URK! MY HEART!
SORRY ABOUT THAT HEART ATTACK.
URK.
DIRTY CARCINOGENIC SMOKE ANGELS, THIS IS ALL YOUR FAULT.
HEY
SHORTLY
OOOH, HEAVEN...

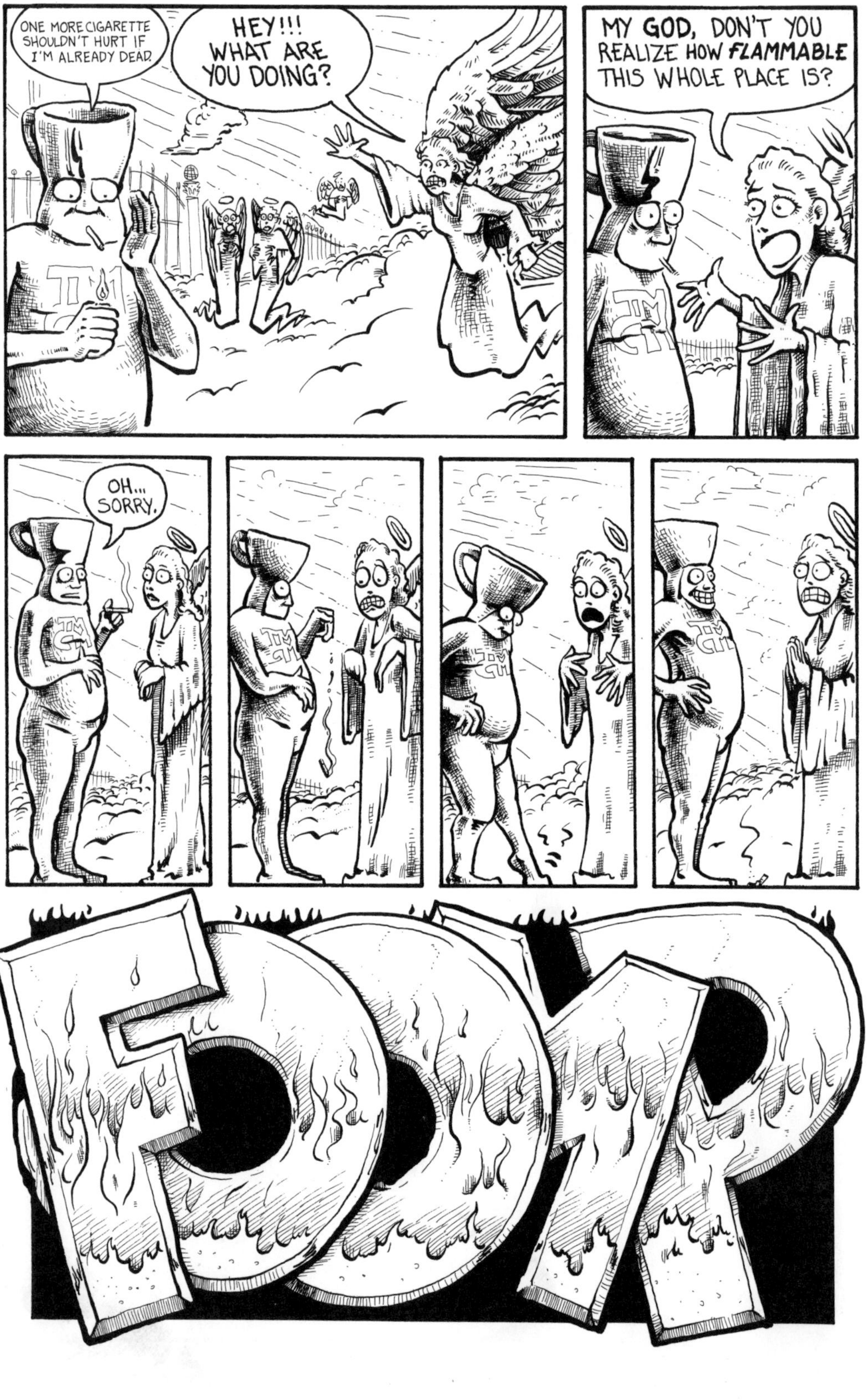
ONE MORE CIGARETTE SHOULDN'T HURT IF I'M ALREADY DEAD.
HEY!!! WHAT ARE YOU DOING?
MY **GOD**, DON'T YOU REALIZE HOW ***FLAMMABLE*** THIS WHOLE PLACE IS?
OH... SORRY.

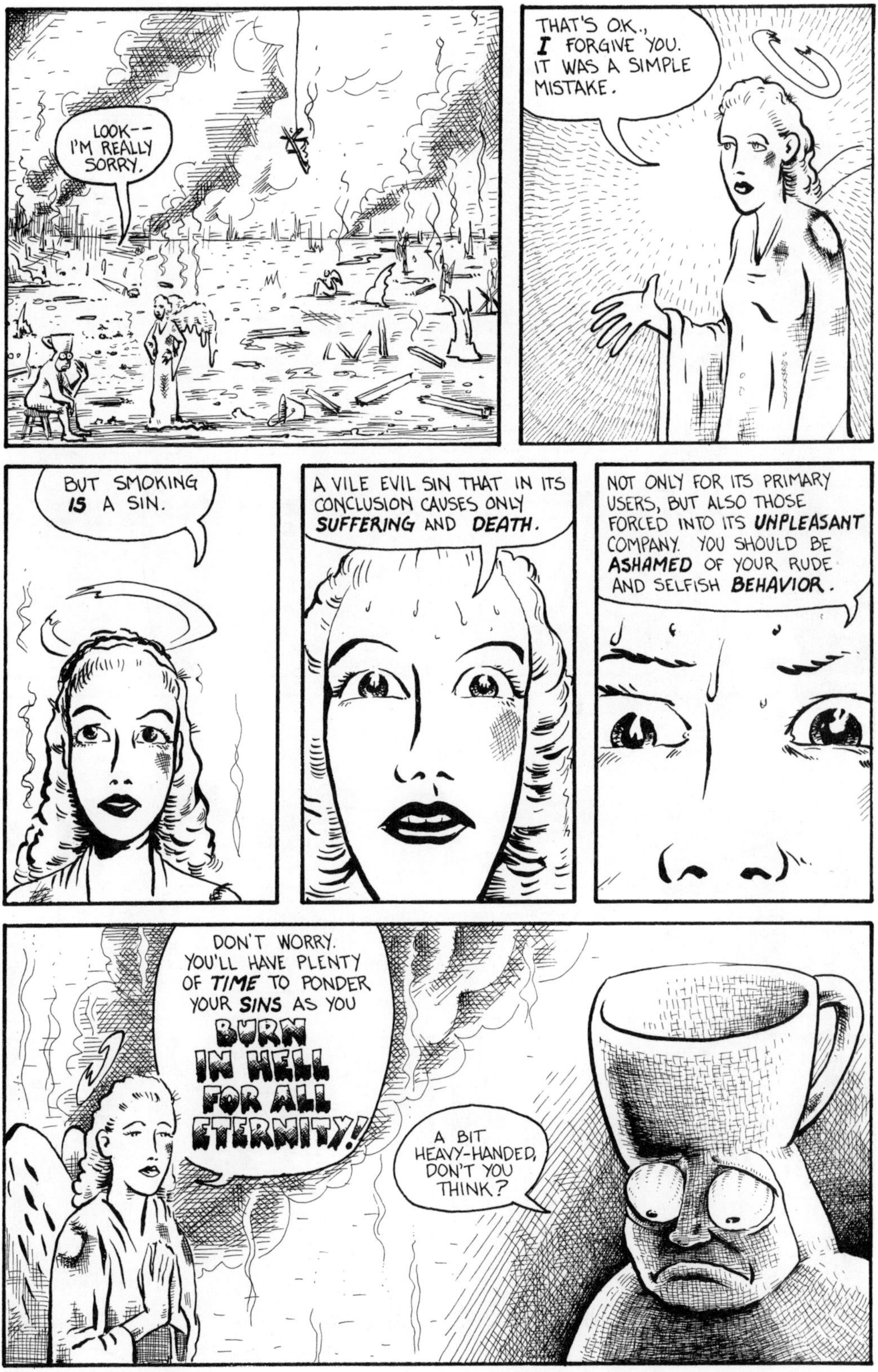
LOOK-- I'M REALLY SORRY.
THAT'S O.K., I FORGIVE YOU. IT WAS A SIMPLE MISTAKE.
BUT SMOKING IS A SIN.
A VILE EVIL SIN THAT IN ITS CONCLUSION CAUSES ONLY SUFFERING AND DEATH.
NOT ONLY FOR ITS PRIMARY USERS, BUT ALSO THOSE FORCED INTO ITS UNPLEASANT COMPANY. YOU SHOULD BE ASHAMED OF YOUR RUDE AND SELFISH BEHAVIOR.
DON'T WORRY. YOU'LL HAVE PLENTY OF TIME TO PONDER YOUR SINS AS YOU BURN IN HELL FOR ALL ETERNITY!
A BIT HEAVY-HANDED, DON'T YOU THINK?

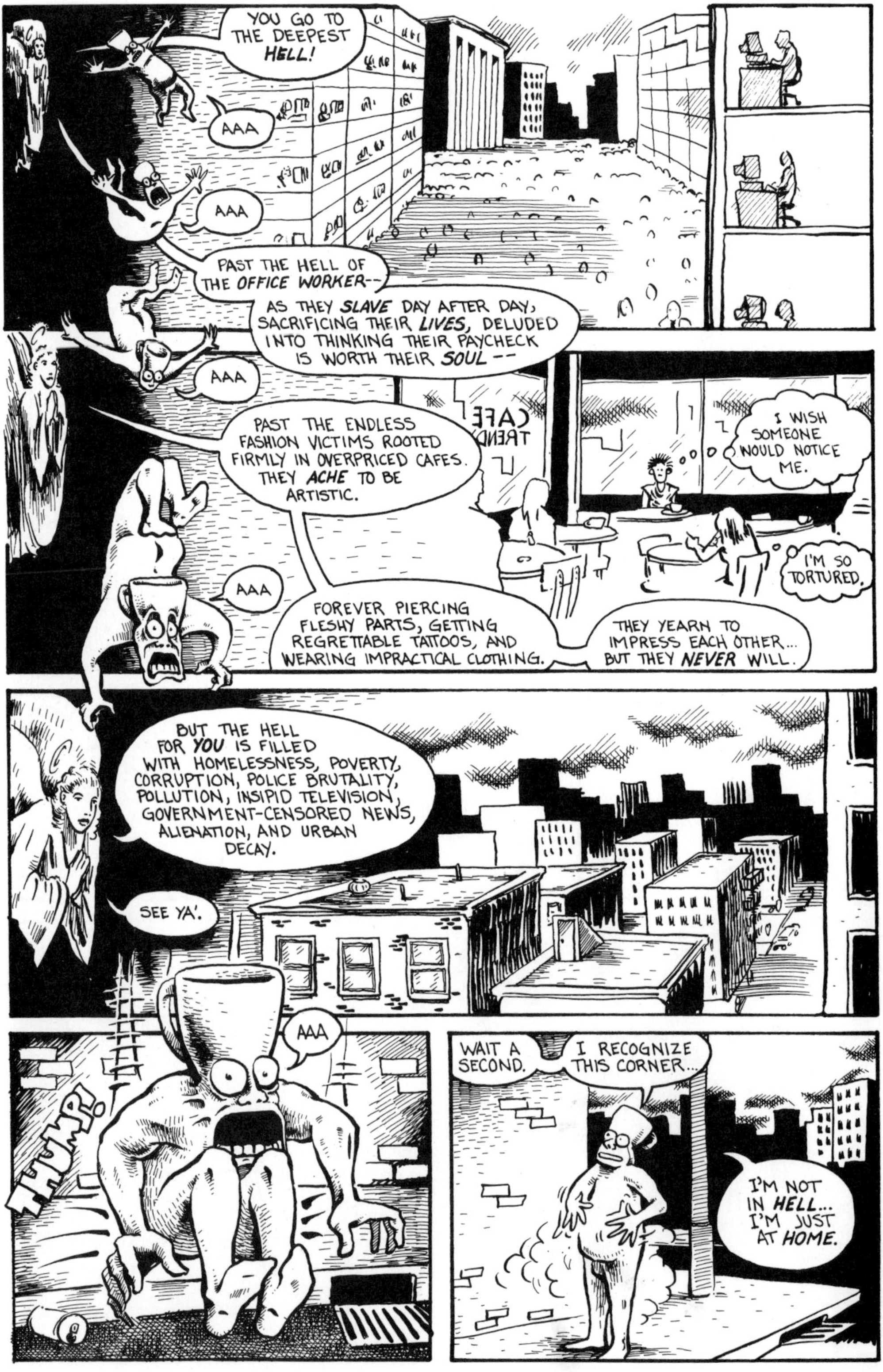

YOU GO TO THE DEEPEST HELL!
AAA
AAA
PAST THE HELL OF THE OFFICE WORKER--
AS THEY SLAVE DAY AFTER DAY, SACRIFICING THEIR LIVES, DELUDED INTO THINKING THEIR PAYCHECK IS WORTH THEIR SOUL--
AAA
PAST THE ENDLESS FASHION VICTIMS ROOTED FIRMLY IN OVERPRICED CAFES. THEY ACHE TO BE ARTISTIC.
CAFE TRENDY
I WISH SOMEONE WOULD NOTICE ME.
I'M SO TORTURED.
AAA
FOREVER PIERCING FLESHY PARTS, GETTING REGRETTABLE TATTOOS, AND WEARING IMPRACTICAL CLOTHING.
THEY YEARN TO IMPRESS EACH OTHER... BUT THEY NEVER WILL.
BUT THE HELL FOR YOU IS FILLED WITH HOMELESSNESS, POVERTY, CORRUPTION, POLICE BRUTALITY, POLLUTION, INSIPID TELEVISION, GOVERNMENT-CENSORED NEWS, ALIENATION, AND URBAN DECAY.
SEE YA'.
AAA
THUMP!
WAIT A SECOND.
I RECOGNIZE THIS CORNER...
I'M NOT IN HELL... I'M JUST AT HOME.

CHAPTER TWO

IN THE LAST EPISODE, *TOO MUCH COFFEE MAN* (TMCM)
MET THE CARCINOGENIC SMOKE ANGELS. THEY HELPED
HIM TAKE A LONG LOOK AT HIS PATHETIC LIFE. WHEN
HE TRIED TO CHEER HIMSELF UP FROM THE RESULTING
DEPRESSION, HE DIED OF A HEART ATTACK. AND
AFTER MANY PAGES OF HILARIOUS, SLAPSTICK
ACTION, *TMCM* FINDS HIMSELF HOME
AGAIN. WE NOW PICK UP THE
NARRATIVE FROM WHERE
WE LAST LEFT IT.

BY SHANNON WHEELER
HOME AT LAST!
HA-HA-HA... HOME... HA-HA-HA... HOME... HA-HA-HA...
COUGH COUGH COUGH
I KEEP MY KEY IN A SECRET FOLD DEEP WITHIN MY SUIT.
OH, MAN. LOOK AT THAT GIANT PILE OF MAIL. I PROBABLY HAVE A TON OF BILLS!
I'LL DEAL WITH THEM LATER.
FIRST, I MUST TAKE CARE OF THE IMPORTANT THINGS ...LIKE WATER MY THIRSTY PLANTS.
FEED THE CAT!
CAT
DO THE DISHES.
ALPHABETIZE MY VINYL COLLECTION.
VACUUM.
ANYTHING TO AVOID PAYING BILLS.
FILE SOME COMICS.
THE KEY TO PRODUCTIVITY IS TO ROTATE YOUR AVOIDANCE TECHNIQUES.
AH. A PHONE MESSAGE, SOMEONE LOVES ME.
BLINK BLINK

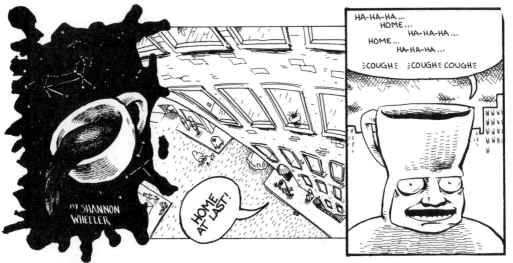

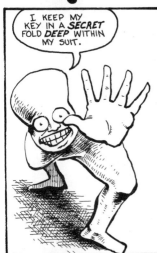

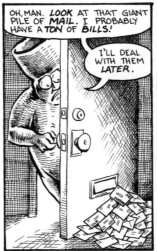

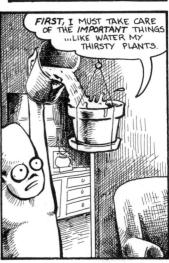

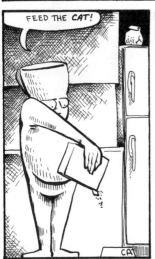

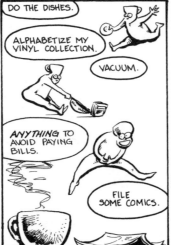

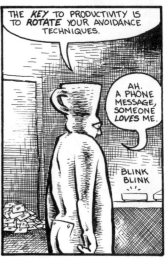

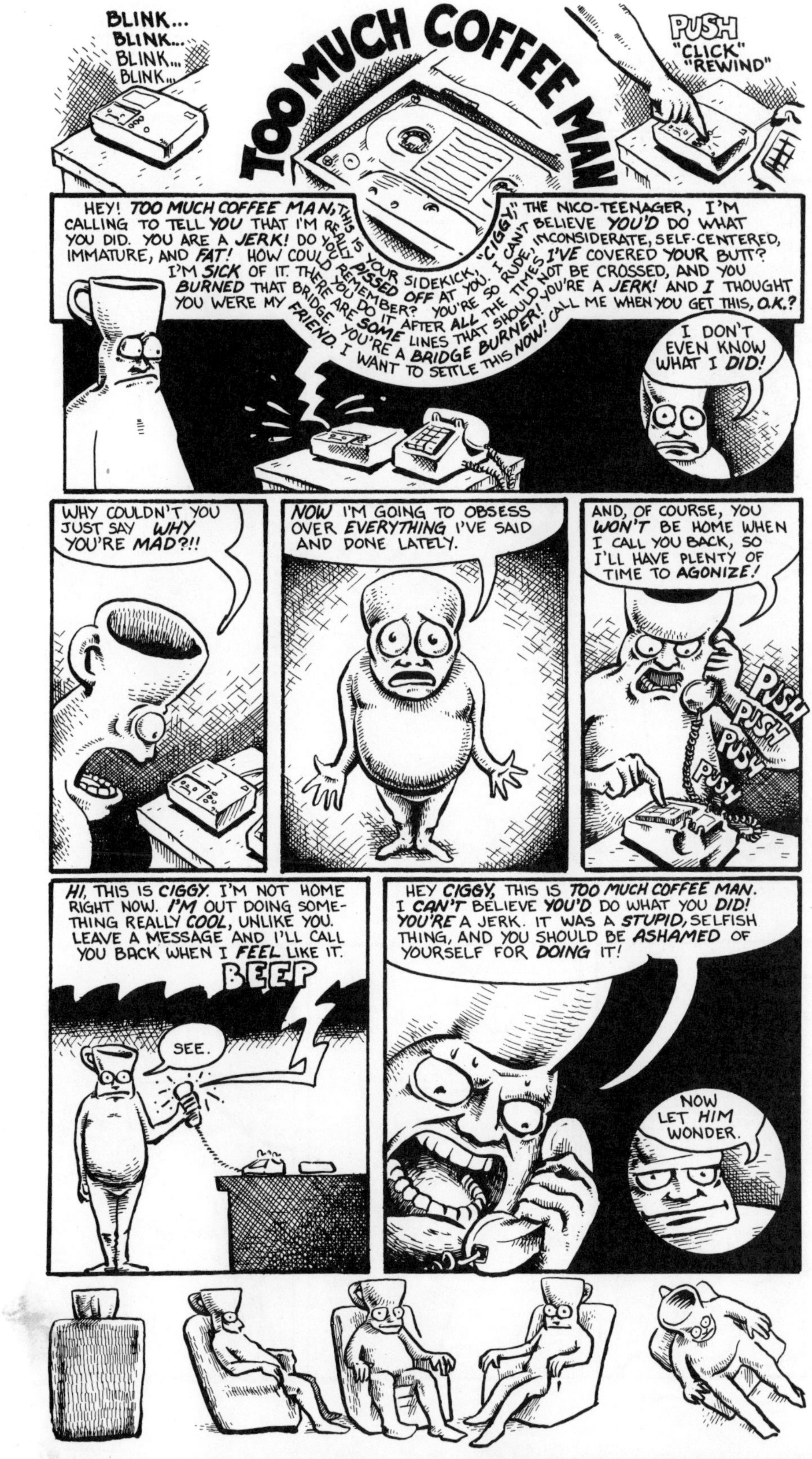
BLINK... BLINK... BLINK... BLINK...
TOO MUCH COFFEE MAN
PUSH
"CLICK" "REWIND"
HEY! TOO MUCH COFFEE MAN, THIS IS YOUR SIDEKICK, "CIGGY," THE NICO-TEENAGER, I'M CALLING TO TELL YOU THAT I'M REALLY PISSED OFF AT YOU. I CAN'T BELIEVE YOU'D DO WHAT YOU DID. YOU ARE A JERK! DO YOU REMEMBER? YOU'RE SO RUDE, INCONSIDERATE, SELF-CENTERED, IMMATURE, AND FAT! HOW COULD YOU DO IT AFTER ALL THE TIMES I'VE COVERED YOUR BUTT? I'M SICK OF IT. THERE ARE SOME LINES THAT SHOULD NOT BE CROSSED, AND YOU BURNED THAT BRIDGE. YOU'RE A BRIDGE BURNER! YOU'RE A JERK! AND I THOUGHT YOU WERE MY FRIEND. I WANT TO SETTLE THIS NOW! CALL ME WHEN YOU GET THIS, O.K.?
I DON'T EVEN KNOW WHAT I DID!
WHY COULDN'T YOU JUST SAY WHY YOU'RE MAD?!!
NOW I'M GOING TO OBSESS OVER EVERYTHING I'VE SAID AND DONE LATELY.
AND, OF COURSE, YOU WON'T BE HOME WHEN I CALL YOU BACK, SO I'LL HAVE PLENTY OF TIME TO AGONIZE!
PUSH PUSH PUSH PUSH
HI, THIS IS CIGGY. I'M NOT HOME RIGHT NOW. I'M OUT DOING SOMETHING REALLY COOL, UNLIKE YOU. LEAVE A MESSAGE AND I'LL CALL YOU BACK WHEN I FEEL LIKE IT.
BEEP
SEE.
HEY CIGGY, THIS IS TOO MUCH COFFEE MAN. I CAN'T BELIEVE YOU'D DO WHAT YOU DID! YOU'RE A JERK. IT WAS A STUPID, SELFISH THING, AND YOU SHOULD BE ASHAMED OF YOURSELF FOR DOING IT!
NOW LET HIM WONDER.

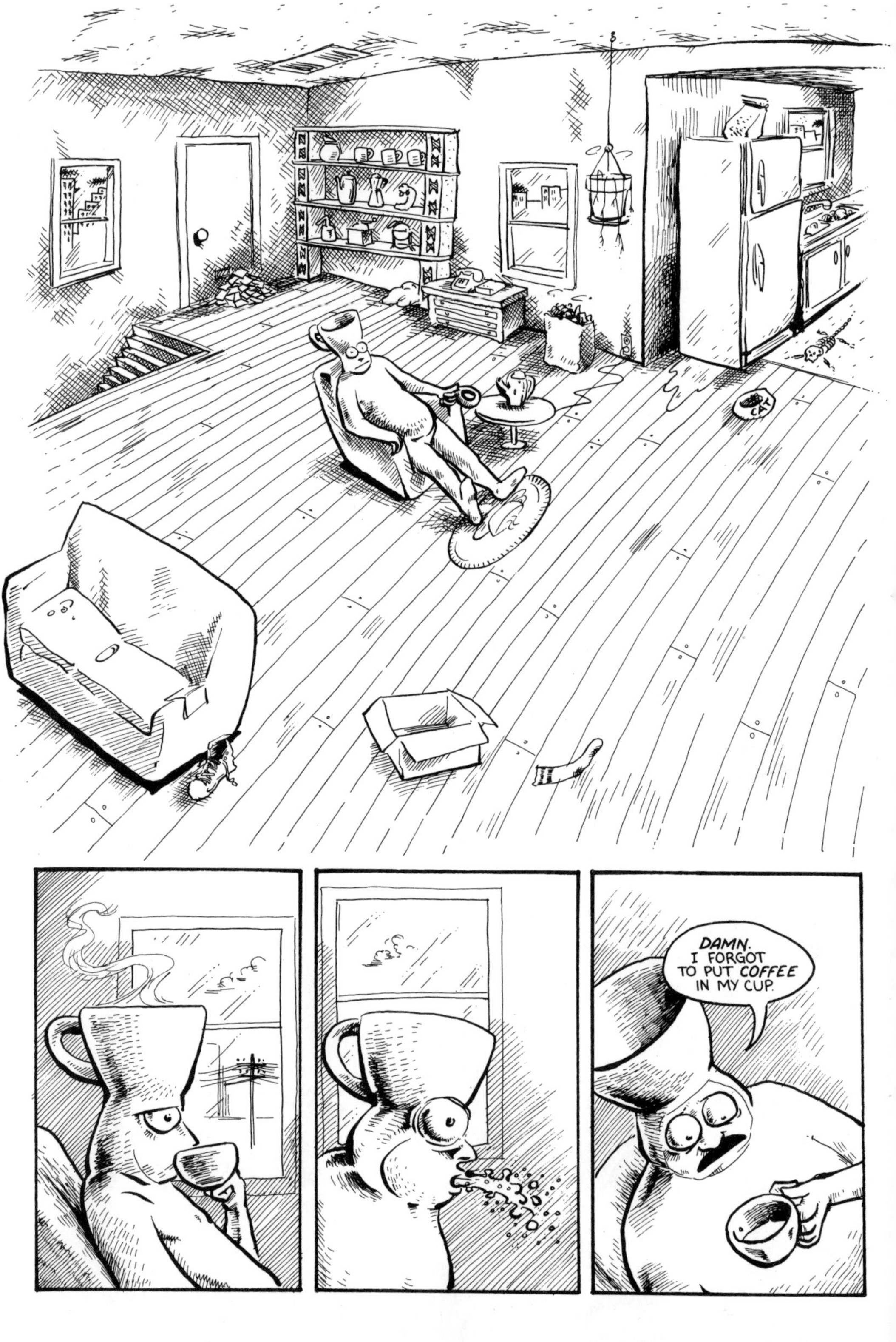
CAT
DAMN. I FORGOT TO PUT COFFEE IN MY CUP.

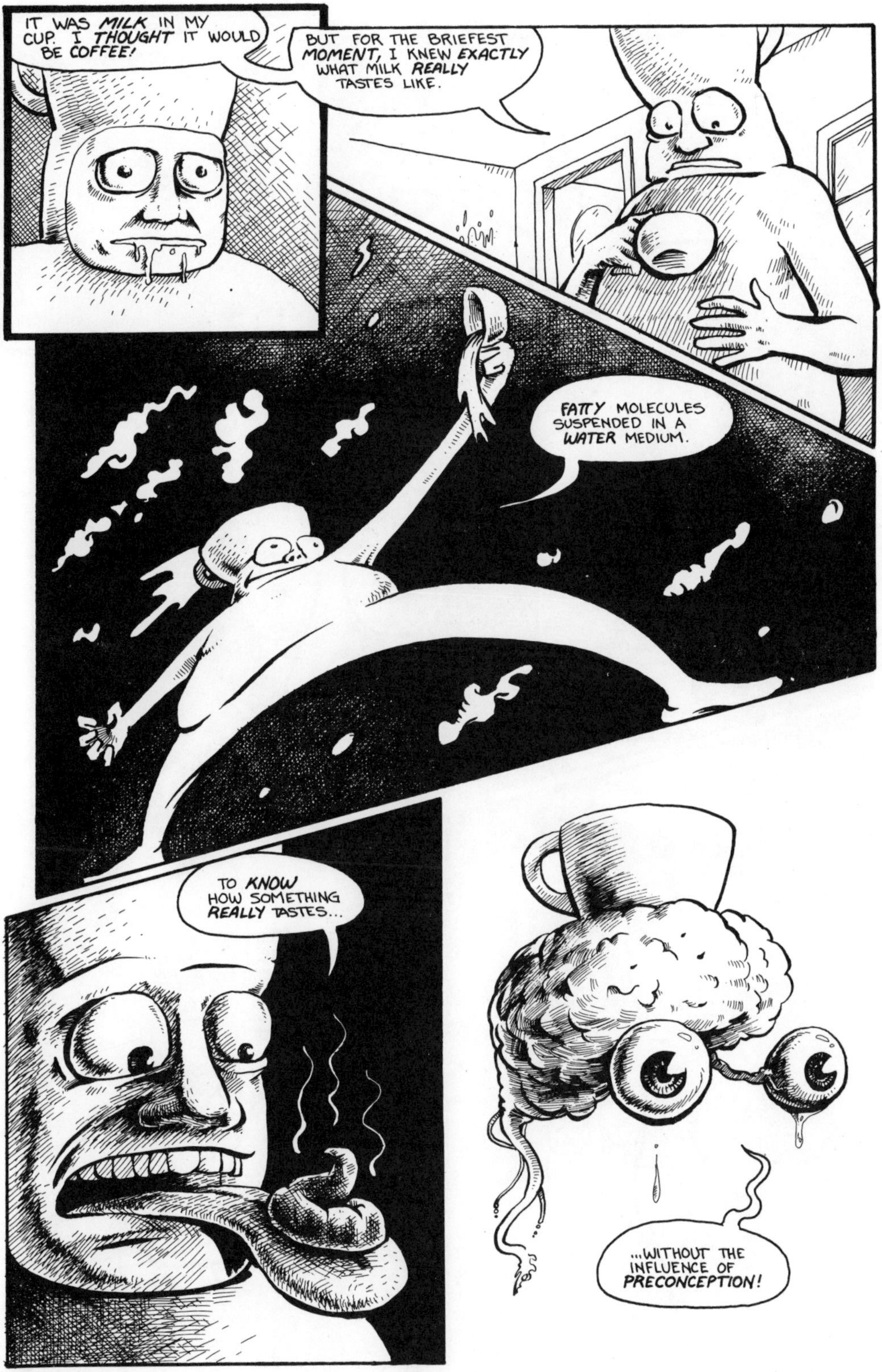
IT WAS MILK IN MY CUP. I THOUGHT IT WOULD BE COFFEE!
BUT FOR THE BRIEFEST MOMENT, I KNEW EXACTLY WHAT MILK REALLY TASTES LIKE.
FATTY MOLECULES SUSPENDED IN A WATER MEDIUM.
TO KNOW HOW SOMETHING REALLY TASTES...
...WITHOUT THE INFLUENCE OF PRECONCEPTION!

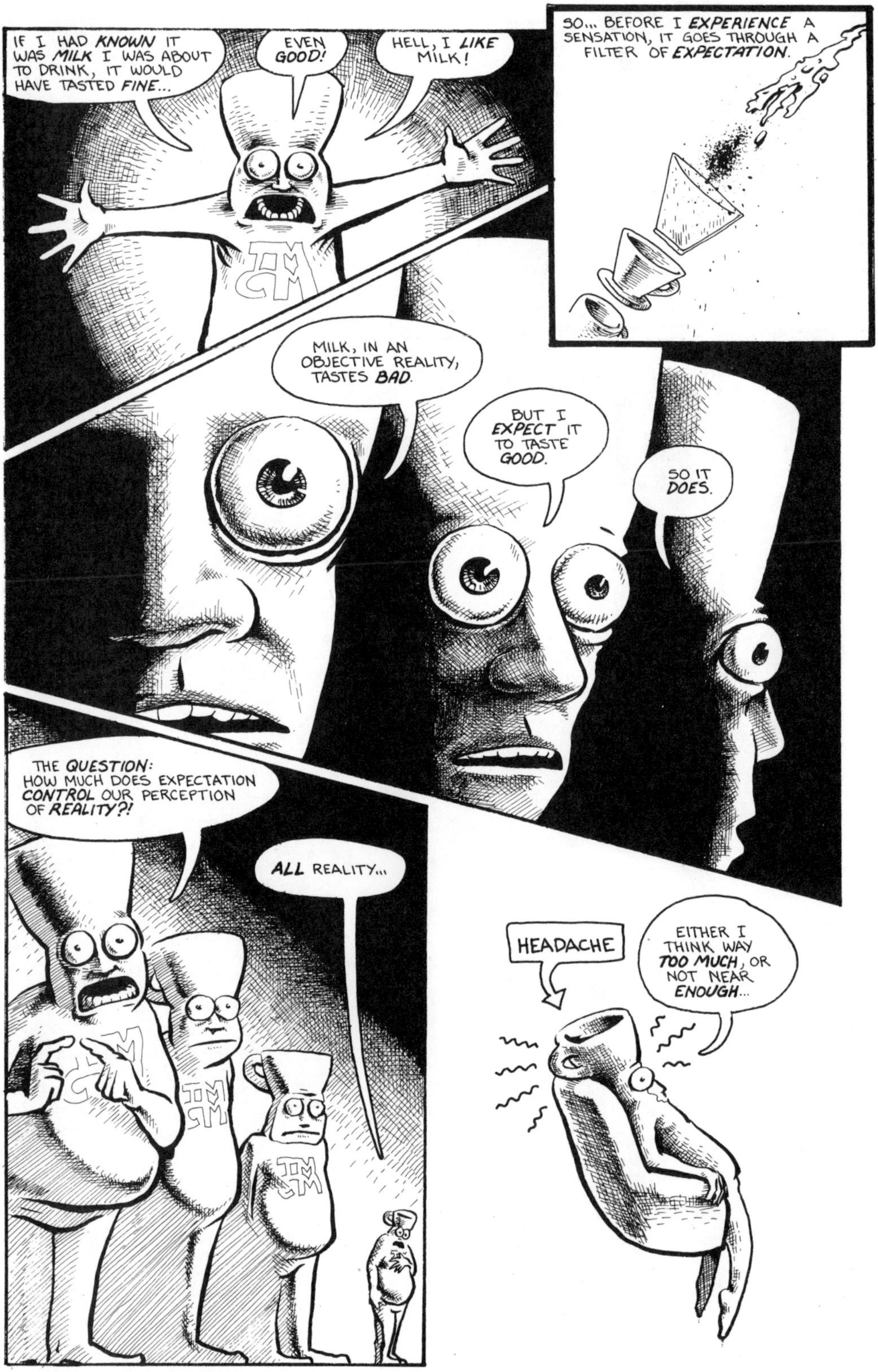
IF I HAD KNOWN IT WAS MILK I WAS ABOUT TO DRINK, IT WOULD HAVE TASTED FINE...
EVEN GOOD!
HELL, I LIKE MILK!
SO... BEFORE I EXPERIENCE A SENSATION, IT GOES THROUGH A FILTER OF EXPECTATION.
MILK, IN AN OBJECTIVE REALITY, TASTES BAD.
BUT I EXPECT IT TO TASTE GOOD.
SO IT DOES.
THE QUESTION: HOW MUCH DOES EXPECTATION CONTROL OUR PERCEPTION OF REALITY?!
ALL REALITY...
HEADACHE
EITHER I THINK WAY TOO MUCH, OR NOT NEAR ENOUGH...

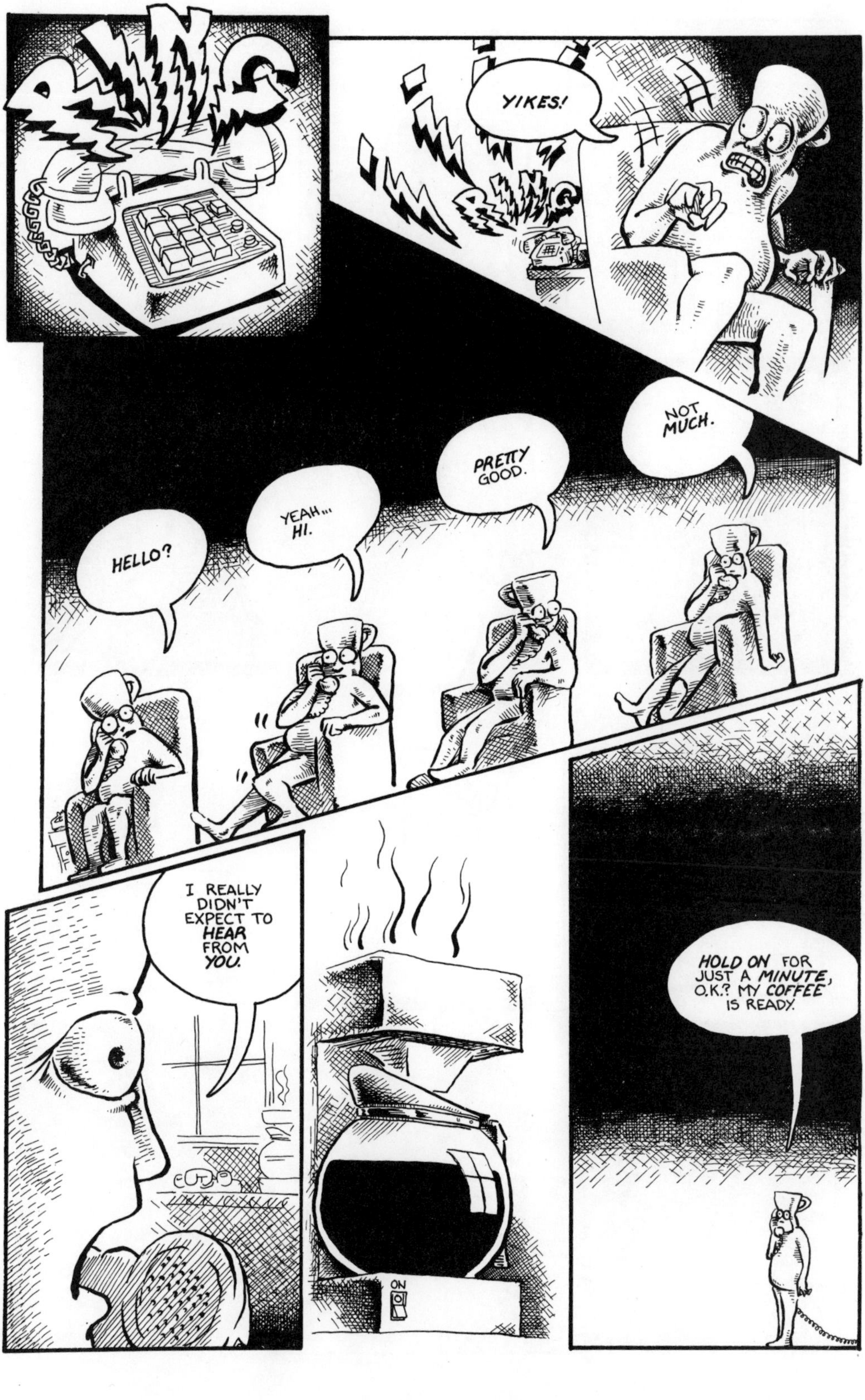
RING
YIKES!
RING
HELLO?
YEAH... HI.
PRETTY GOOD.
NOT MUCH.
I REALLY DIDN'T EXPECT TO HEAR FROM YOU.
ON
HOLD ON FOR JUST A MINUTE, O.K.? MY COFFEE IS READY.

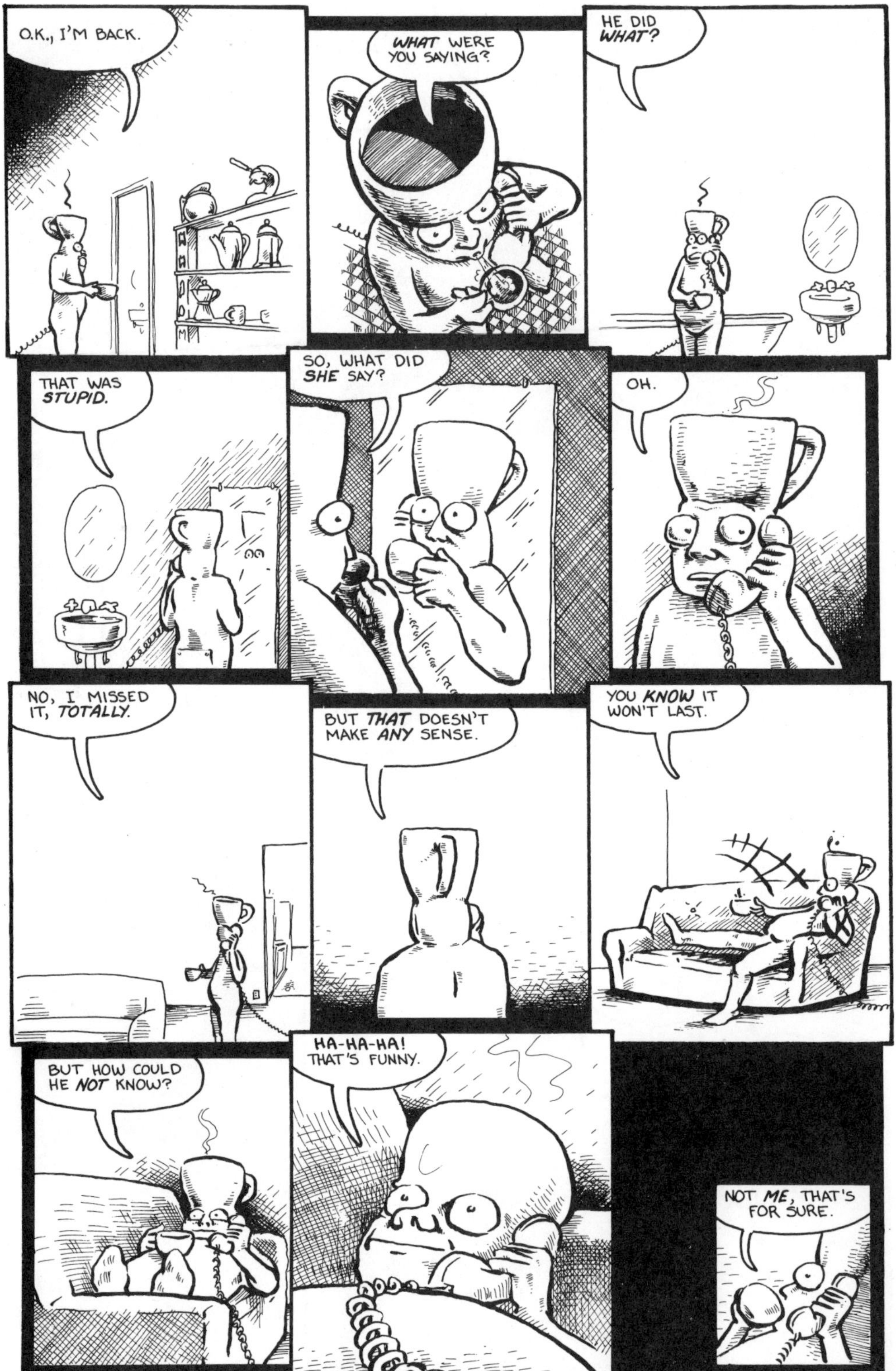
O.K., I'M BACK.
WHAT WERE YOU SAYING?
HE DID WHAT?
THAT WAS STUPID.
SO, WHAT DID SHE SAY?
OH.
NO, I MISSED IT, TOTALLY.
BUT THAT DOESN'T MAKE ANY SENSE.
YOU KNOW IT WON'T LAST.
BUT HOW COULD HE NOT KNOW?
HA-HA-HA! THAT'S FUNNY.
NOT ME, THAT'S FOR SURE.

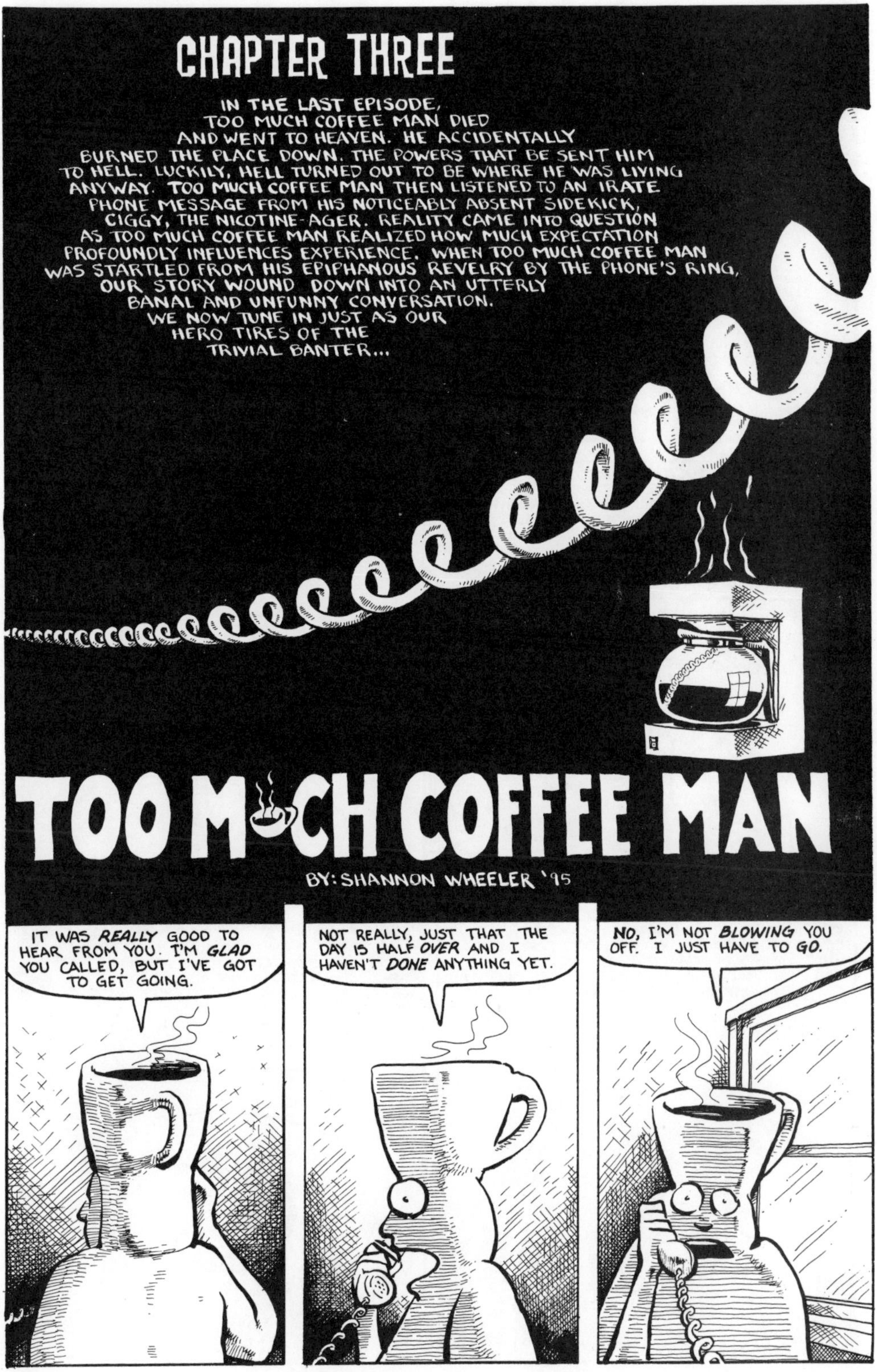
CHAPTER THREE
IN THE LAST EPISODE, TOO MUCH COFFEE MAN DIED AND WENT TO HEAVEN. HE ACCIDENTALLY BURNED THE PLACE DOWN. THE POWERS THAT BE SENT HIM TO HELL. LUCKILY, HELL TURNED OUT TO BE WHERE HE WAS LIVING ANYWAY. TOO MUCH COFFEE MAN THEN LISTENED TO AN IRATE PHONE MESSAGE FROM HIS NOTICEABLY ABSENT SIDEKICK, CIGGY, THE NICOTINE-AGER. REALITY CAME INTO QUESTION AS TOO MUCH COFFEE MAN REALIZED HOW MUCH EXPECTATION PROFOUNDLY INFLUENCES EXPERIENCE. WHEN TOO MUCH COFFEE MAN WAS STARTLED FROM HIS EPIPHANOUS REVELRY BY THE PHONE'S RING, OUR STORY WOUND DOWN INTO AN UTTERLY BANAL AND UNFUNNY CONVERSATION. WE NOW TUNE IN JUST AS OUR HERO TIRES OF THE TRIVIAL BANTER...
TOO MUCH COFFEE MAN
BY: SHANNON WHEELER '95
IT WAS *REALLY* GOOD TO HEAR FROM YOU. I'M *GLAD* YOU CALLED, BUT I'VE GOT TO GET GOING.
NOT REALLY, JUST THAT THE DAY IS HALF *OVER* AND I HAVEN'T *DONE* ANYTHING YET.
NO, I'M NOT *BLOWING* YOU OFF. I JUST HAVE TO *GO*.

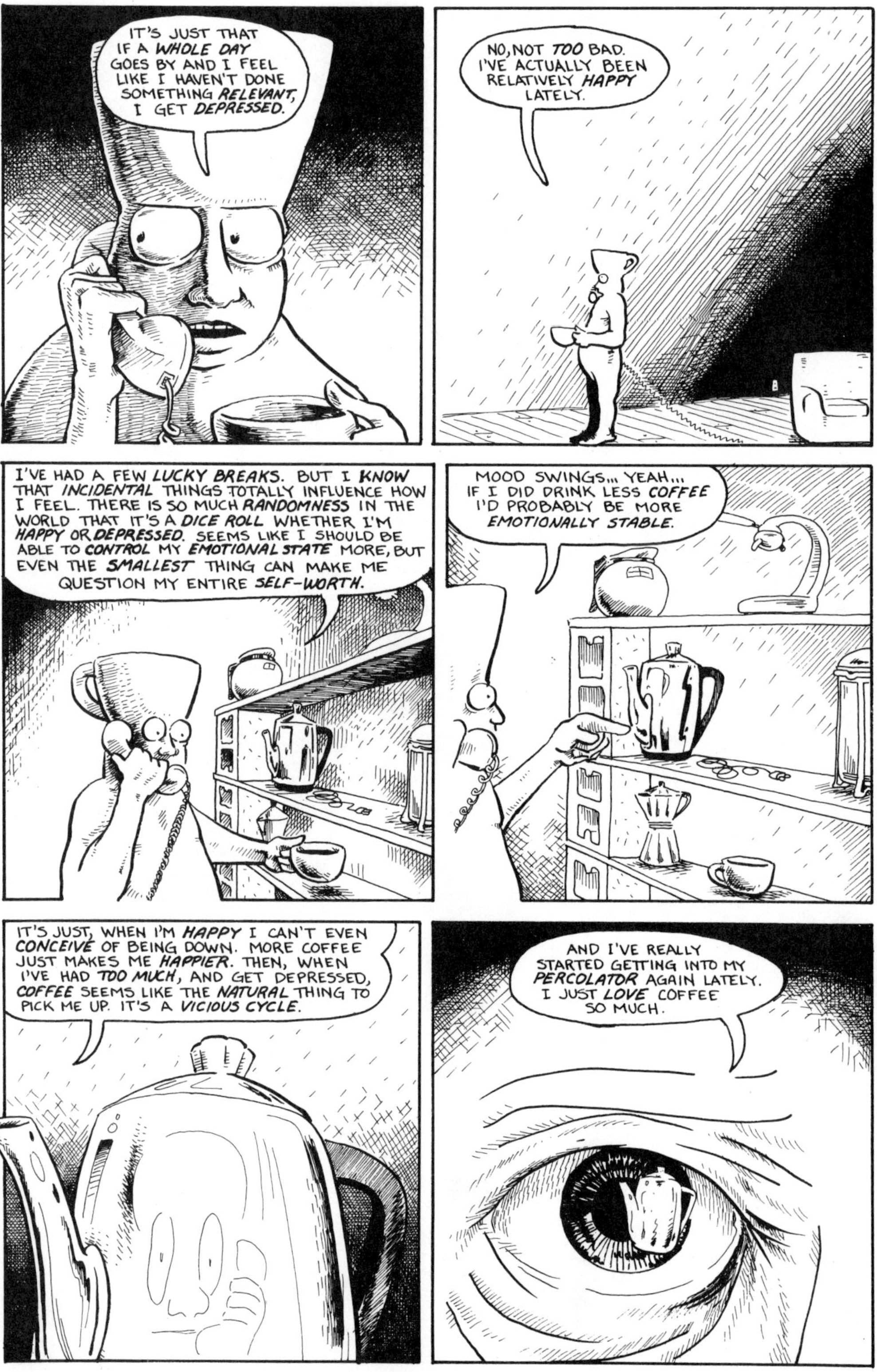
IT'S JUST THAT IF A WHOLE DAY GOES BY AND I FEEL LIKE I HAVEN'T DONE SOMETHING RELEVANT, I GET DEPRESSED.
NO, NOT TOO BAD. I'VE ACTUALLY BEEN RELATIVELY HAPPY LATELY.
I'VE HAD A FEW LUCKY BREAKS. BUT I KNOW THAT INCIDENTAL THINGS TOTALLY INFLUENCE HOW I FEEL. THERE IS SO MUCH RANDOMNESS IN THE WORLD THAT IT'S A DICE ROLL WHETHER I'M HAPPY OR DEPRESSED. SEEMS LIKE I SHOULD BE ABLE TO CONTROL MY EMOTIONAL STATE MORE, BUT EVEN THE SMALLEST THING CAN MAKE ME QUESTION MY ENTIRE SELF-WORTH.
MOOD SWINGS... YEAH... IF I DID DRINK LESS COFFEE I'D PROBABLY BE MORE EMOTIONALLY STABLE.
IT'S JUST, WHEN I'M HAPPY I CAN'T EVEN CONCEIVE OF BEING DOWN. MORE COFFEE JUST MAKES ME HAPPIER. THEN, WHEN I'VE HAD TOO MUCH, AND GET DEPRESSED, COFFEE SEEMS LIKE THE NATURAL THING TO PICK ME UP. IT'S A VICIOUS CYCLE.
AND I'VE REALLY STARTED GETTING INTO MY PERCOLATOR AGAIN LATELY. I JUST LOVE COFFEE SO MUCH.

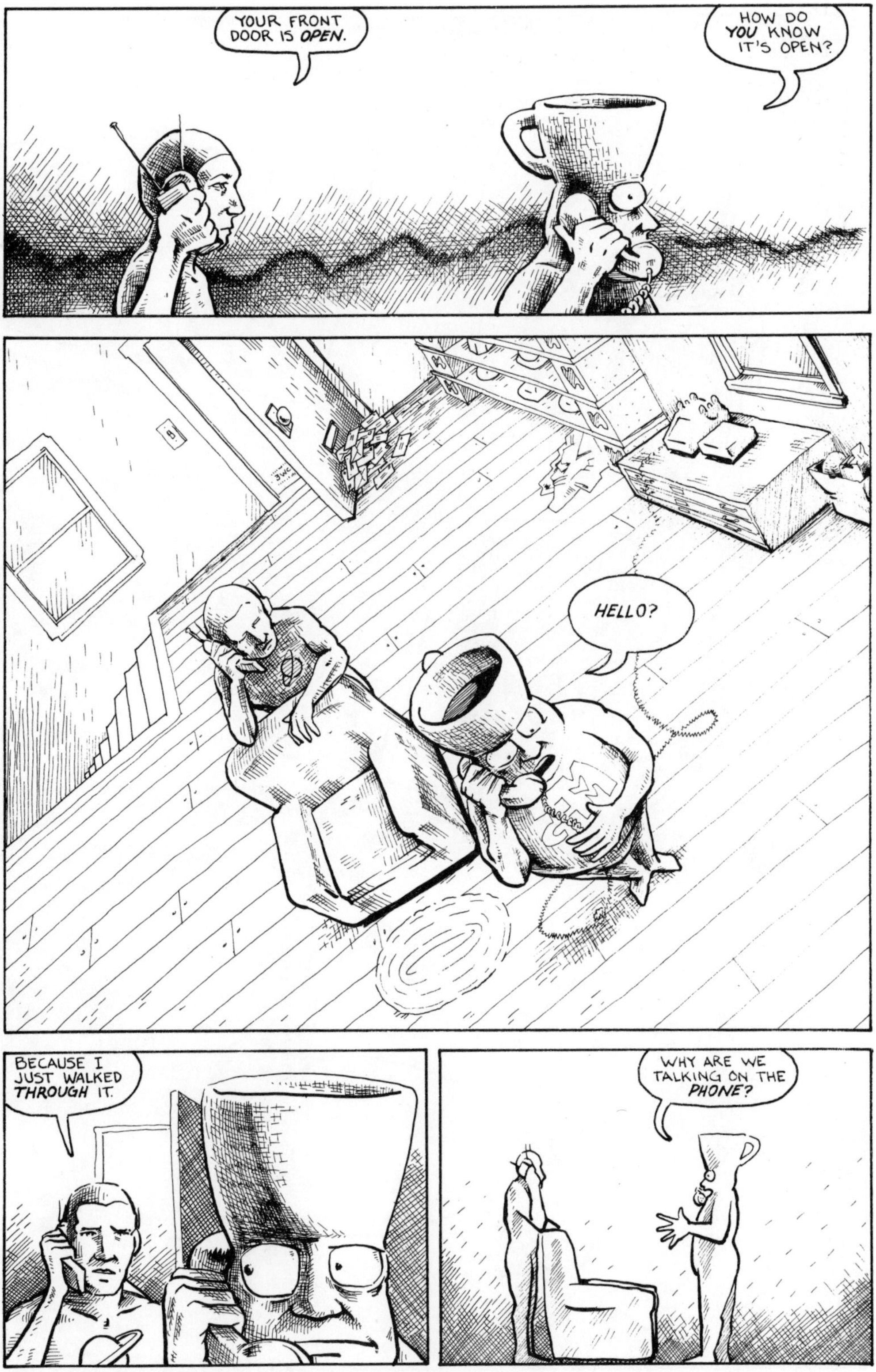
YOUR FRONT DOOR IS OPEN.
HOW DO YOU KNOW IT'S OPEN?
HELLO?
BECAUSE I JUST WALKED THROUGH IT.
WHY ARE WE TALKING ON THE PHONE?

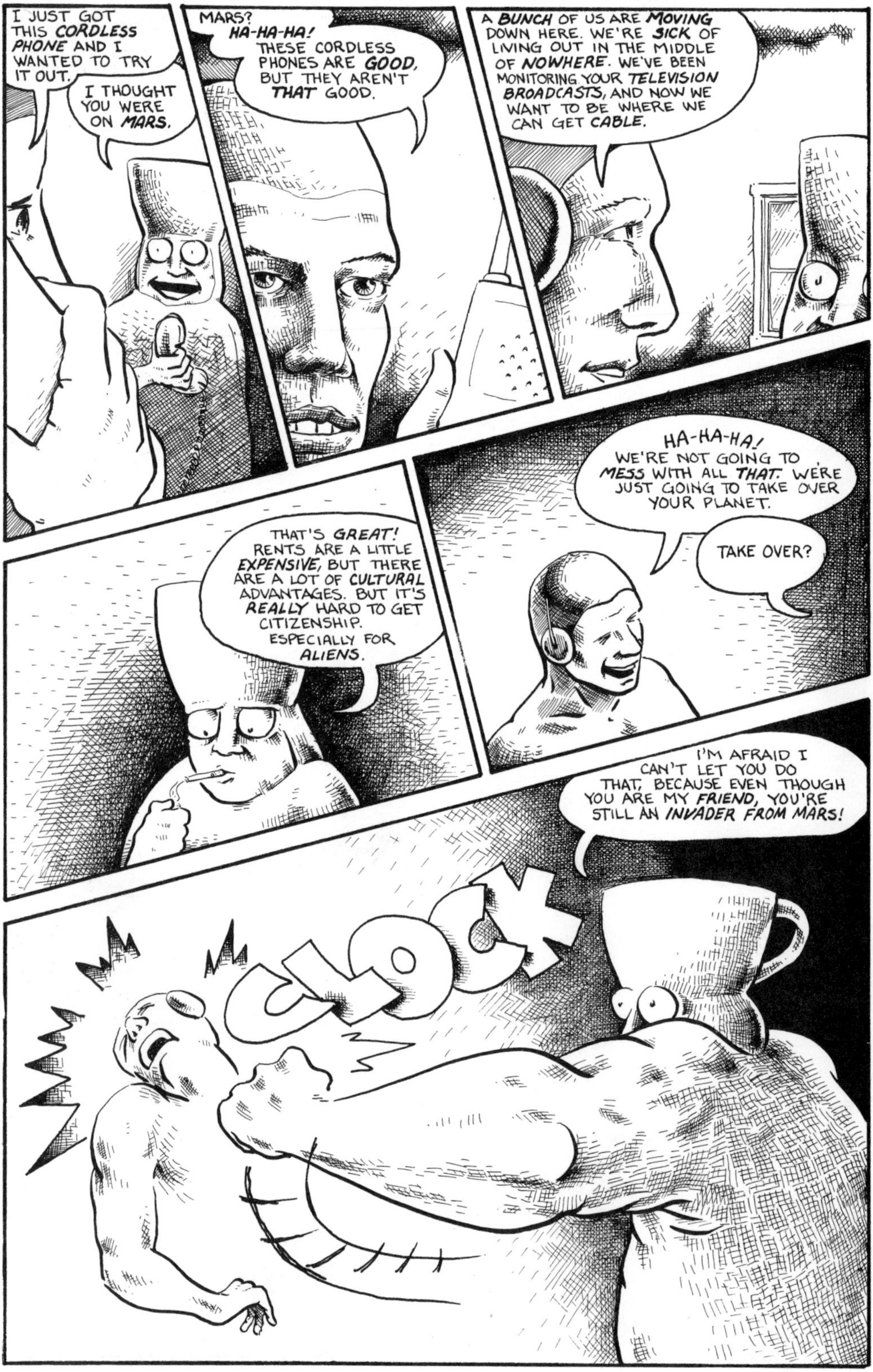
I JUST GOT THIS CORDLESS PHONE AND I WANTED TO TRY IT OUT.
I THOUGHT YOU WERE ON MARS.
MARS? HA-HA-HA! THESE CORDLESS PHONES ARE GOOD, BUT THEY AREN'T THAT GOOD.
A BUNCH OF US ARE MOVING DOWN HERE. WE'RE SICK OF LIVING OUT IN THE MIDDLE OF NOWHERE. WE'VE BEEN MONITORING YOUR TELEVISION BROADCASTS, AND NOW WE WANT TO BE WHERE WE CAN GET CABLE.
THAT'S GREAT! RENTS ARE A LITTLE EXPENSIVE, BUT THERE ARE A LOT OF CULTURAL ADVANTAGES. BUT IT'S REALLY HARD TO GET CITIZENSHIP. ESPECIALLY FOR ALIENS.
HA-HA-HA! WE'RE NOT GOING TO MESS WITH ALL THAT. WE'RE JUST GOING TO TAKE OVER YOUR PLANET.
TAKE OVER?
I'M AFRAID I CAN'T LET YOU DO THAT, BECAUSE EVEN THOUGH YOU ARE MY FRIEND, YOU'RE STILL AN INVADER FROM MARS!
CLOCK

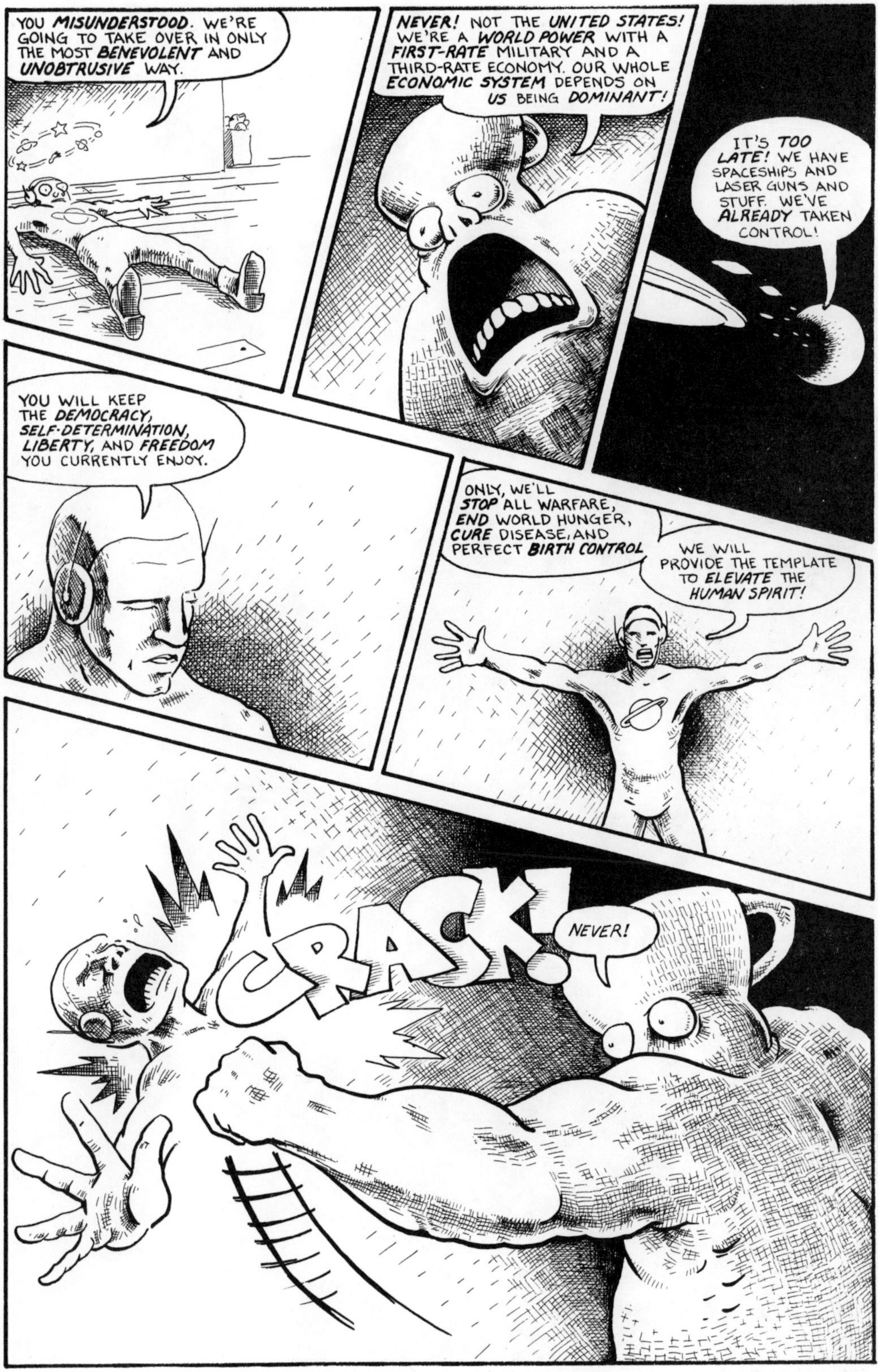
YOU MISUNDERSTOOD. WE'RE GOING TO TAKE OVER IN ONLY THE MOST BENEVOLENT AND UNOBTRUSIVE WAY.
NEVER! NOT THE UNITED STATES! WE'RE A WORLD POWER WITH A FIRST-RATE MILITARY AND A THIRD-RATE ECONOMY. OUR WHOLE ECONOMIC SYSTEM DEPENDS ON US BEING DOMINANT!
IT'S TOO LATE! WE HAVE SPACESHIPS AND LASER GUNS AND STUFF. WE'VE ALREADY TAKEN CONTROL!
YOU WILL KEEP THE DEMOCRACY, SELF-DETERMINATION, LIBERTY, AND FREEDOM YOU CURRENTLY ENJOY.
ONLY, WE'LL STOP ALL WARFARE, END WORLD HUNGER, CURE DISEASE, AND PERFECT BIRTH CONTROL
WE WILL PROVIDE THE TEMPLATE TO ELEVATE THE HUMAN SPIRIT!
CRACK!
NEVER!

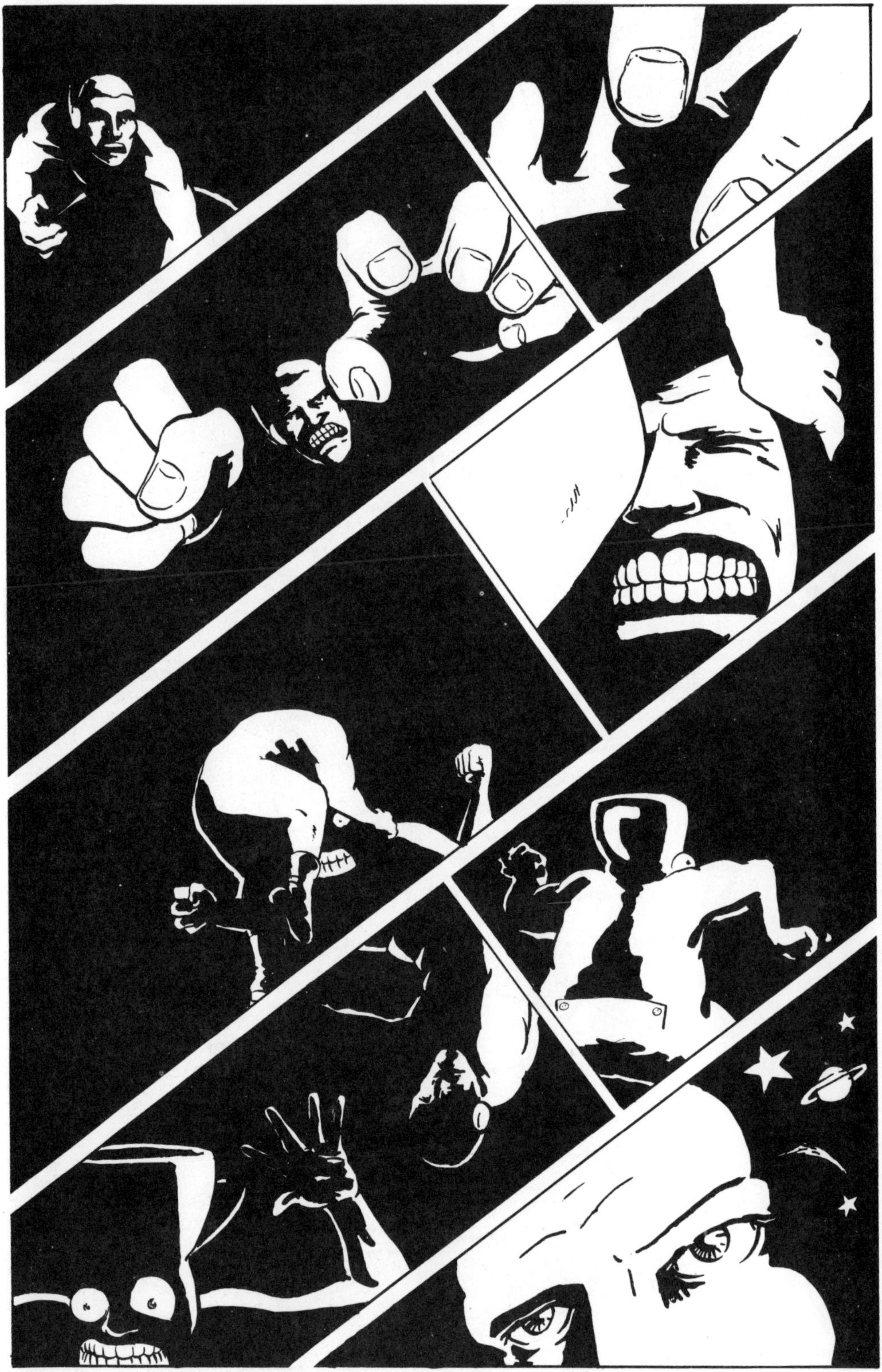

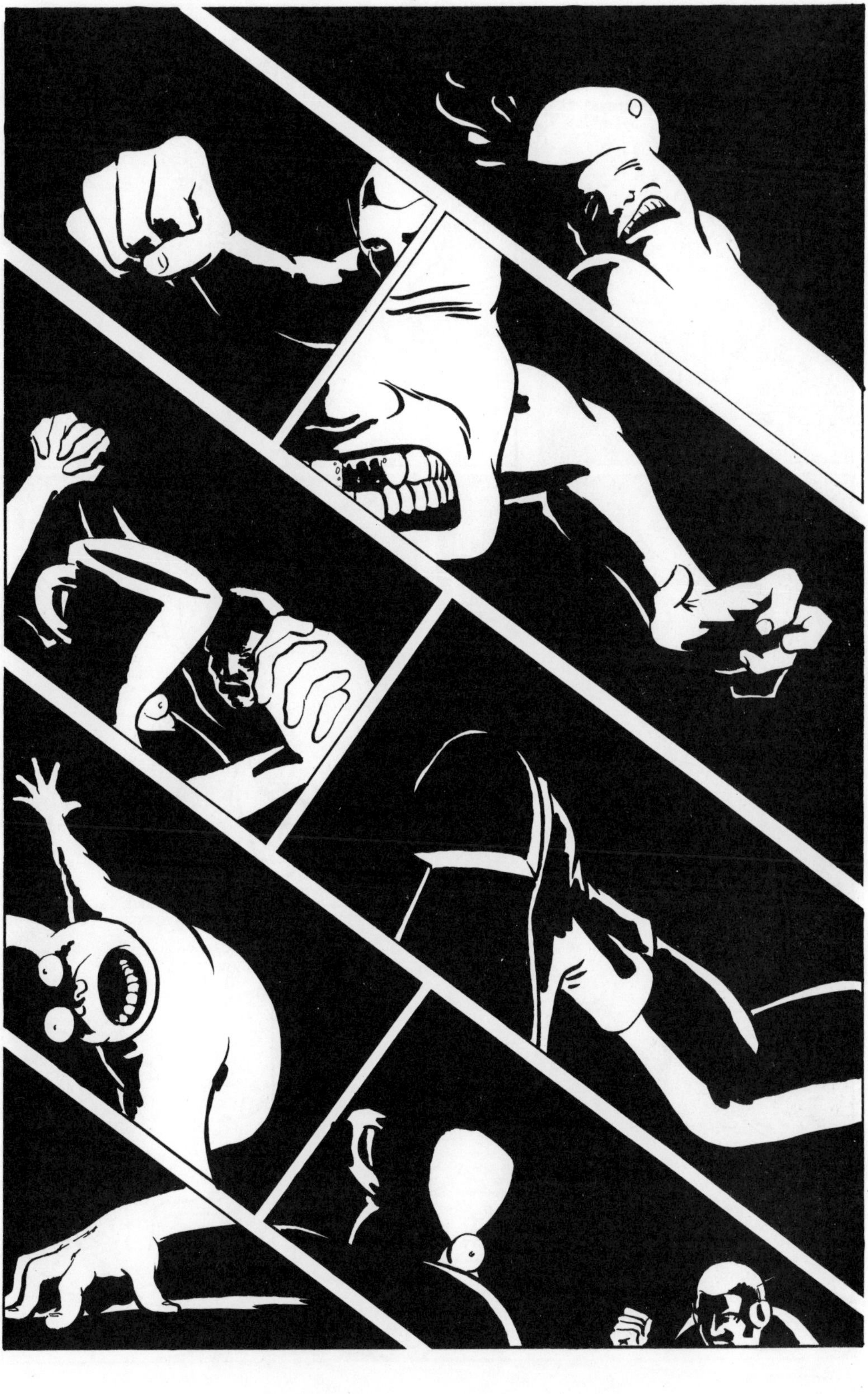

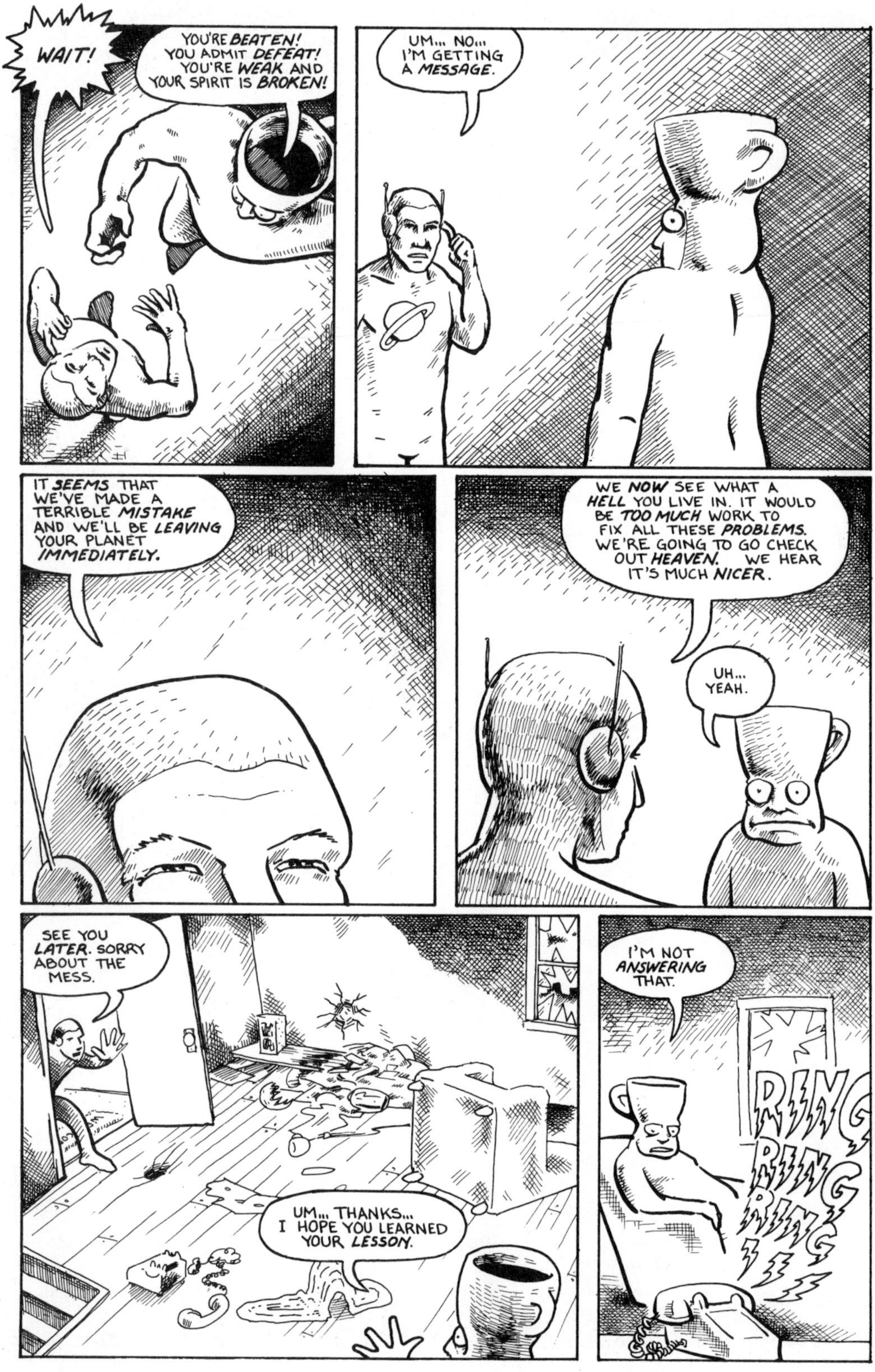
WAIT!
YOU'RE BEATEN! YOU ADMIT DEFEAT! YOU'RE WEAK AND YOUR SPIRIT IS BROKEN!
UM... NO... I'M GETTING A MESSAGE.
IT SEEMS THAT WE'VE MADE A TERRIBLE MISTAKE AND WE'LL BE LEAVING YOUR PLANET IMMEDIATELY.
WE NOW SEE WHAT A HELL YOU LIVE IN. IT WOULD BE TOO MUCH WORK TO FIX ALL THESE PROBLEMS. WE'RE GOING TO GO CHECK OUT HEAVEN. WE HEAR IT'S MUCH NICER.
UH... YEAH.
SEE YOU LATER. SORRY ABOUT THE MESS.
UM... THANKS... I HOPE YOU LEARNED YOUR LESSON.
I'M NOT ANSWERING THAT.
RING
RING
RING

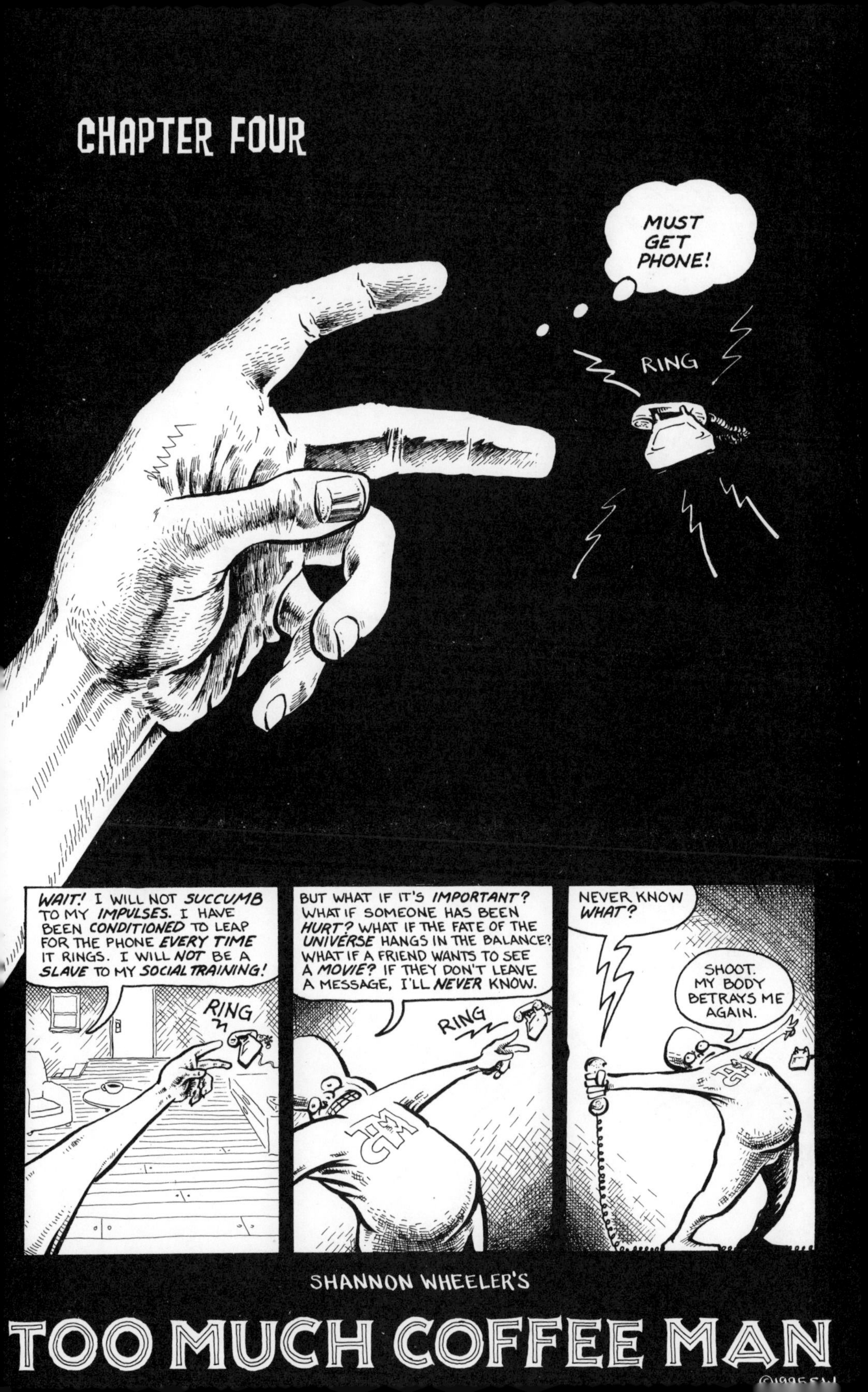
CHAPTER FOUR
MUST GET PHONE!
RING
WAIT! I WILL NOT SUCCUMB TO MY IMPULSES. I HAVE BEEN CONDITIONED TO LEAP FOR THE PHONE EVERY TIME IT RINGS. I WILL NOT BE A SLAVE TO MY SOCIAL TRAINING!
RING
BUT WHAT IF IT'S IMPORTANT? WHAT IF SOMEONE HAS BEEN HURT? WHAT IF THE FATE OF THE UNIVERSE HANGS IN THE BALANCE? WHAT IF A FRIEND WANTS TO SEE A MOVIE? IF THEY DON'T LEAVE A MESSAGE, I'LL NEVER KNOW.
RING
NEVER KNOW WHAT?
SHOOT. MY BODY BETRAYS ME AGAIN.
SHANNON WHEELER'S
TOO MUCH COFFEE MAN

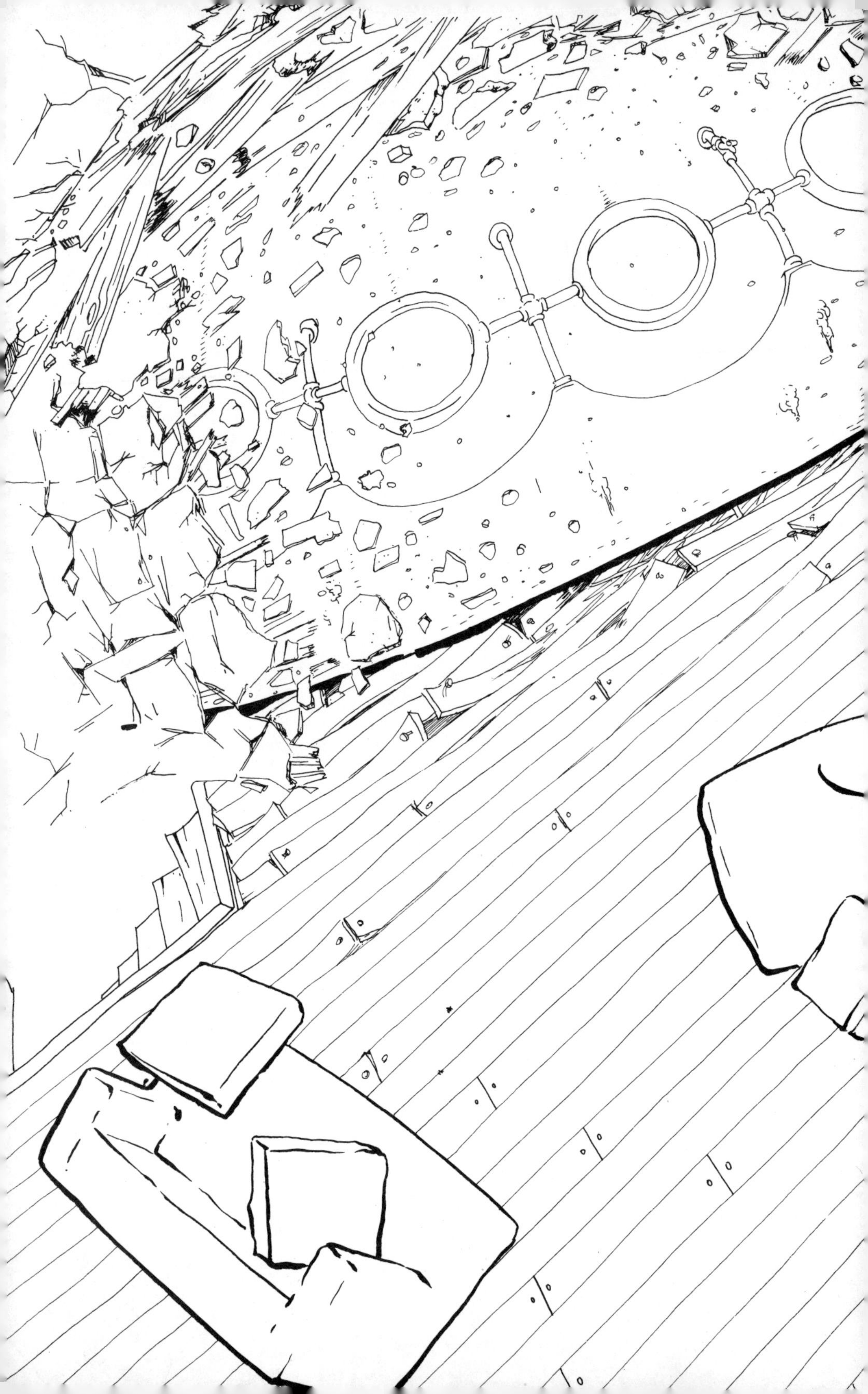

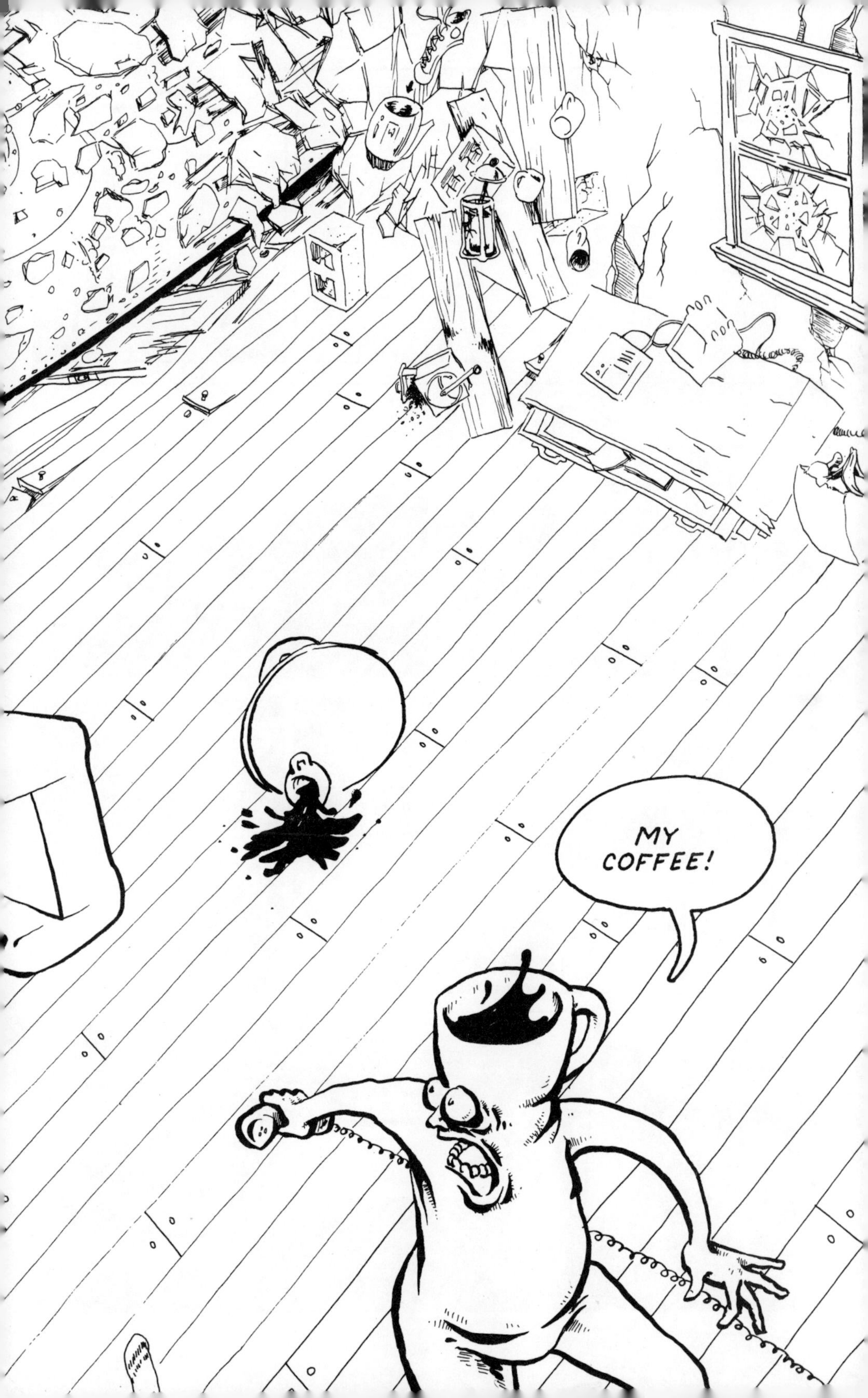
MY COFFEE!

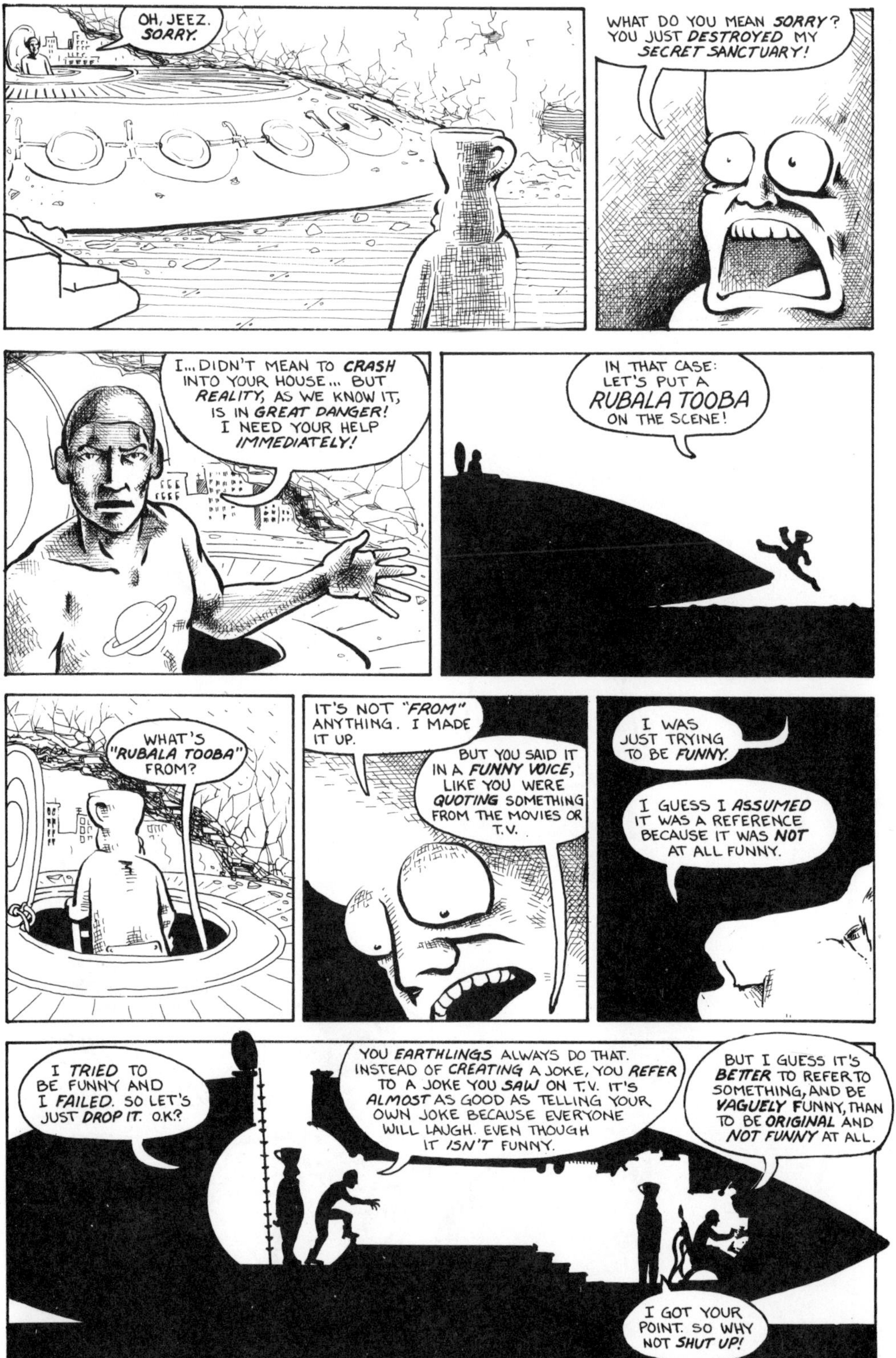

OH, JEEZ. SORRY.
WHAT DO YOU MEAN SORRY? YOU JUST DESTROYED MY SECRET SANCTUARY!
I... DIDN'T MEAN TO CRASH INTO YOUR HOUSE... BUT REALITY, AS WE KNOW IT, IS IN GREAT DANGER! I NEED YOUR HELP IMMEDIATELY!
IN THAT CASE: LET'S PUT A RUBALA TOOBA ON THE SCENE!
WHAT'S "RUBALA TOOBA" FROM?
IT'S NOT "FROM" ANYTHING. I MADE IT UP.
BUT YOU SAID IT IN A FUNNY VOICE, LIKE YOU WERE QUOTING SOMETHING FROM THE MOVIES OR T.V.
I WAS JUST TRYING TO BE FUNNY.
I GUESS I ASSUMED IT WAS A REFERENCE BECAUSE IT WAS NOT AT ALL FUNNY.
I TRIED TO BE FUNNY AND I FAILED. SO LET'S JUST DROP IT. O.K.?
YOU EARTHLINGS ALWAYS DO THAT. INSTEAD OF CREATING A JOKE, YOU REFER TO A JOKE YOU SAW ON T.V. IT'S ALMOST AS GOOD AS TELLING YOUR OWN JOKE BECAUSE EVERYONE WILL LAUGH. EVEN THOUGH IT ISN'T FUNNY.
BUT I GUESS IT'S BETTER TO REFER TO SOMETHING, AND BE VAGUELY FUNNY, THAN TO BE ORIGINAL AND NOT FUNNY AT ALL.
I GOT YOUR POINT. SO WHY NOT SHUT UP!

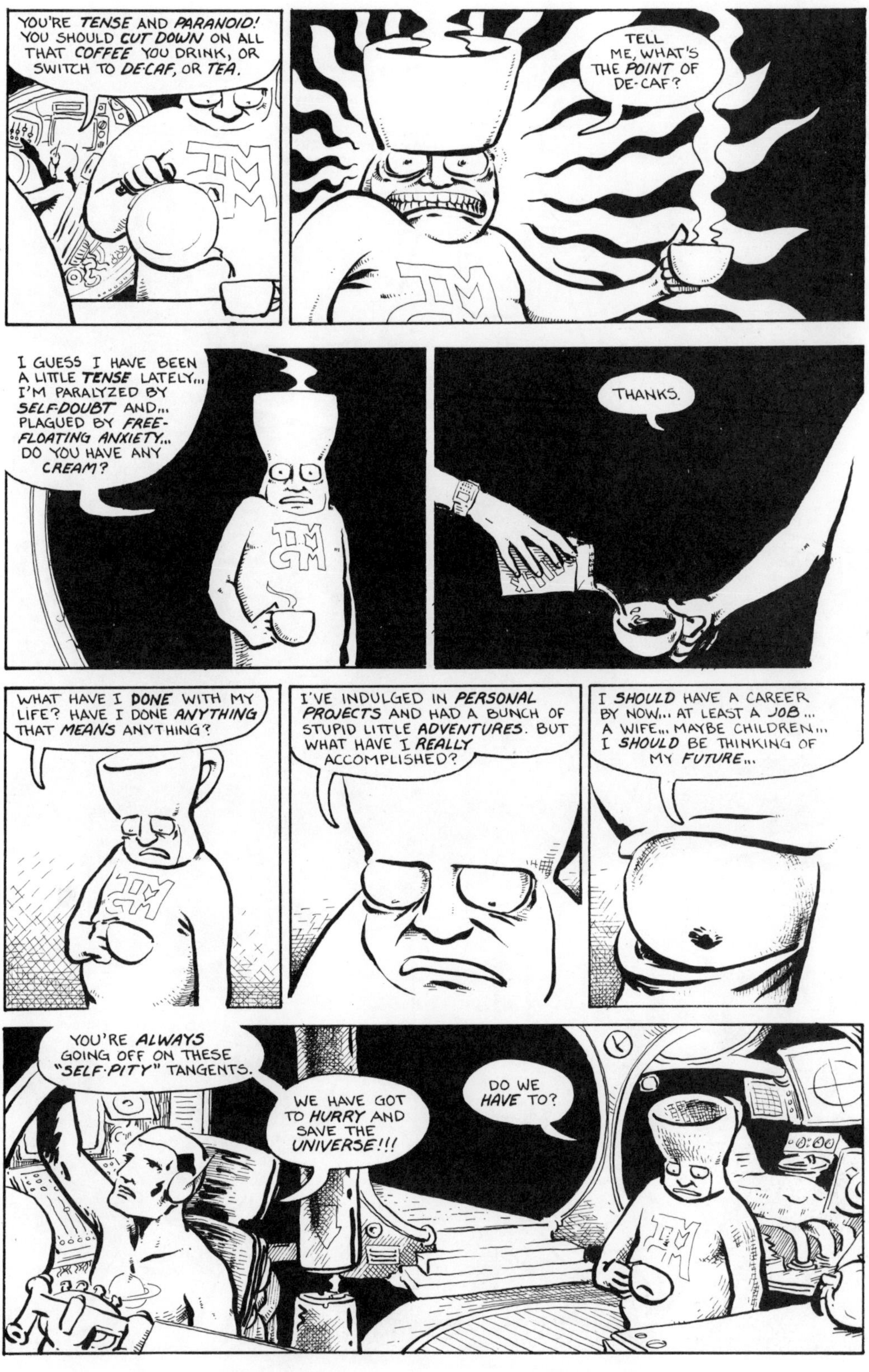
YOU'RE TENSE AND PARANOID! YOU SHOULD CUT DOWN ON ALL THAT COFFEE YOU DRINK, OR SWITCH TO DE-CAF, OR TEA.
TELL ME, WHAT'S THE POINT OF DE-CAF?
I GUESS I HAVE BEEN A LITTLE TENSE LATELY... I'M PARALYZED BY SELF-DOUBT AND... PLAGUED BY FREE-FLOATING ANXIETY... DO YOU HAVE ANY CREAM?
THANKS.
WHAT HAVE I DONE WITH MY LIFE? HAVE I DONE ANYTHING THAT MEANS ANYTHING?
I'VE INDULGED IN PERSONAL PROJECTS AND HAD A BUNCH OF STUPID LITTLE ADVENTURES. BUT WHAT HAVE I REALLY ACCOMPLISHED?
I SHOULD HAVE A CAREER BY NOW... AT LEAST A JOB... A WIFE... MAYBE CHILDREN... I SHOULD BE THINKING OF MY FUTURE...
YOU'RE ALWAYS GOING OFF ON THESE "SELF-PITY" TANGENTS.
WE HAVE GOT TO HURRY AND SAVE THE UNIVERSE!!!
DO WE HAVE TO?

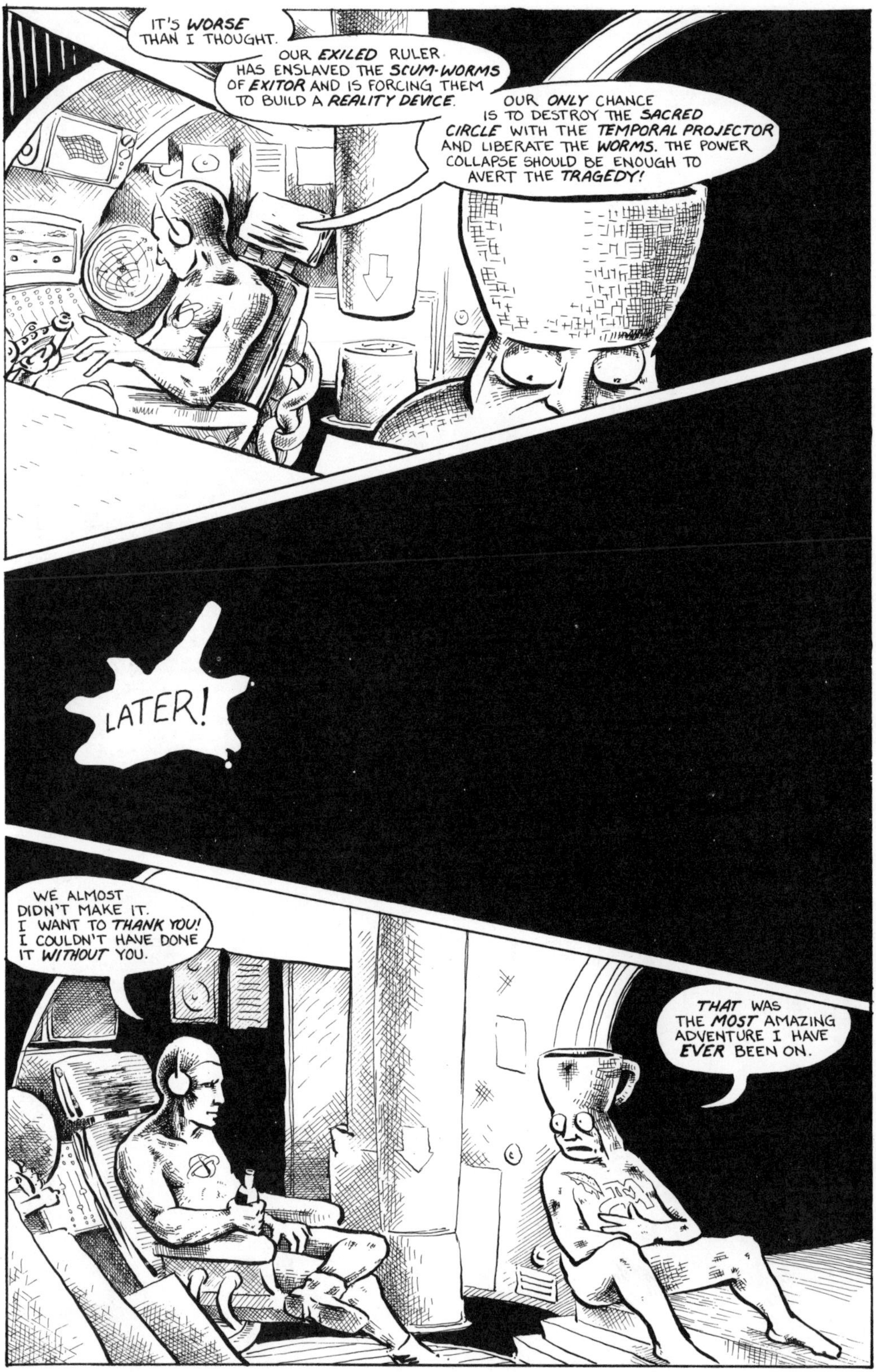
IT'S WORSE THAN I THOUGHT.
OUR EXILED RULER HAS ENSLAVED THE SCUM-WORMS OF EXITOR AND IS FORCING THEM TO BUILD A REALITY DEVICE.
OUR ONLY CHANCE IS TO DESTROY THE SACRED CIRCLE WITH THE TEMPORAL PROJECTOR AND LIBERATE THE WORMS. THE POWER COLLAPSE SHOULD BE ENOUGH TO AVERT THE TRAGEDY!
LATER!
WE ALMOST DIDN'T MAKE IT. I WANT TO THANK YOU! I COULDN'T HAVE DONE IT WITHOUT YOU.
THAT WAS THE MOST AMAZING ADVENTURE I HAVE EVER BEEN ON.

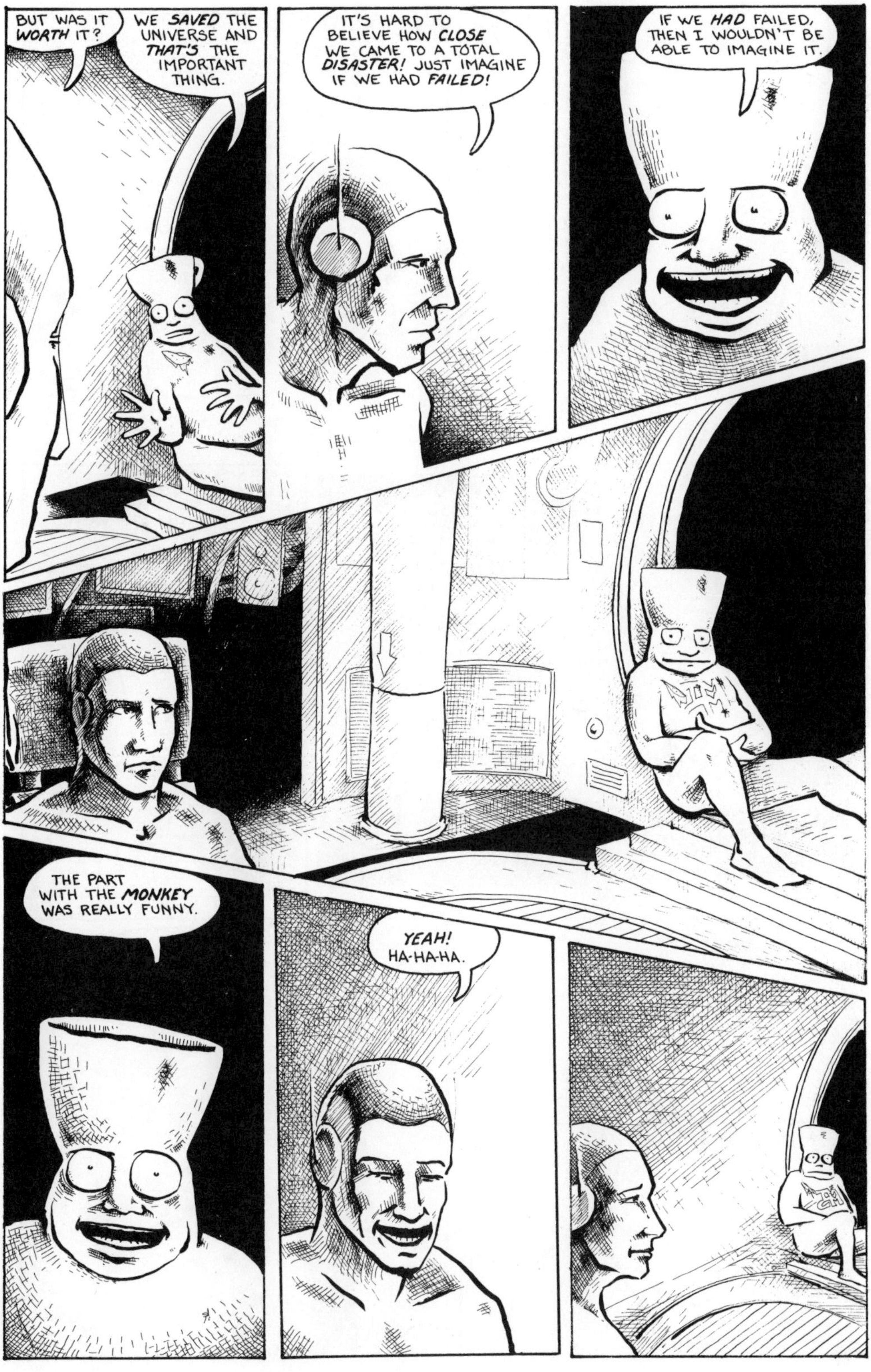

BUT WAS IT WORTH IT?
WE SAVED THE UNIVERSE AND THAT'S THE IMPORTANT THING.
IT'S HARD TO BELIEVE HOW CLOSE WE CAME TO A TOTAL DISASTER! JUST IMAGINE IF WE HAD FAILED!
IF WE HAD FAILED, THEN I WOULDN'T BE ABLE TO IMAGINE IT.
THE PART WITH THE MONKEY WAS REALLY FUNNY.
YEAH! HA-HA-HA.

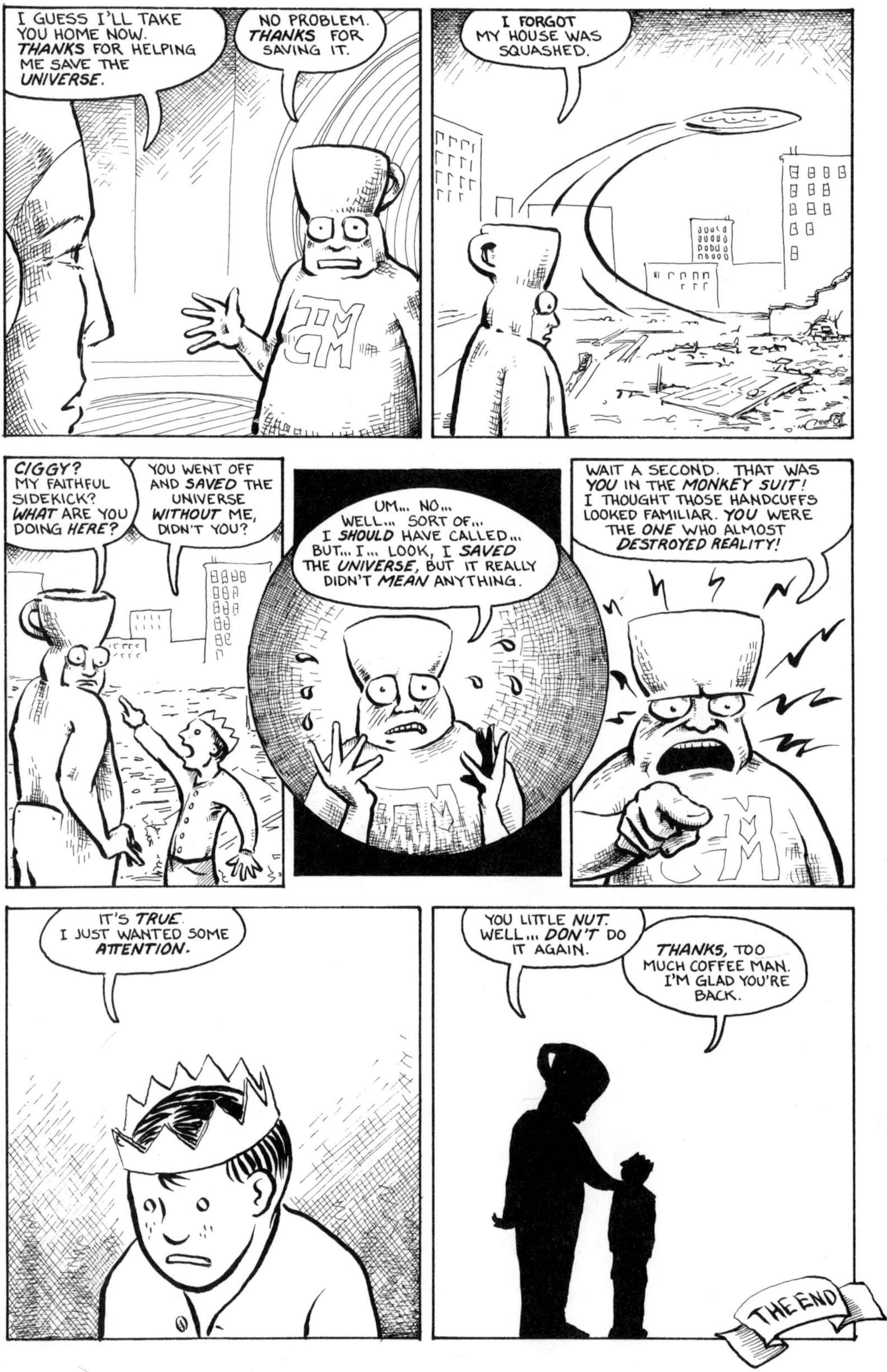
I GUESS I'LL TAKE YOU HOME NOW. THANKS FOR HELPING ME SAVE THE UNIVERSE.
NO PROBLEM. THANKS FOR SAVING IT.
I FORGOT MY HOUSE WAS SQUASHED.
CIGGY? MY FAITHFUL SIDEKICK? WHAT ARE YOU DOING HERE?
YOU WENT OFF AND SAVED THE UNIVERSE WITHOUT ME, DIDN'T YOU?
UM... NO... WELL... SORT OF... I SHOULD HAVE CALLED... BUT... I... LOOK, I SAVED THE UNIVERSE, BUT IT REALLY DIDN'T MEAN ANYTHING.
WAIT A SECOND. THAT WAS YOU IN THE MONKEY SUIT! I THOUGHT THOSE HANDCUFFS LOOKED FAMILIAR. YOU WERE THE ONE WHO ALMOST DESTROYED REALITY!
IT'S TRUE. I JUST WANTED SOME ATTENTION.
YOU LITTLE NUT. WELL... DON'T DO IT AGAIN.
THANKS, TOO MUCH COFFEE MAN. I'M GLAD YOU'RE BACK.
THE END

BULLET HOLE STORY

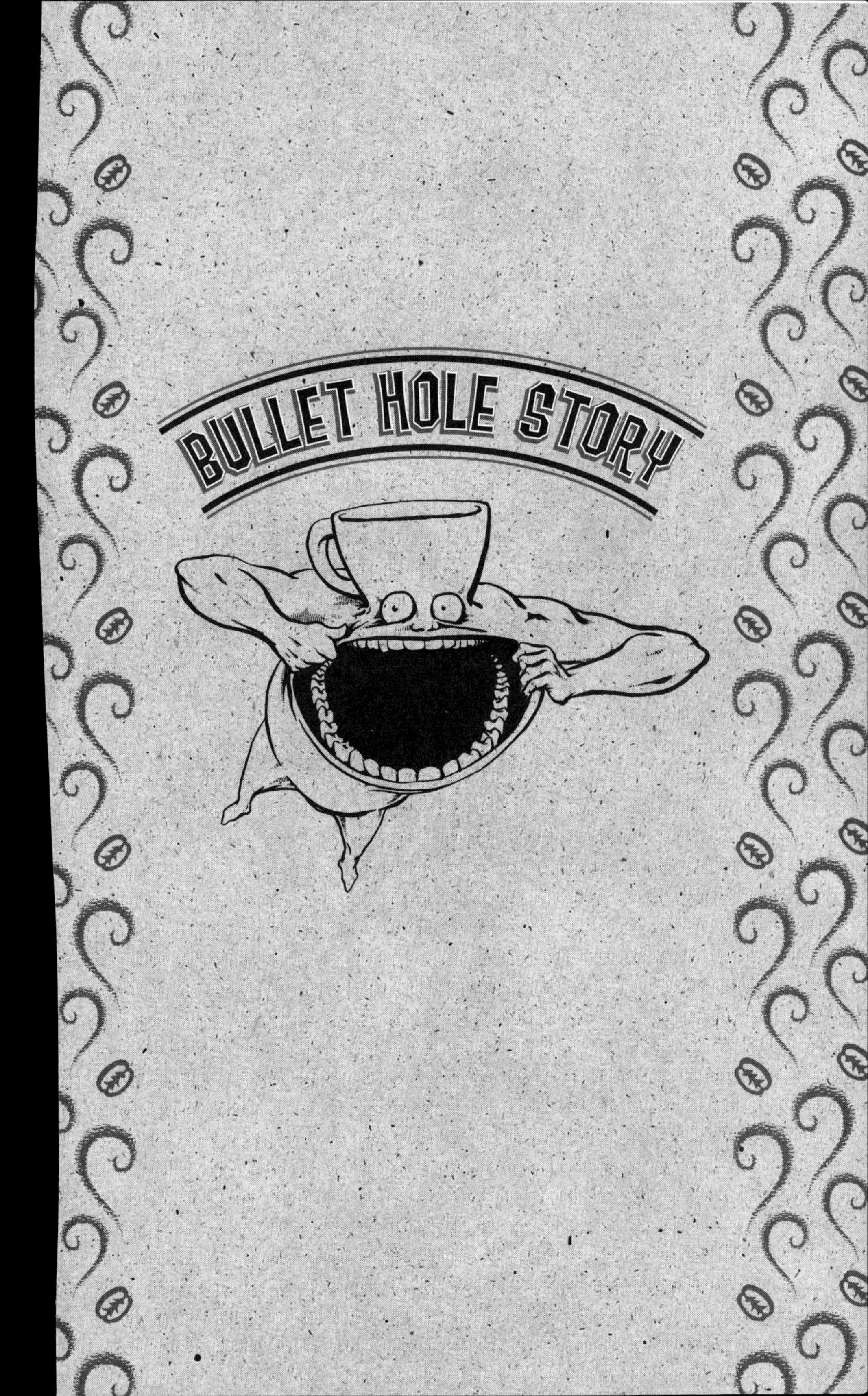

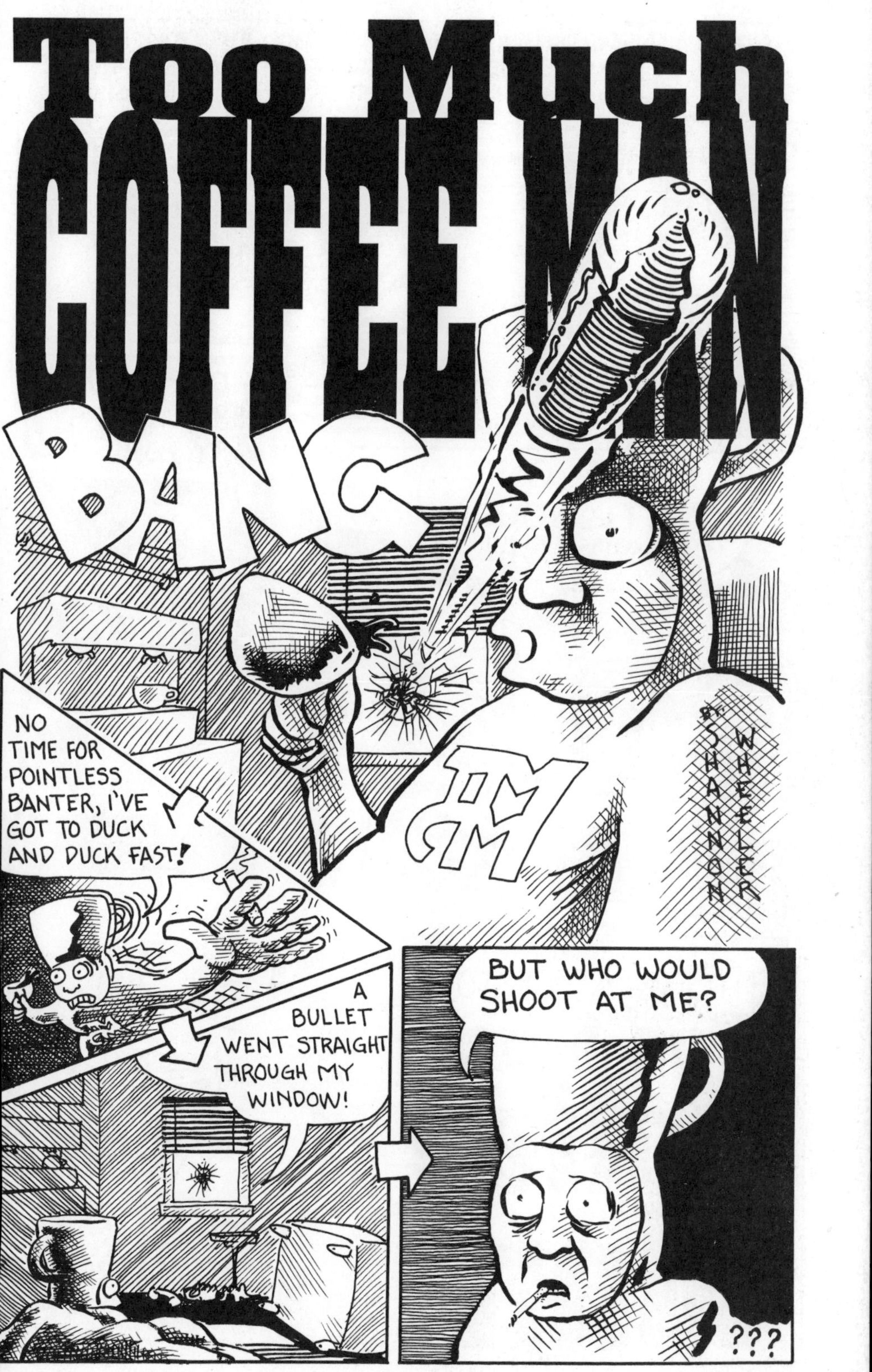

Too Much
COFFEE MAN
BANG
BY SHANNON WHEELER
NO TIME FOR POINTLESS BANTER, I'VE GOT TO DUCK AND DUCK FAST!
A BULLET WENT STRAIGHT THROUGH MY WINDOW!
BUT WHO WOULD SHOOT AT ME?
???

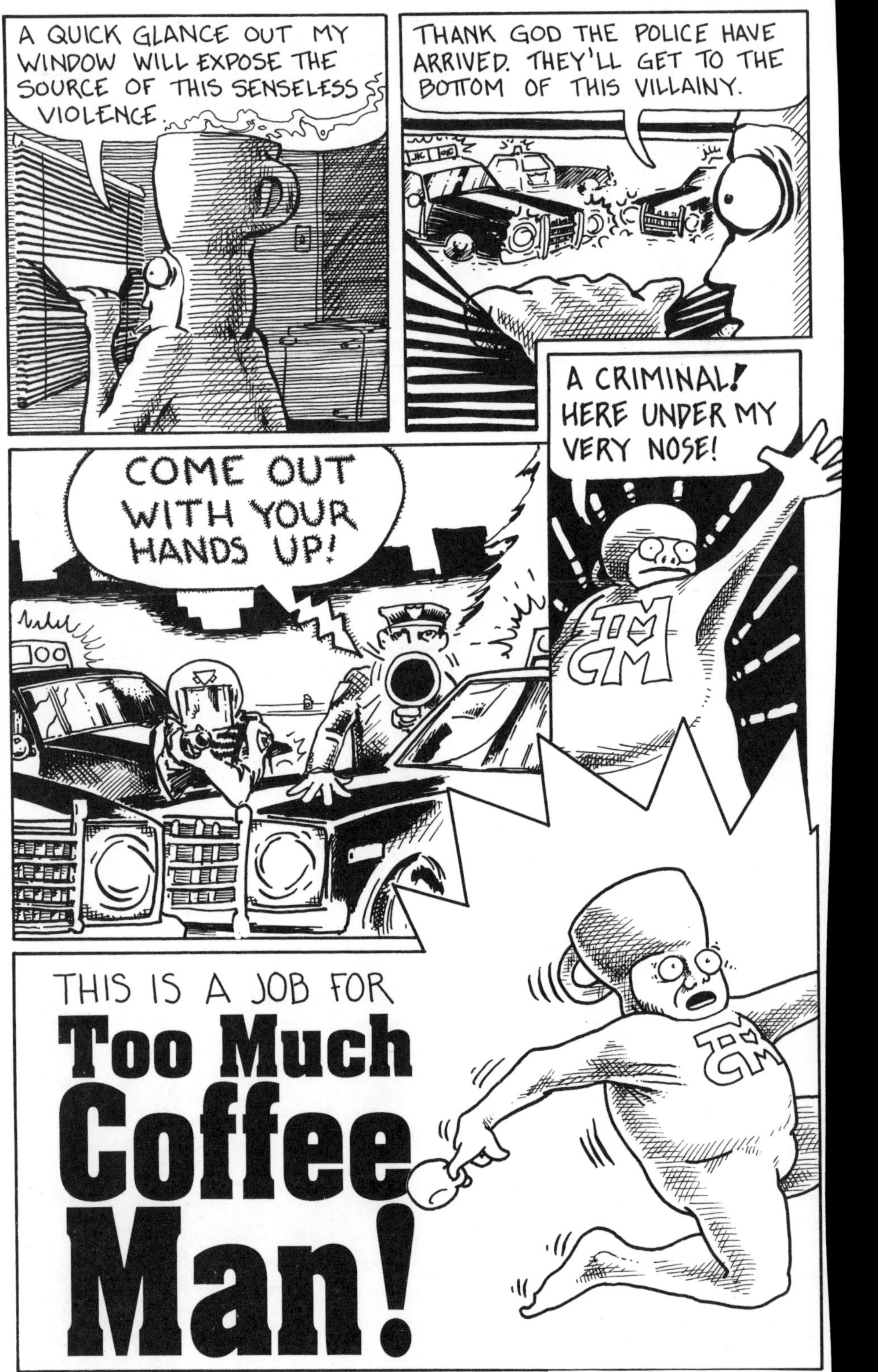
A QUICK GLANCE OUT MY WINDOW WILL EXPOSE THE SOURCE OF THIS SENSELESS VIOLENCE.
THANK GOD THE POLICE HAVE ARRIVED. THEY'LL GET TO THE BOTTOM OF THIS VILLAINY.
A CRIMINAL! HERE UNDER MY VERY NOSE!
COME OUT WITH YOUR HANDS UP!
THIS IS A JOB FOR
Too Much Coffee Man!

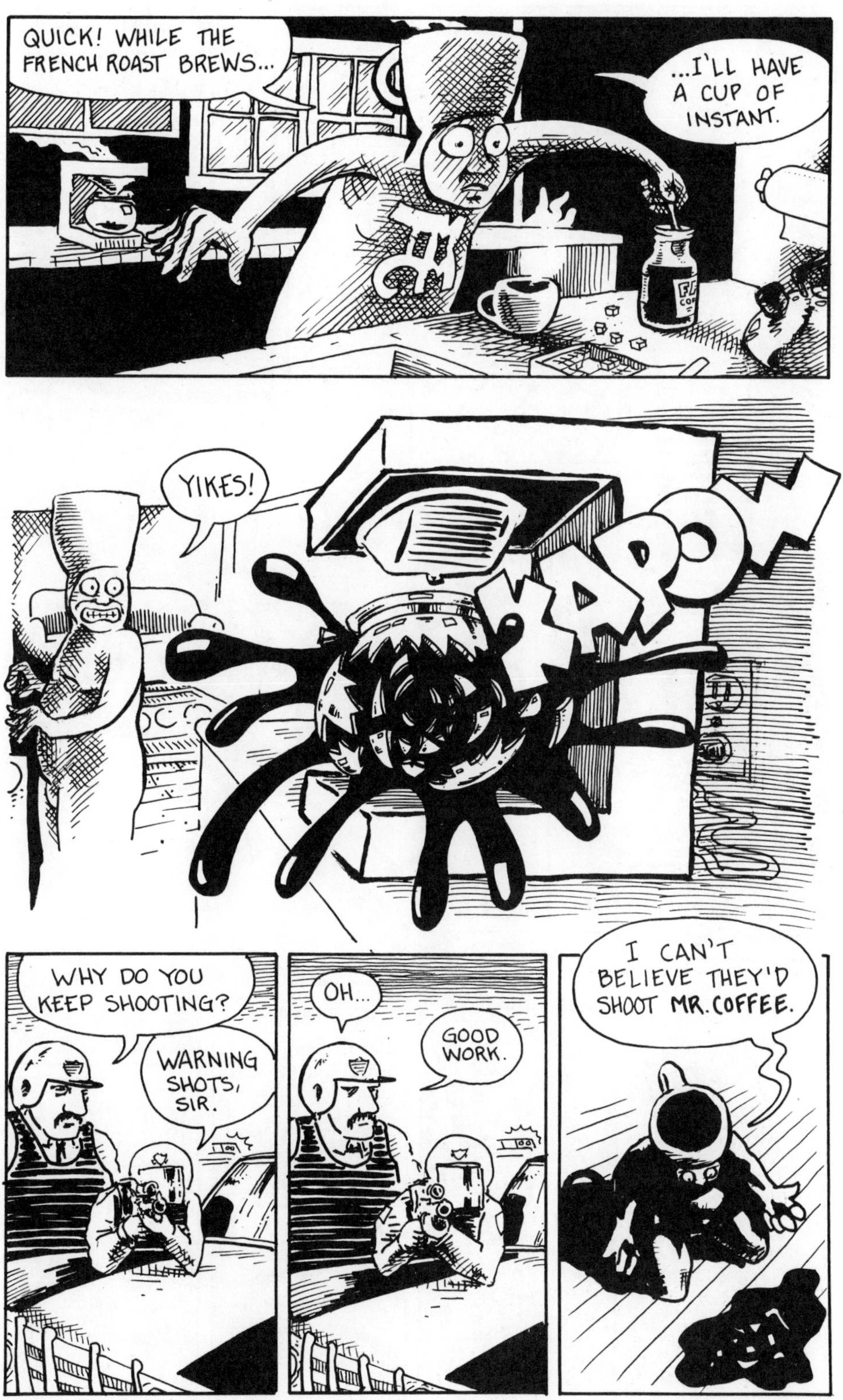
QUICK! WHILE THE FRENCH ROAST BREWS...
...I'LL HAVE A CUP OF INSTANT.
YIKES!
KAPOW
WHY DO YOU KEEP SHOOTING?
WARNING SHOTS, SIR.
OH...
GOOD WORK.
I CAN'T BELIEVE THEY'D SHOOT MR. COFFEE.

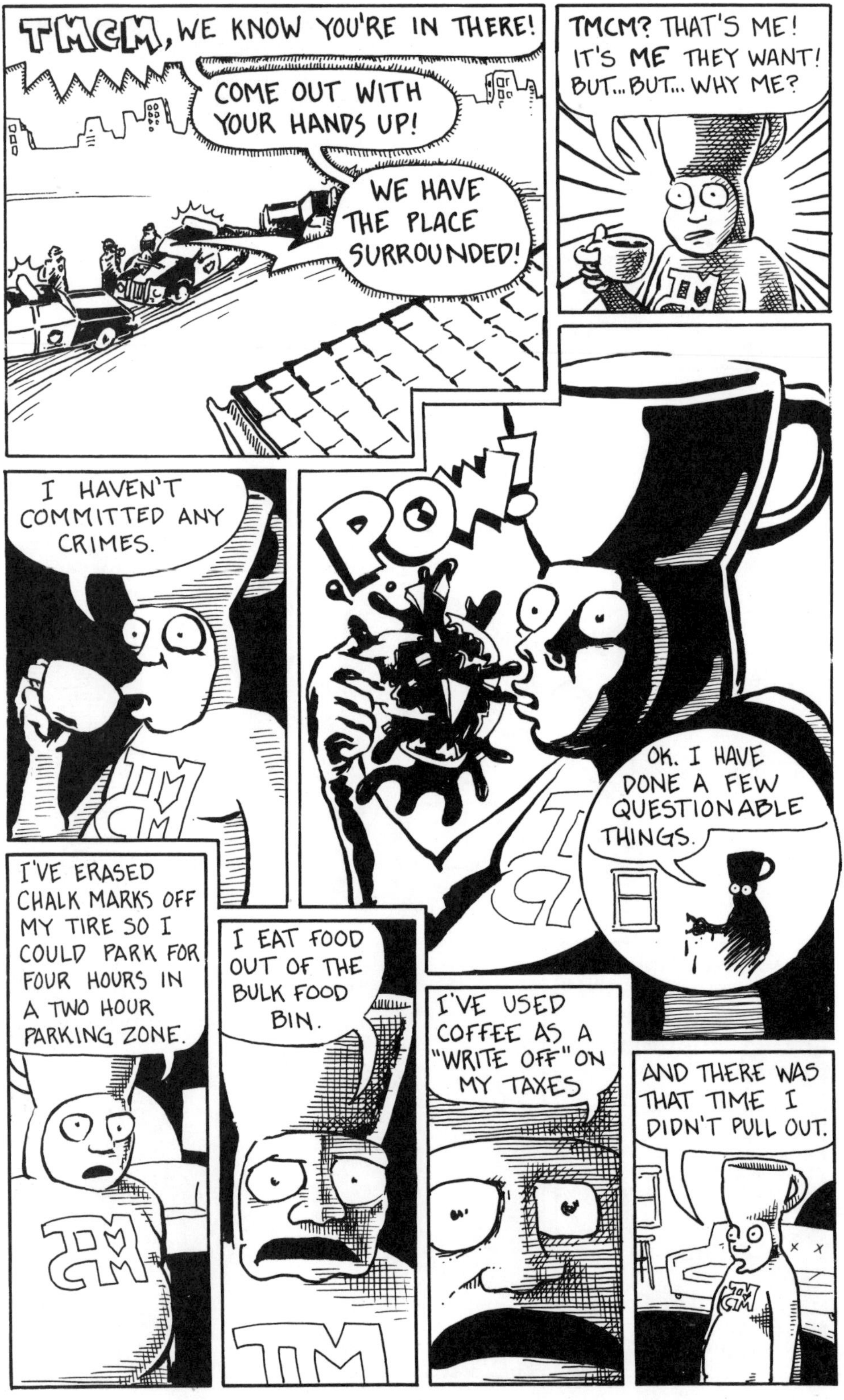
TMCM, WE KNOW YOU'RE IN THERE!
COME OUT WITH YOUR HANDS UP!
WE HAVE THE PLACE SURROUNDED!
TMCM? THAT'S ME! IT'S ME THEY WANT! BUT... BUT... WHY ME?
I HAVEN'T COMMITTED ANY CRIMES.
POW!
OK. I HAVE DONE A FEW QUESTIONABLE THINGS.
I'VE ERASED CHALK MARKS OFF MY TIRE SO I COULD PARK FOR FOUR HOURS IN A TWO HOUR PARKING ZONE.
I EAT FOOD OUT OF THE BULK FOOD BIN.
I'VE USED COFFEE AS A "WRITE OFF" ON MY TAXES
AND THERE WAS THAT TIME I DIDN'T PULL OUT.

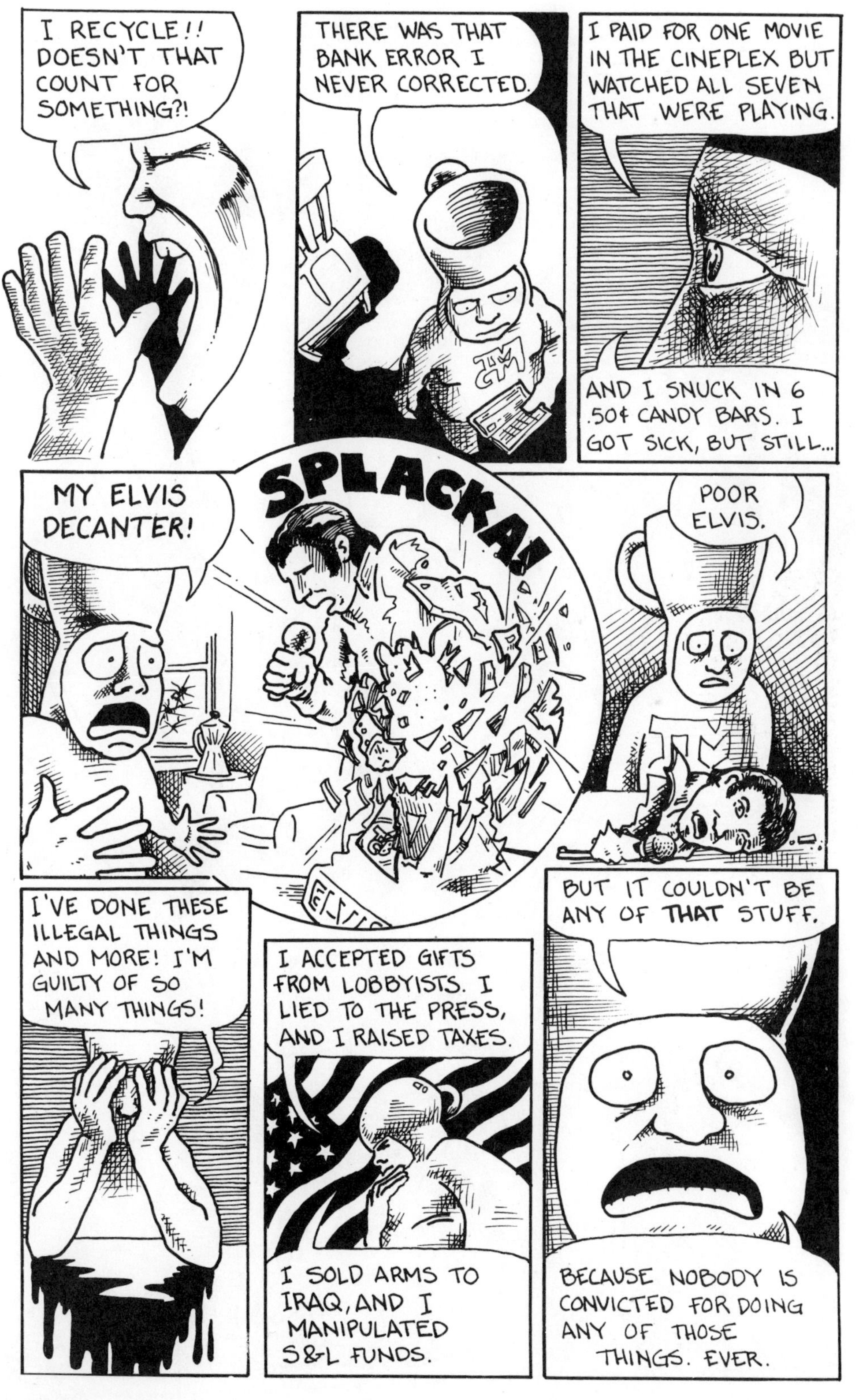
I RECYCLE!! DOESN'T THAT COUNT FOR SOMETHING?!
THERE WAS THAT BANK ERROR I NEVER CORRECTED.
I PAID FOR ONE MOVIE IN THE CINEPLEX BUT WATCHED ALL SEVEN THAT WERE PLAYING.
AND I SNUCK IN 6 .50¢ CANDY BARS. I GOT SICK, BUT STILL...
SPLACKA!
MY ELVIS DECANTER!
POOR ELVIS.
I'VE DONE THESE ILLEGAL THINGS AND MORE! I'M GUILTY OF SO MANY THINGS!
I ACCEPTED GIFTS FROM LOBBYISTS. I LIED TO THE PRESS, AND I RAISED TAXES.
I SOLD ARMS TO IRAQ, AND I MANIPULATED S&L FUNDS.
BUT IT COULDN'T BE ANY OF THAT STUFF.
BECAUSE NOBODY IS CONVICTED FOR DOING ANY OF THOSE THINGS. EVER.

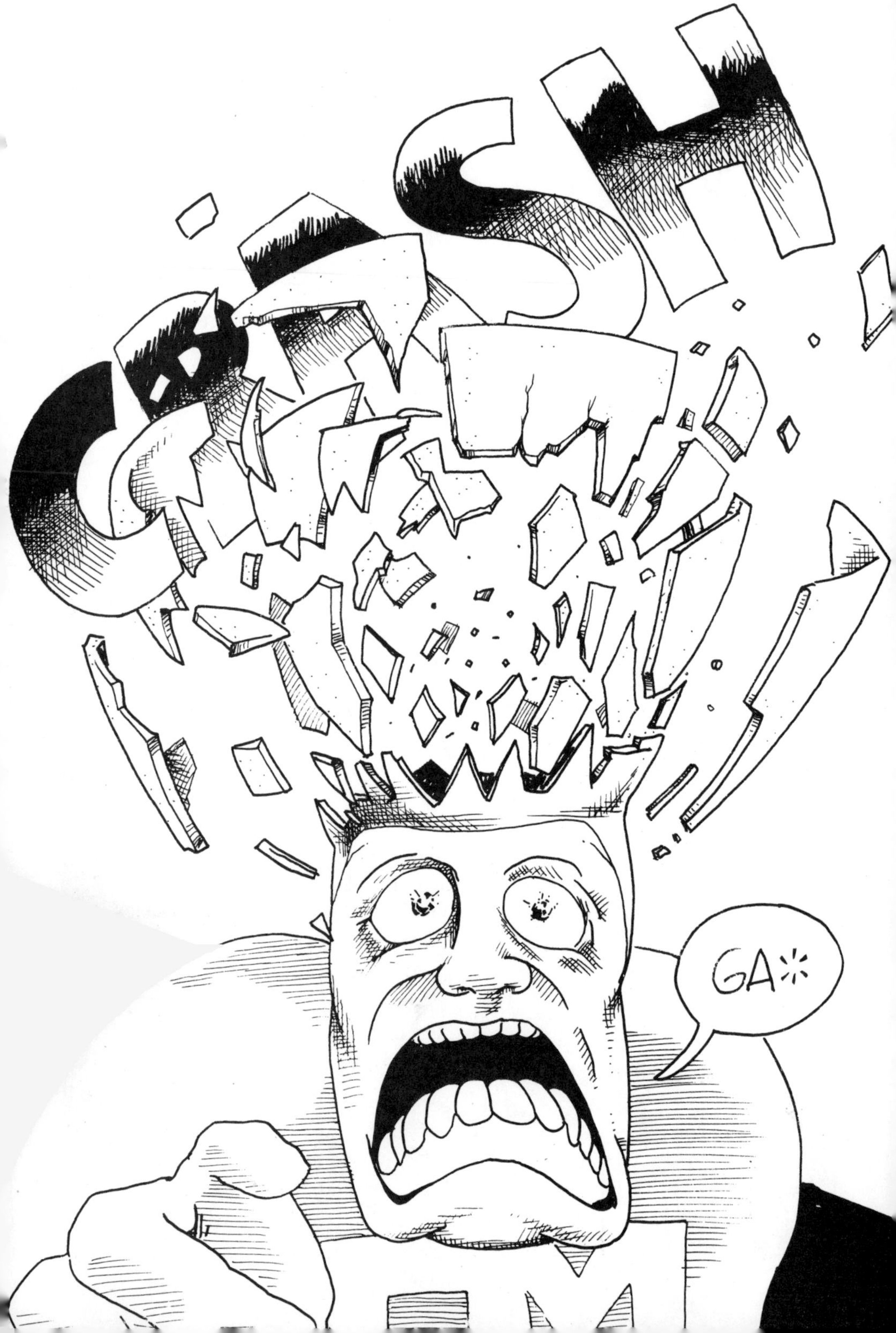
CRASH
GA

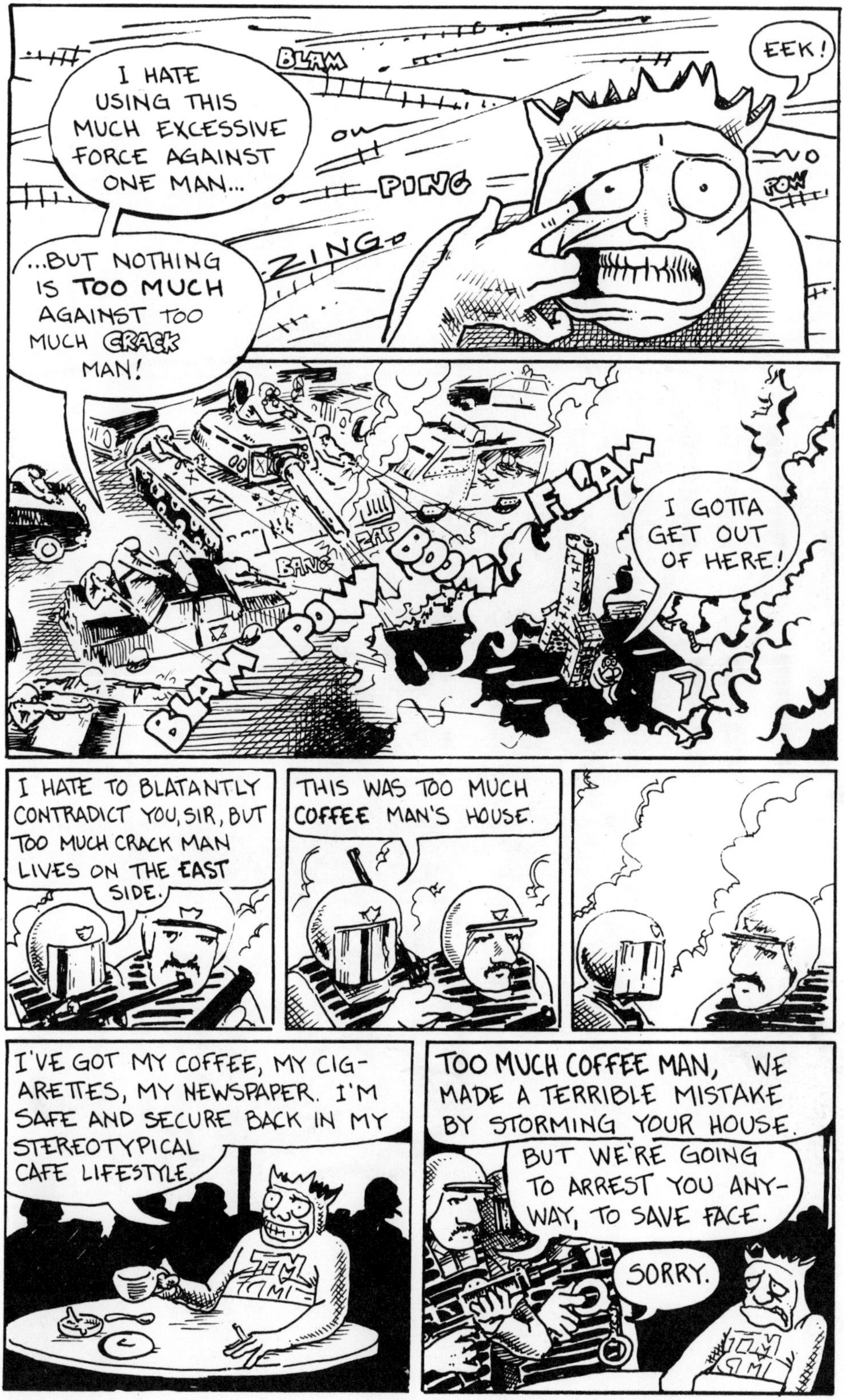

BLAM
I HATE USING THIS MUCH EXCESSIVE FORCE AGAINST ONE MAN...
EEK!
PING
POW
ZING
...BUT NOTHING IS TOO MUCH AGAINST TOO MUCH CRACK MAN!
FLAM
I GOTTA GET OUT OF HERE!
ZAP
BANG
BOOM
POW
BLAM
I HATE TO BLATANTLY CONTRADICT YOU, SIR, BUT TOO MUCH CRACK MAN LIVES ON THE EAST SIDE.
THIS WAS TOO MUCH COFFEE MAN'S HOUSE.
I'VE GOT MY COFFEE, MY CIG-ARETTES, MY NEWSPAPER. I'M SAFE AND SECURE BACK IN MY STEREOTYPICAL CAFE LIFESTYLE.
TOO MUCH COFFEE MAN, WE MADE A TERRIBLE MISTAKE BY STORMING YOUR HOUSE.
BUT WE'RE GOING TO ARREST YOU ANY-WAY, TO SAVE FACE.
SORRY.

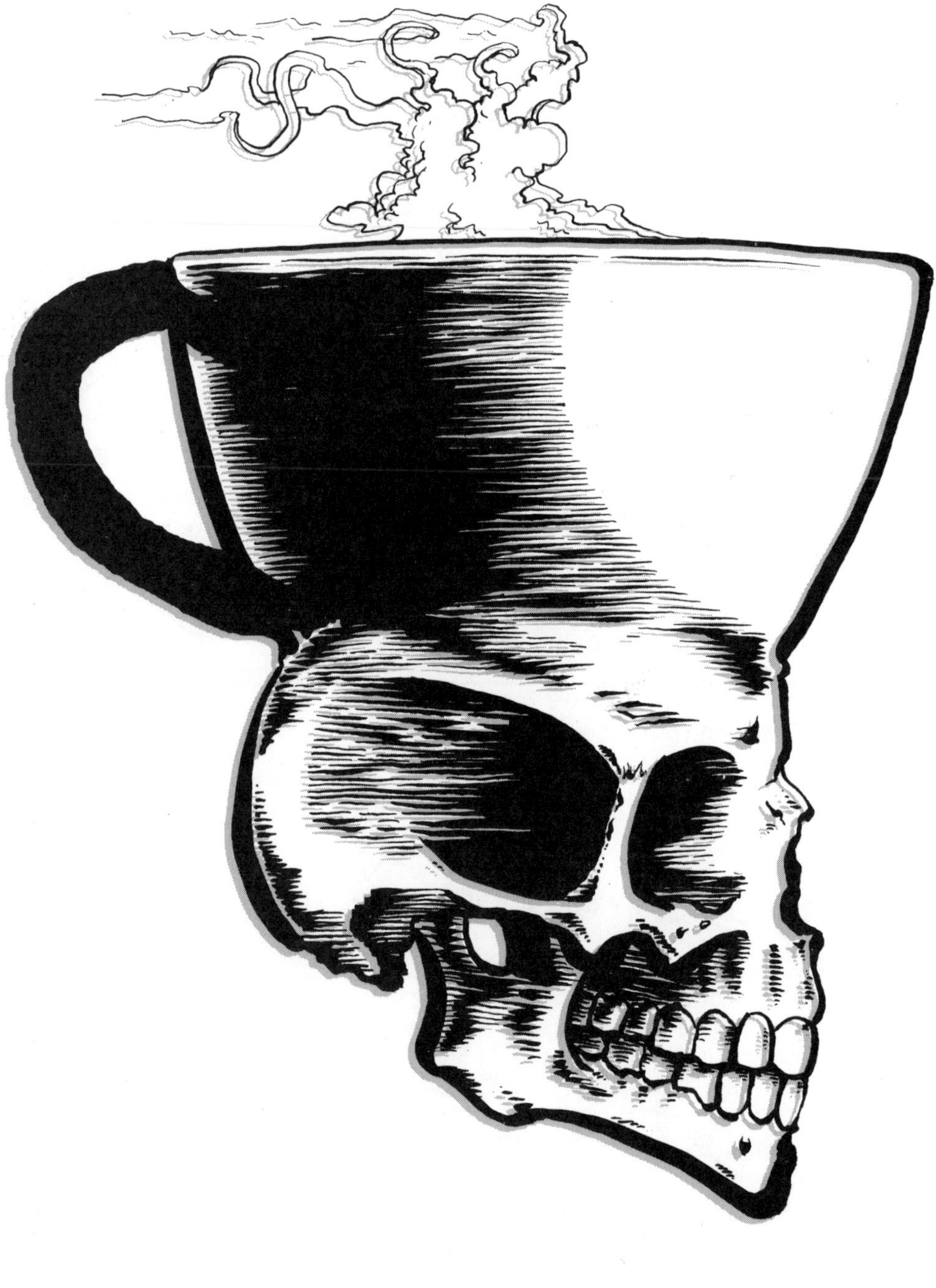

NEWSPAPER COMIC STRIPS

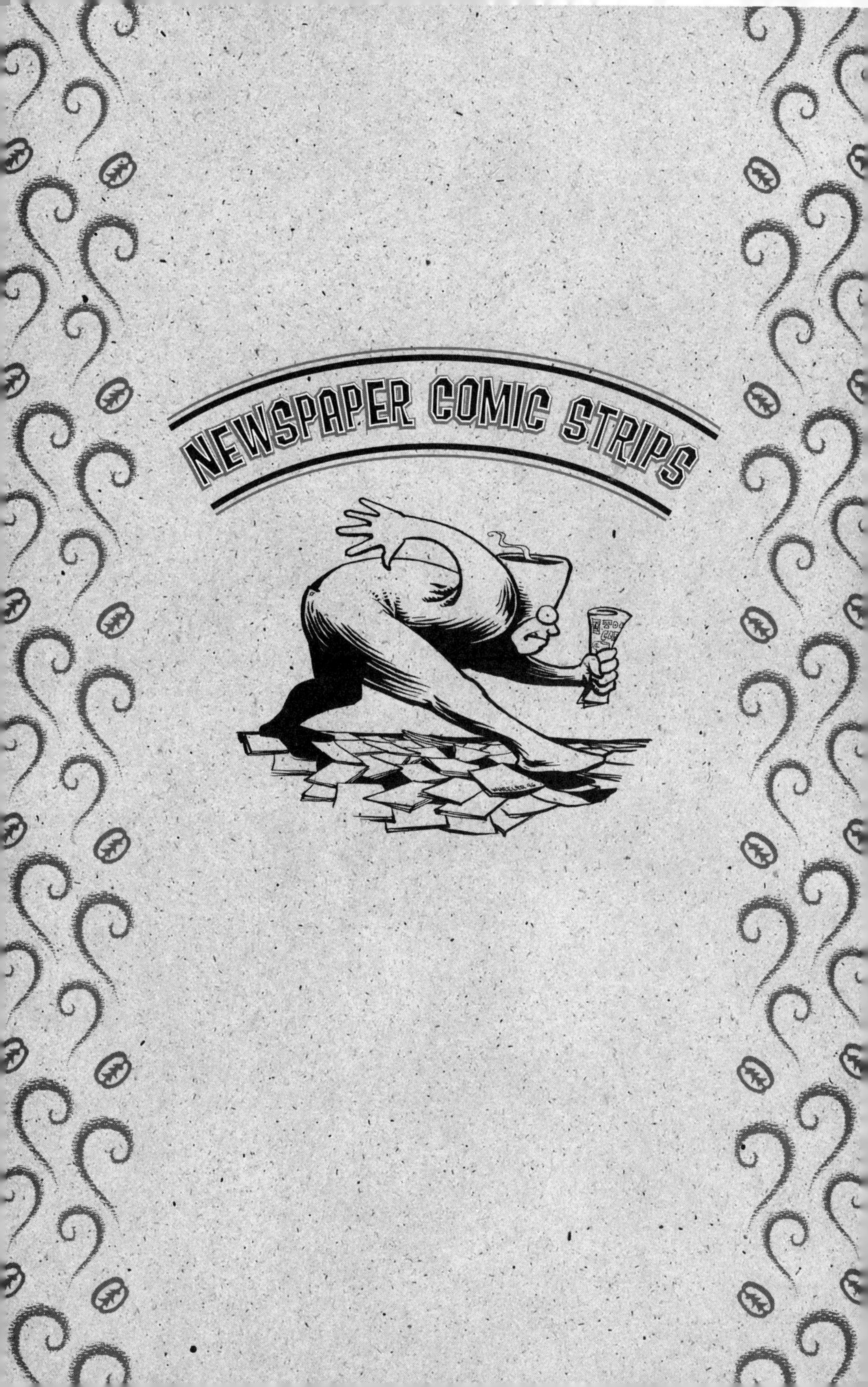

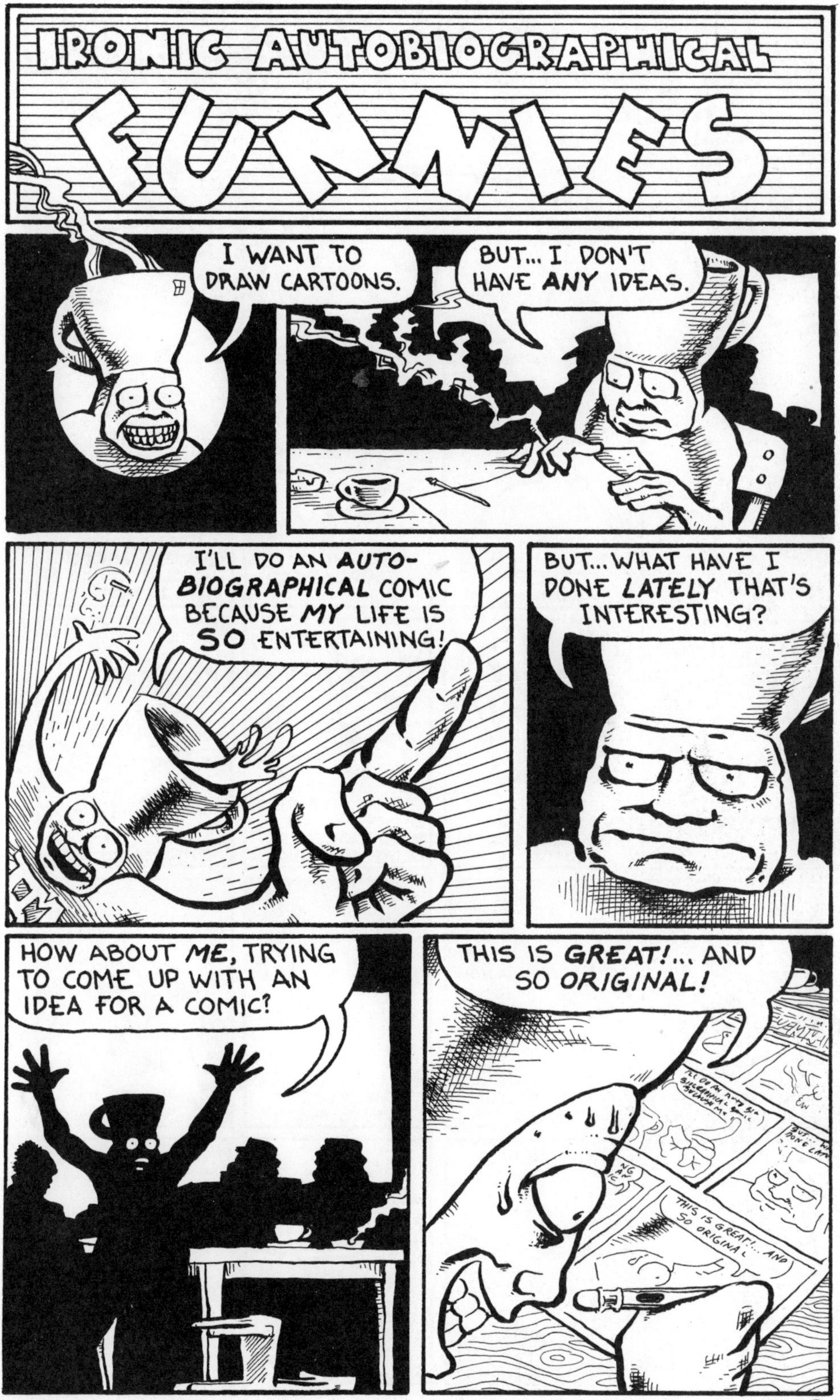
IRONIC AUTOBIOGRAPHICAL FUNNIES
I WANT TO DRAW CARTOONS.
BUT... I DON'T HAVE ANY IDEAS.
I'LL DO AN AUTO-BIOGRAPHICAL COMIC BECAUSE MY LIFE IS SO ENTERTAINING!
BUT... WHAT HAVE I DONE LATELY THAT'S INTERESTING?
HOW ABOUT ME, TRYING TO COME UP WITH AN IDEA FOR A COMIC?
THIS IS GREAT!... AND SO ORIGINAL!
THIS IS GREAT!... AND SO ORIGINAL
END.

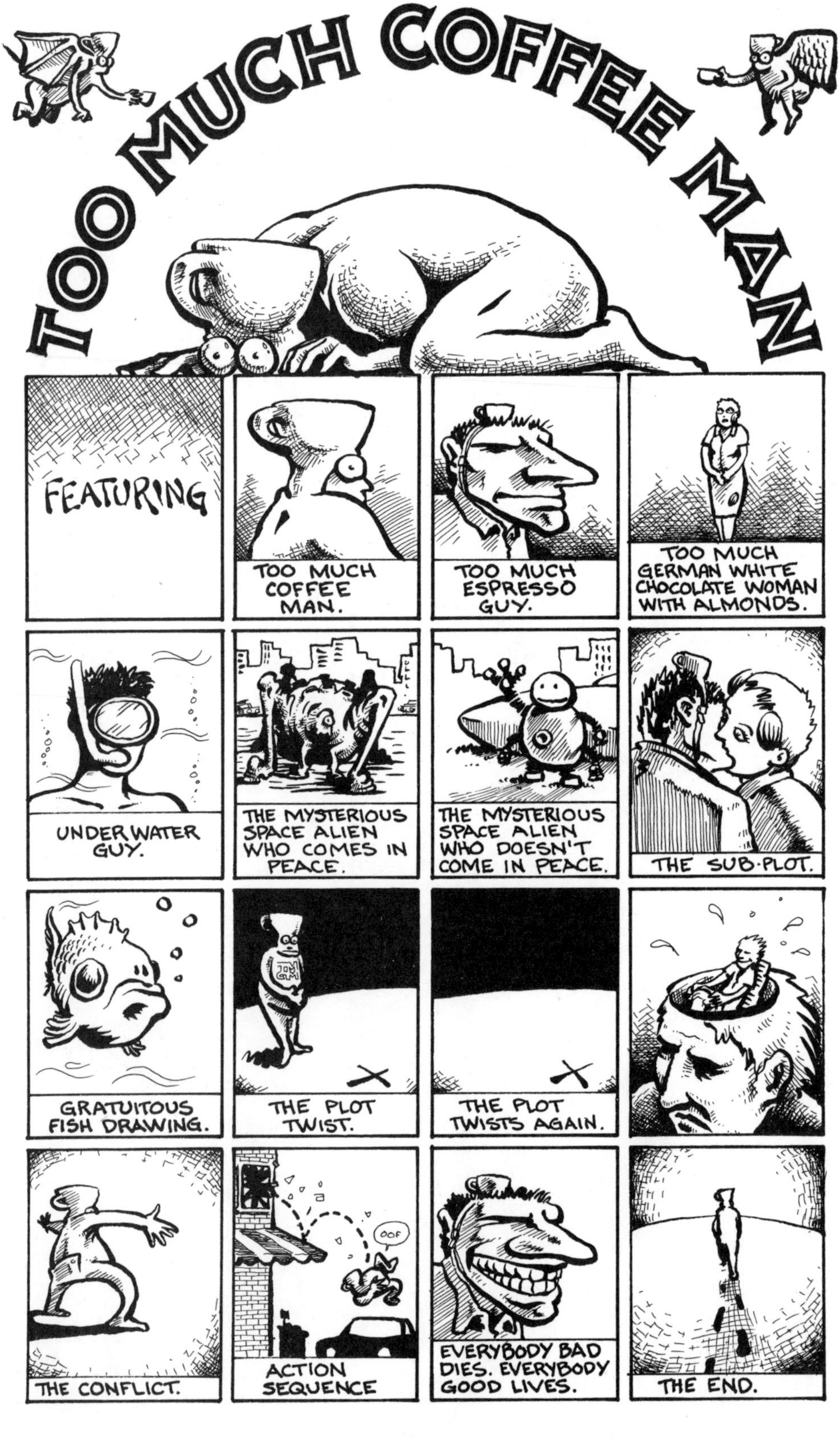
TOO MUCH COFFEE MAN
FEATURING
TOO MUCH COFFEE MAN.
TOO MUCH ESPRESSO GUY.
TOO MUCH GERMAN WHITE CHOCOLATE WOMAN WITH ALMONDS.
UNDERWATER GUY.
THE MYSTERIOUS SPACE ALIEN WHO COMES IN PEACE.
THE MYSTERIOUS SPACE ALIEN WHO DOESN'T COME IN PEACE.
THE SUB-PLOT.
GRATUITOUS FISH DRAWING.
THE PLOT TWIST.
THE PLOT TWISTS AGAIN.
THE CONFLICT.
OOF
ACTION SEQUENCE
EVERYBODY BAD DIES. EVERYBODY GOOD LIVES.
THE END.

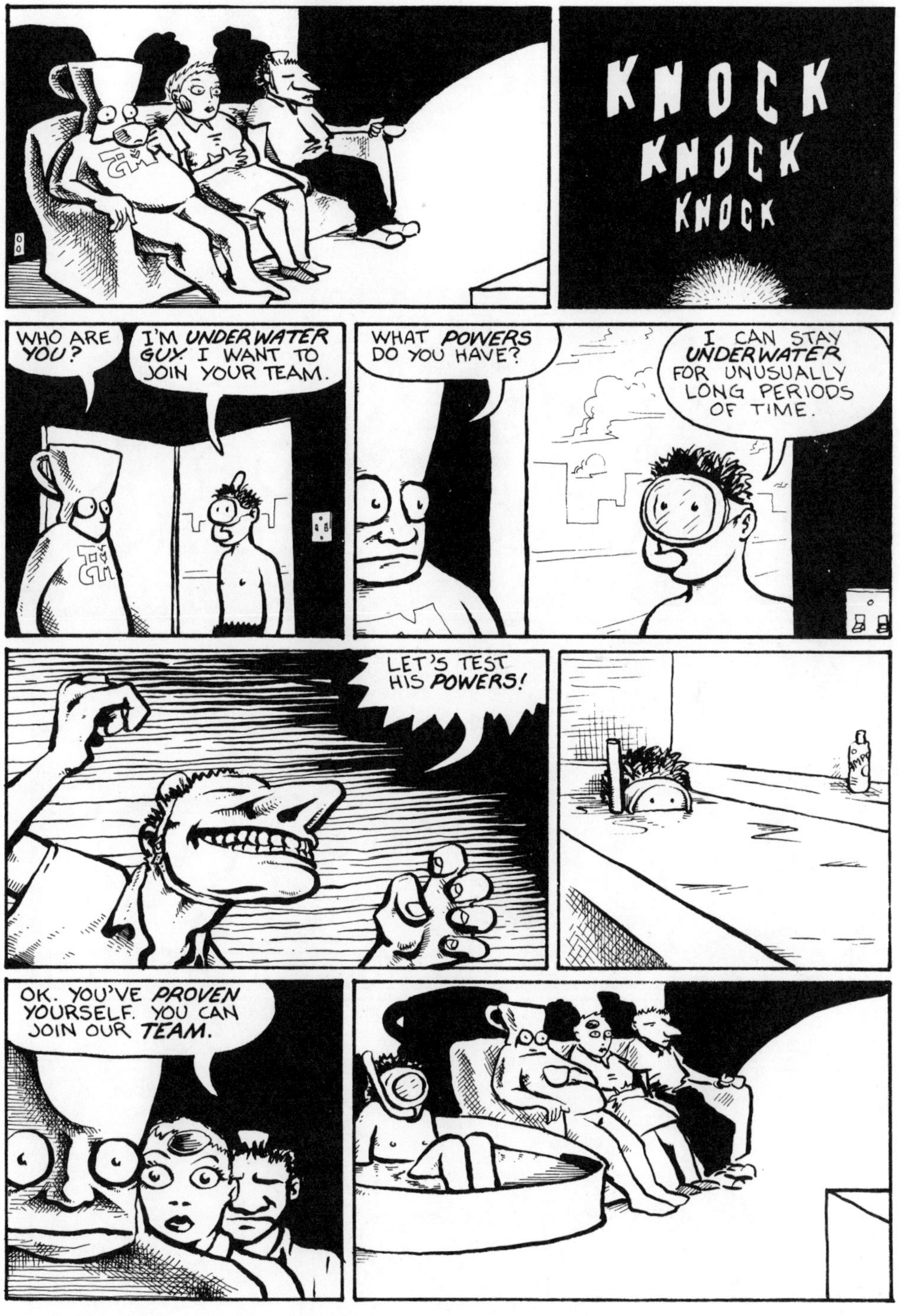
KNOCK
KNOCK
KNOCK
WHO ARE YOU?
I'M UNDERWATER GUY. I WANT TO JOIN YOUR TEAM.
WHAT POWERS DO YOU HAVE?
I CAN STAY UNDERWATER FOR UNUSUALLY LONG PERIODS OF TIME.
LET'S TEST HIS POWERS!
OK. YOU'VE PROVEN YOURSELF. YOU CAN JOIN OUR TEAM.

TOO MUCH COFFEE MAN

Shannon Wheeler

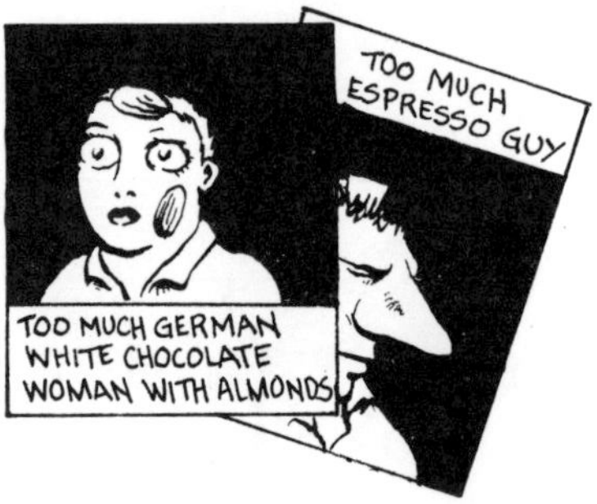
TOO MUCH GERMAN WHITE CHOCOLATE WOMAN WITH ALMONDS
TOO MUCH ESPRESSO GUY

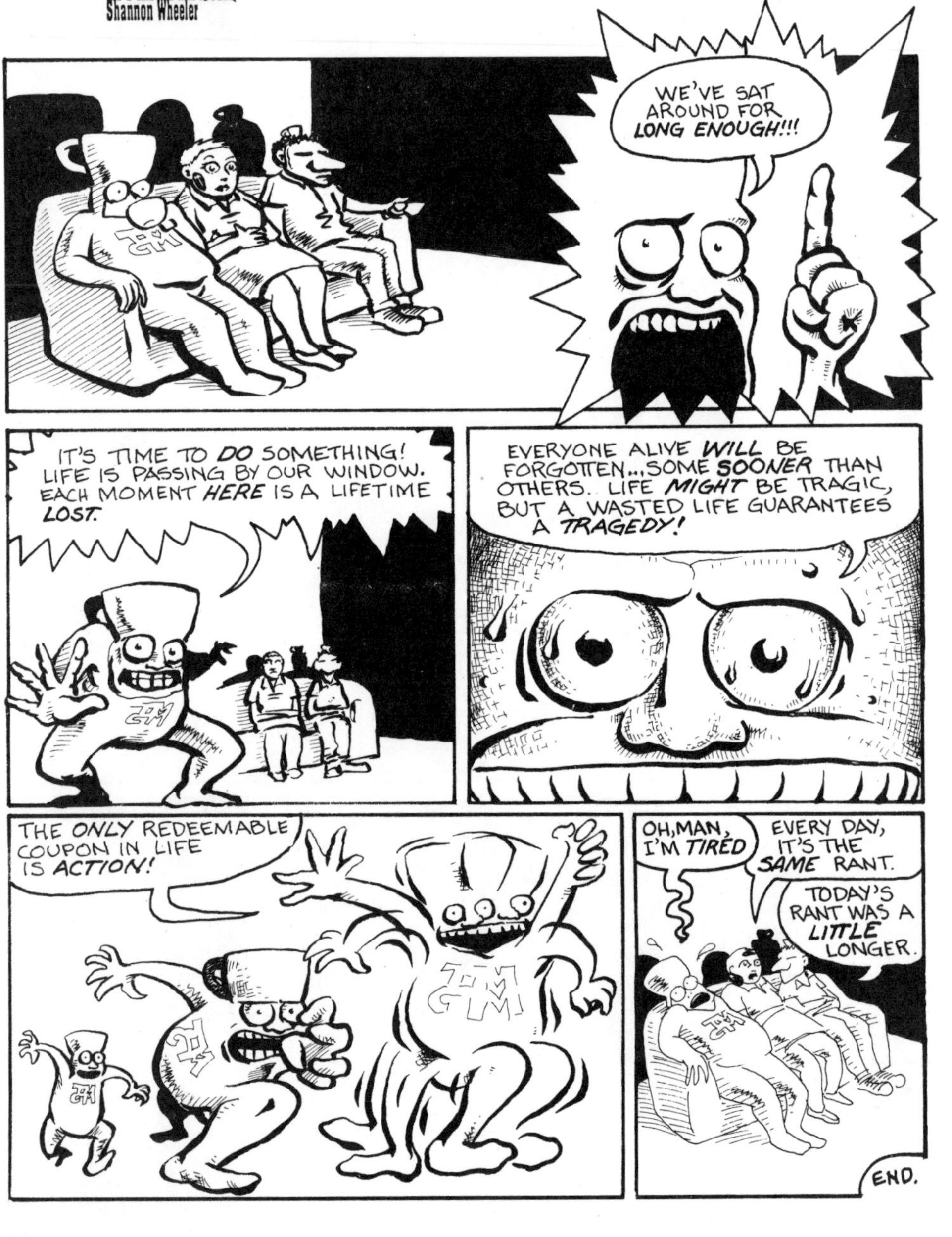
WE'VE SAT AROUND FOR LONG ENOUGH!!!
IT'S TIME TO DO SOMETHING! LIFE IS PASSING BY OUR WINDOW. EACH MOMENT HERE IS A LIFETIME LOST.
EVERYONE ALIVE WILL BE FORGOTTEN...SOME SOONER THAN OTHERS. LIFE MIGHT BE TRAGIC, BUT A WASTED LIFE GUARANTEES A TRAGEDY!
THE ONLY REDEEMABLE COUPON IN LIFE IS ACTION!
OH,MAN, I'M TIRED
EVERY DAY, IT'S THE SAME RANT.
TODAY'S RANT WAS A LITTLE LONGER.
END.

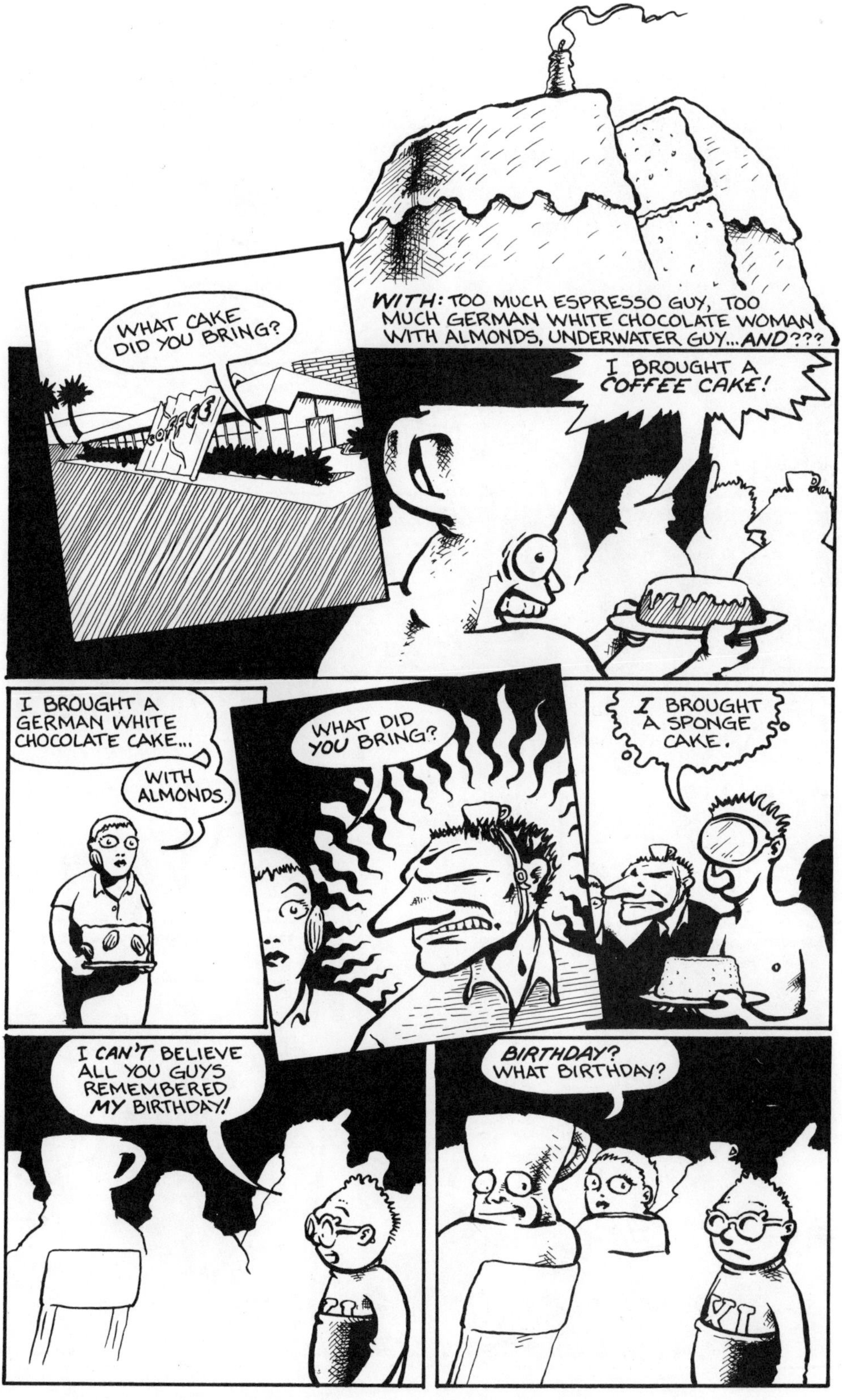
WITH: TOO MUCH ESPRESSO GUY, TOO MUCH GERMAN WHITE CHOCOLATE WOMAN WITH ALMONDS, UNDERWATER GUY... AND???
WHAT CAKE DID YOU BRING?
COFFEE
I BROUGHT A COFFEE CAKE!
I BROUGHT A GERMAN WHITE CHOCOLATE CAKE...
WITH ALMONDS.
WHAT DID YOU BRING?
I BROUGHT A SPONGE CAKE.
I CAN'T BELIEVE ALL YOU GUYS REMEMBERED MY BIRTHDAY!
BIRTHDAY? WHAT BIRTHDAY?

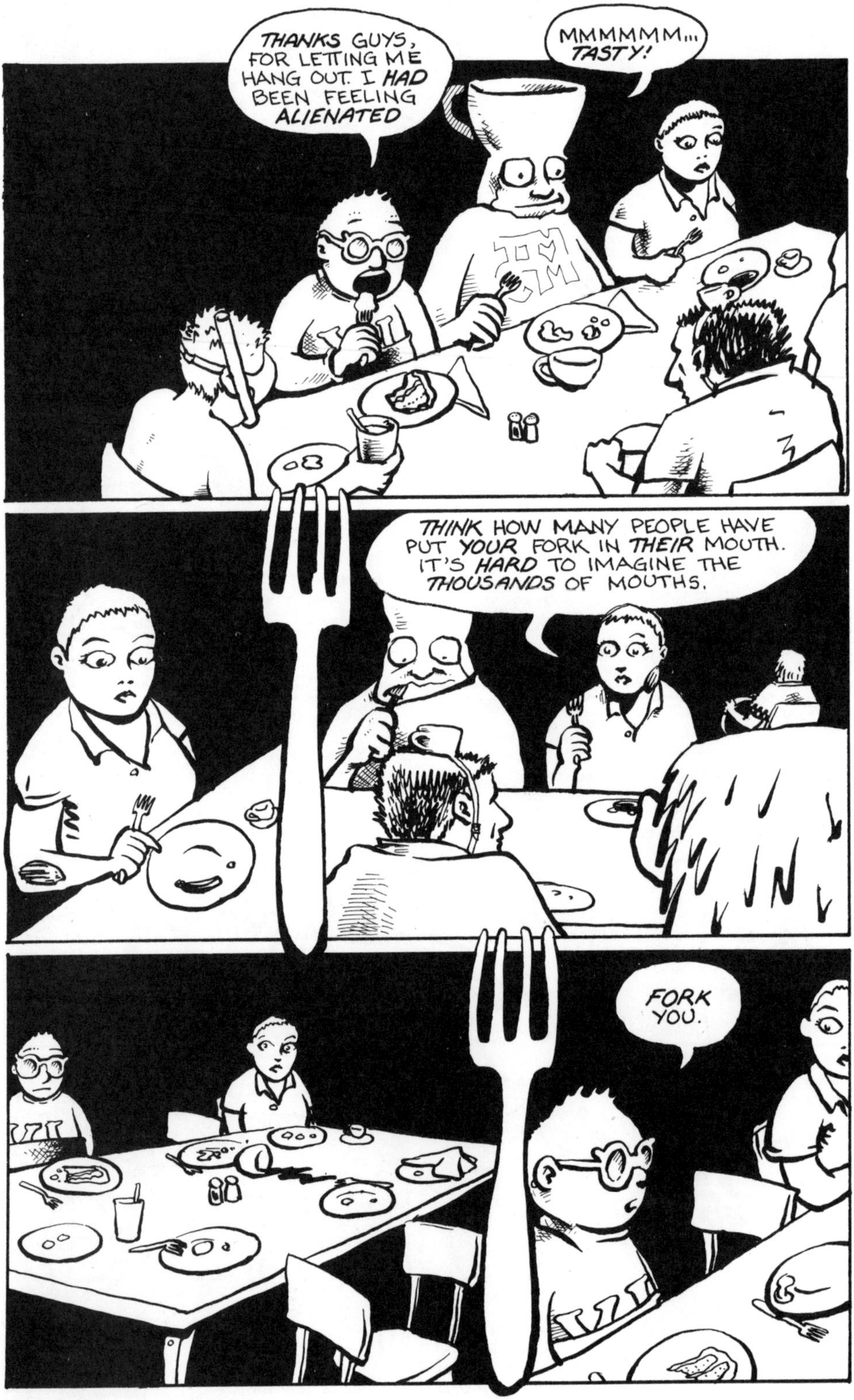
THANKS GUYS, FOR LETTING ME HANG OUT. I HAD BEEN FEELING ALIENATED
MMMMMM... TASTY!
THINK HOW MANY PEOPLE HAVE PUT YOUR FORK IN THEIR MOUTH. IT'S HARD TO IMAGINE THE THOUSANDS OF MOUTHS.
FORK YOU.

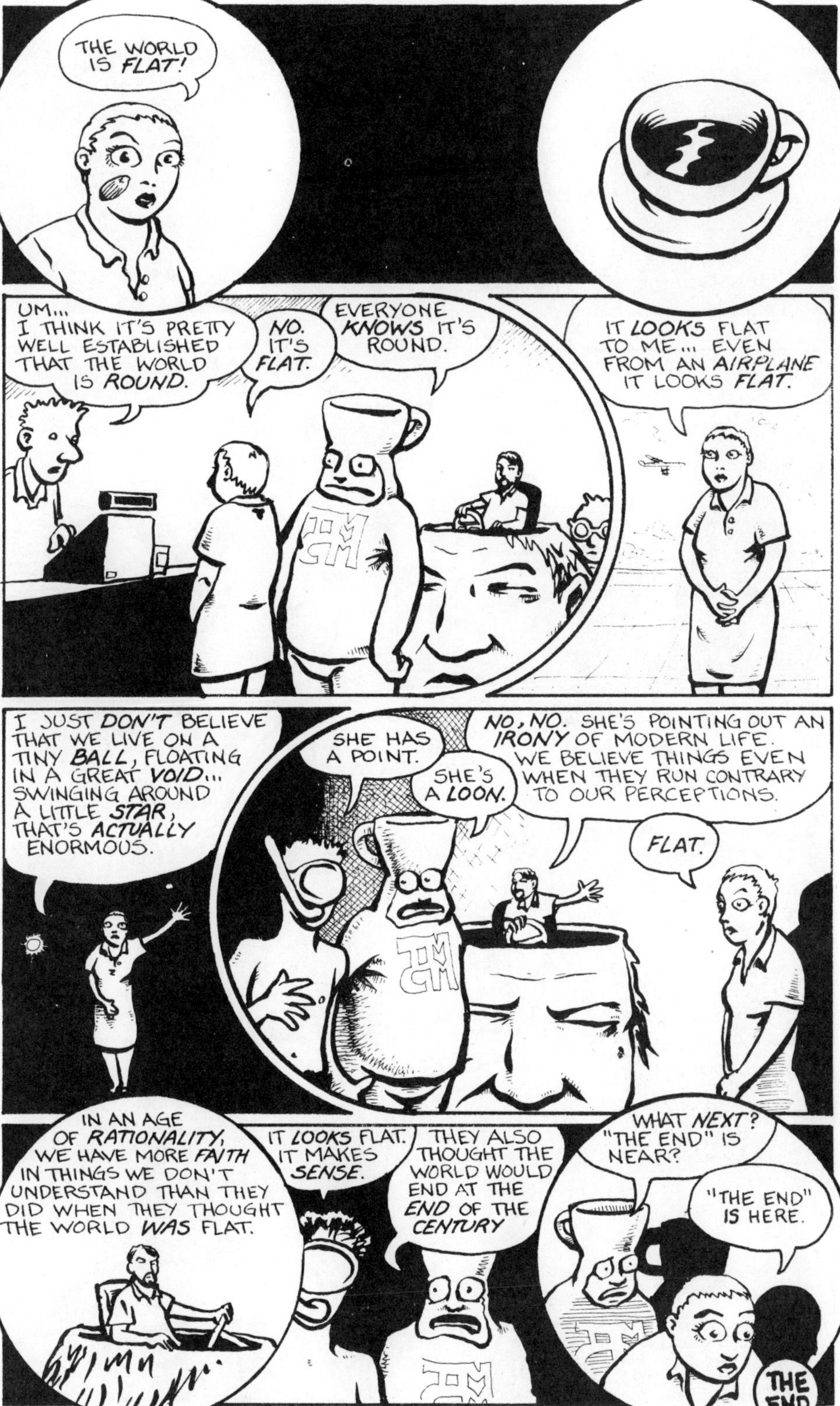
THE WORLD IS FLAT!
UM... I THINK IT'S PRETTY WELL ESTABLISHED THAT THE WORLD IS ROUND.
NO. IT'S FLAT.
EVERYONE KNOWS IT'S ROUND.
IT LOOKS FLAT TO ME... EVEN FROM AN AIRPLANE IT LOOKS FLAT.
I JUST DON'T BELIEVE THAT WE LIVE ON A TINY BALL, FLOATING IN A GREAT VOID... SWINGING AROUND A LITTLE STAR, THAT'S ACTUALLY ENORMOUS.
SHE HAS A POINT.
SHE'S A LOON.
NO, NO. SHE'S POINTING OUT AN IRONY OF MODERN LIFE. WE BELIEVE THINGS EVEN WHEN THEY RUN CONTRARY TO OUR PERCEPTIONS.
FLAT.
IN AN AGE OF RATIONALITY, WE HAVE MORE FAITH IN THINGS WE DON'T UNDERSTAND THAN THEY DID WHEN THEY THOUGHT THE WORLD WAS FLAT.
IT LOOKS FLAT. IT MAKES SENSE.
THEY ALSO THOUGHT THE WORLD WOULD END AT THE END OF THE CENTURY
WHAT NEXT? "THE END" IS NEAR?
"THE END" IS HERE.
THE END

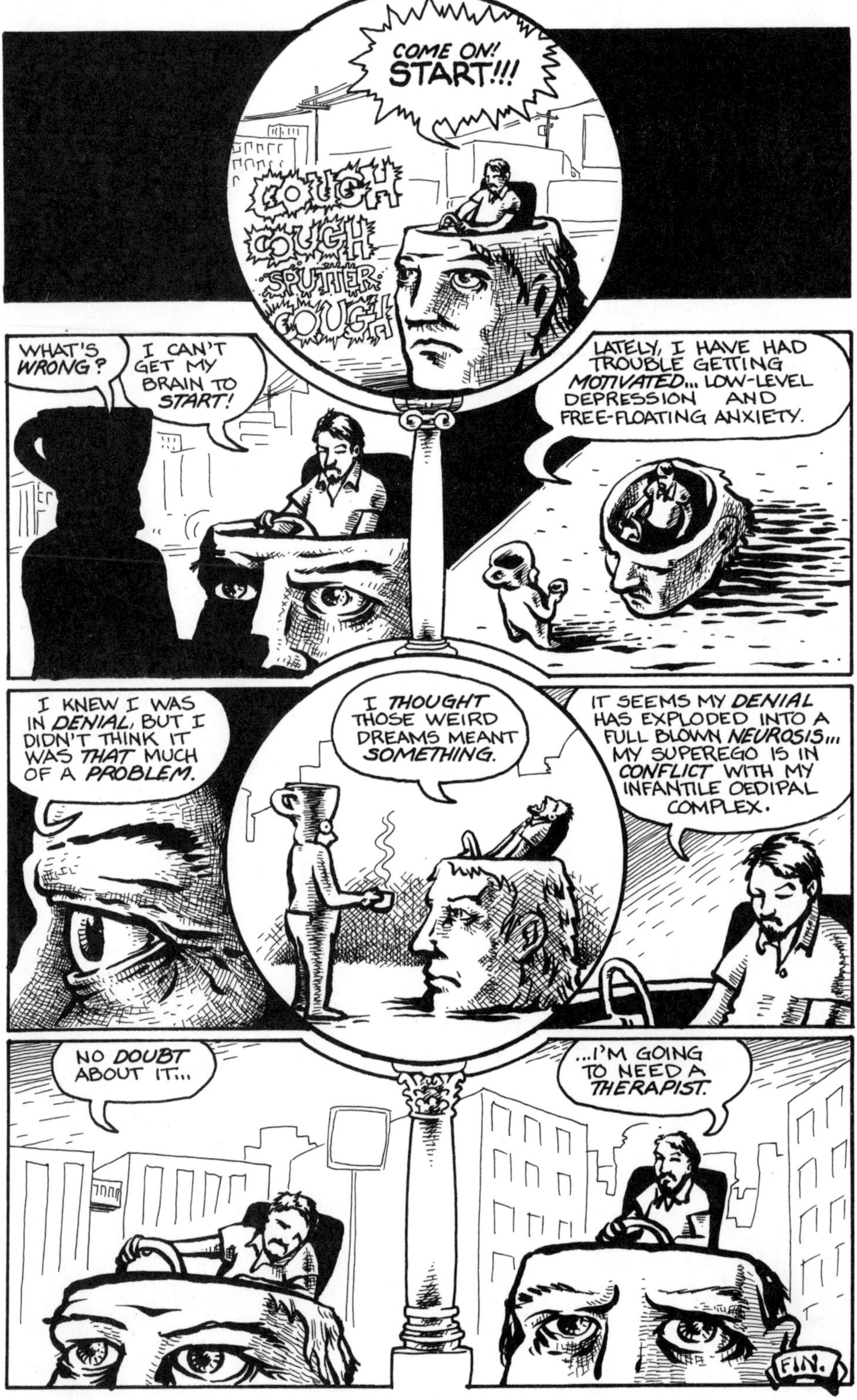
COME ON! START!!!
COUGH COUGH SPUTTER COUGH
WHAT'S WRONG?
I CAN'T GET MY BRAIN TO START!
LATELY, I HAVE HAD TROUBLE GETTING MOTIVATED... LOW-LEVEL DEPRESSION AND FREE-FLOATING ANXIETY.
I KNEW I WAS IN DENIAL, BUT I DIDN'T THINK IT WAS THAT MUCH OF A PROBLEM.
I THOUGHT THOSE WEIRD DREAMS MEANT SOMETHING.
IT SEEMS MY DENIAL HAS EXPLODED INTO A FULL BLOWN NEUROSIS... MY SUPEREGO IS IN CONFLICT WITH MY INFANTILE OEDIPAL COMPLEX.
NO DOUBT ABOUT IT...
...I'M GOING TO NEED A THERAPIST.
FIN.

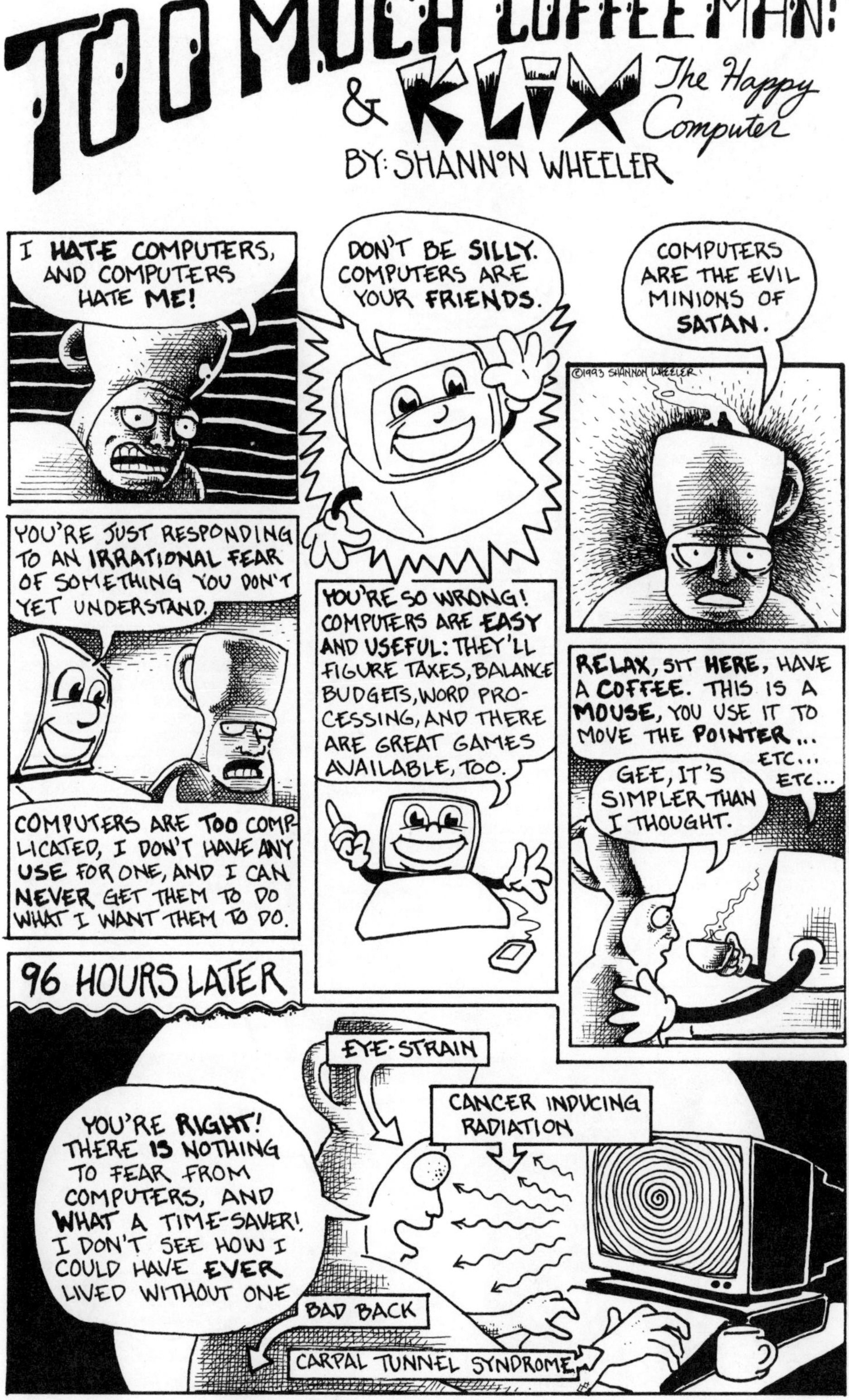

TOO MUCH COFFEE MAN: & KLIX The Happy Computer
BY: SHANNON WHEELER
I HATE COMPUTERS, AND COMPUTERS HATE ME!
DON'T BE SILLY. COMPUTERS ARE YOUR FRIENDS.
COMPUTERS ARE THE EVIL MINIONS OF SATAN.
©1993 SHANNON WHEELER
YOU'RE JUST RESPONDING TO AN IRRATIONAL FEAR OF SOMETHING YOU DON'T YET UNDERSTAND.
COMPUTERS ARE TOO COMPLICATED, I DON'T HAVE ANY USE FOR ONE, AND I CAN NEVER GET THEM TO DO WHAT I WANT THEM TO DO.
YOU'RE SO WRONG! COMPUTERS ARE EASY AND USEFUL: THEY'LL FIGURE TAXES, BALANCE BUDGETS, WORD PROCESSING, AND THERE ARE GREAT GAMES AVAILABLE, TOO.
RELAX, SIT HERE, HAVE A COFFEE. THIS IS A MOUSE, YOU USE IT TO MOVE THE POINTER... ETC... ETC...
GEE, IT'S SIMPLER THAN I THOUGHT.
96 HOURS LATER
EYE-STRAIN
CANCER INDUCING RADIATION
YOU'RE RIGHT! THERE IS NOTHING TO FEAR FROM COMPUTERS, AND WHAT A TIME-SAVER! I DON'T SEE HOW I COULD HAVE EVER LIVED WITHOUT ONE
BAD BACK
CARPAL TUNNEL SYNDROME

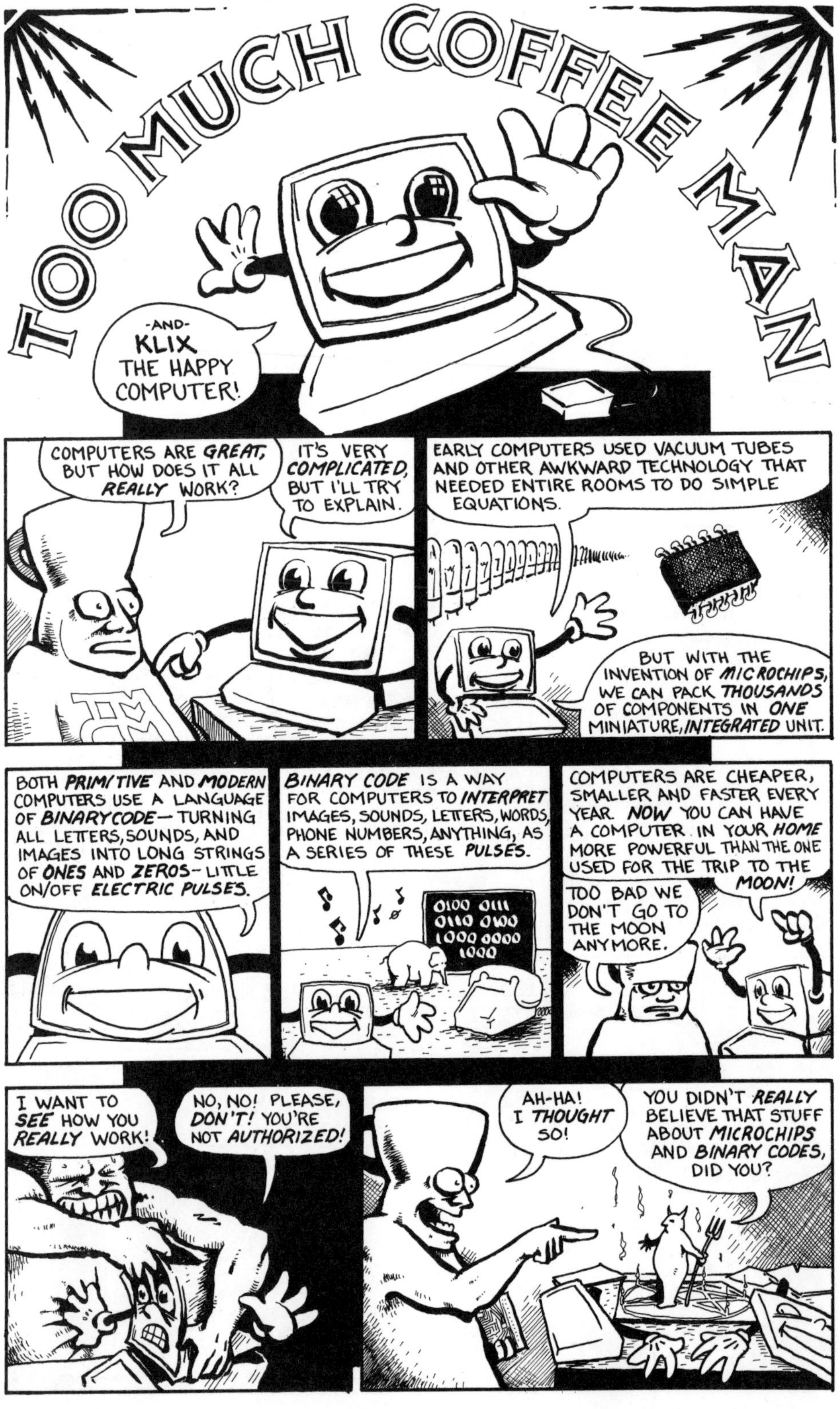
TOO MUCH COFFEE MAN
-AND- KLIX THE HAPPY COMPUTER!
COMPUTERS ARE GREAT, BUT HOW DOES IT ALL REALLY WORK?
IT'S VERY COMPLICATED, BUT I'LL TRY TO EXPLAIN.
EARLY COMPUTERS USED VACUUM TUBES AND OTHER AWKWARD TECHNOLOGY THAT NEEDED ENTIRE ROOMS TO DO SIMPLE EQUATIONS.
BUT WITH THE INVENTION OF MICROCHIPS, WE CAN PACK THOUSANDS OF COMPONENTS IN ONE MINIATURE, INTEGRATED UNIT.
BOTH PRIMITIVE AND MODERN COMPUTERS USE A LANGUAGE OF BINARY CODE— TURNING ALL LETTERS, SOUNDS, AND IMAGES INTO LONG STRINGS OF ONES AND ZEROS– LITTLE ON/OFF ELECTRIC PULSES.
BINARY CODE IS A WAY FOR COMPUTERS TO INTERPRET IMAGES, SOUNDS, LETTERS, WORDS, PHONE NUMBERS, ANYTHING, AS A SERIES OF THESE PULSES.
0100 0111
0110 0100
1000 0000
1000
COMPUTERS ARE CHEAPER, SMALLER AND FASTER EVERY YEAR. NOW YOU CAN HAVE A COMPUTER IN YOUR HOME MORE POWERFUL THAN THE ONE USED FOR THE TRIP TO THE MOON!
TOO BAD WE DON'T GO TO THE MOON ANYMORE.
I WANT TO SEE HOW YOU REALLY WORK!
NO, NO! PLEASE, DON'T! YOU'RE NOT AUTHORIZED!
AH-HA! I THOUGHT SO!
YOU DIDN'T REALLY BELIEVE THAT STUFF ABOUT MICROCHIPS AND BINARY CODES, DID YOU?

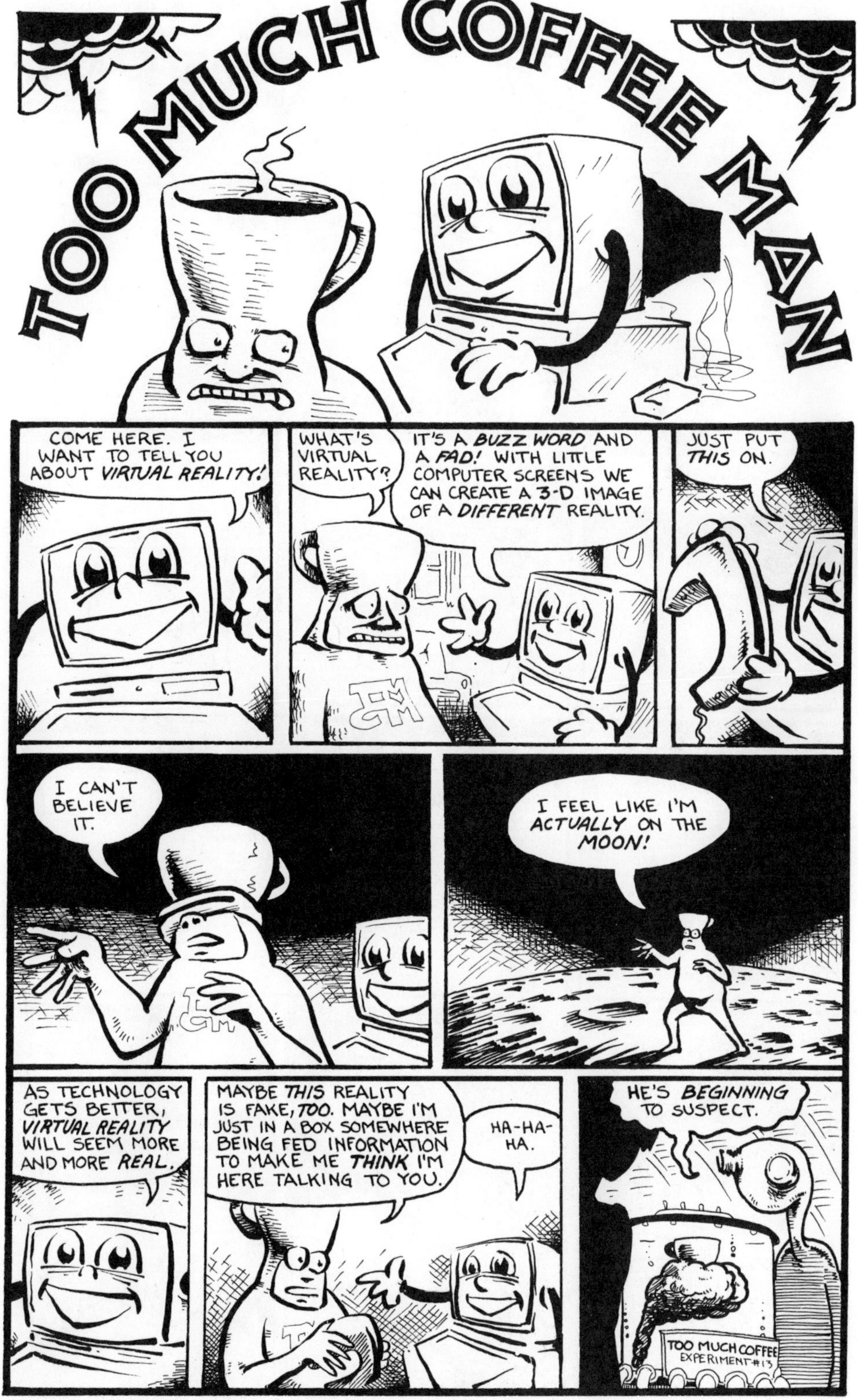
TOO MUCH COFFEE MAN
COME HERE. I WANT TO TELL YOU ABOUT VIRTUAL REALITY!
WHAT'S VIRTUAL REALITY?
IT'S A BUZZ WORD AND A FAD! WITH LITTLE COMPUTER SCREENS WE CAN CREATE A 3-D IMAGE OF A DIFFERENT REALITY.
JUST PUT THIS ON.
I CAN'T BELIEVE IT.
I FEEL LIKE I'M ACTUALLY ON THE MOON!
AS TECHNOLOGY GETS BETTER, VIRTUAL REALITY WILL SEEM MORE AND MORE REAL.
MAYBE THIS REALITY IS FAKE, TOO. MAYBE I'M JUST IN A BOX SOMEWHERE BEING FED INFORMATION TO MAKE ME THINK I'M HERE TALKING TO YOU.
HA-HA-HA.
HE'S BEGINNING TO SUSPECT.
TOO MUCH COFFEE EXPERIMENT #13

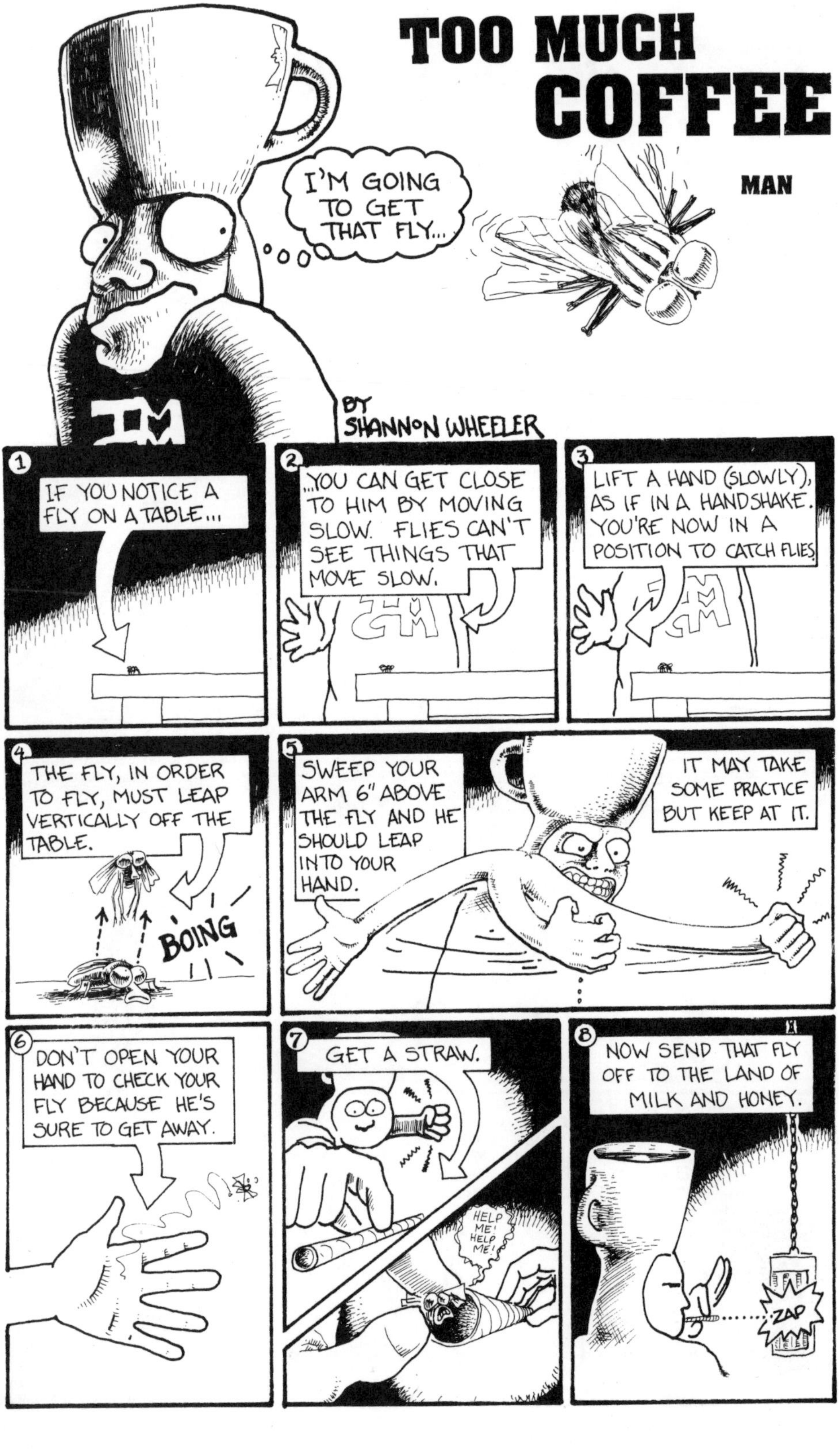

TOO MUCH COFFEE MAN
I'M GOING TO GET THAT FLY...
BY SHANNON WHEELER
IM
1
IF YOU NOTICE A FLY ON A TABLE...
2
...YOU CAN GET CLOSE TO HIM BY MOVING SLOW. FLIES CAN'T SEE THINGS THAT MOVE SLOW.
3
LIFT A HAND (SLOWLY), AS IF IN A HANDSHAKE. YOU'RE NOW IN A POSITION TO CATCH FLIES.
4
THE FLY, IN ORDER TO FLY, MUST LEAP VERTICALLY OFF THE TABLE.
BOING
5
SWEEP YOUR ARM 6" ABOVE THE FLY AND HE SHOULD LEAP INTO YOUR HAND.
IT MAY TAKE SOME PRACTICE BUT KEEP AT IT.
6
DON'T OPEN YOUR HAND TO CHECK YOUR FLY BECAUSE HE'S SURE TO GET AWAY.
7
GET A STRAW.
HELP ME! HELP ME!
8
NOW SEND THAT FLY OFF TO THE LAND OF MILK AND HONEY.
ZAP

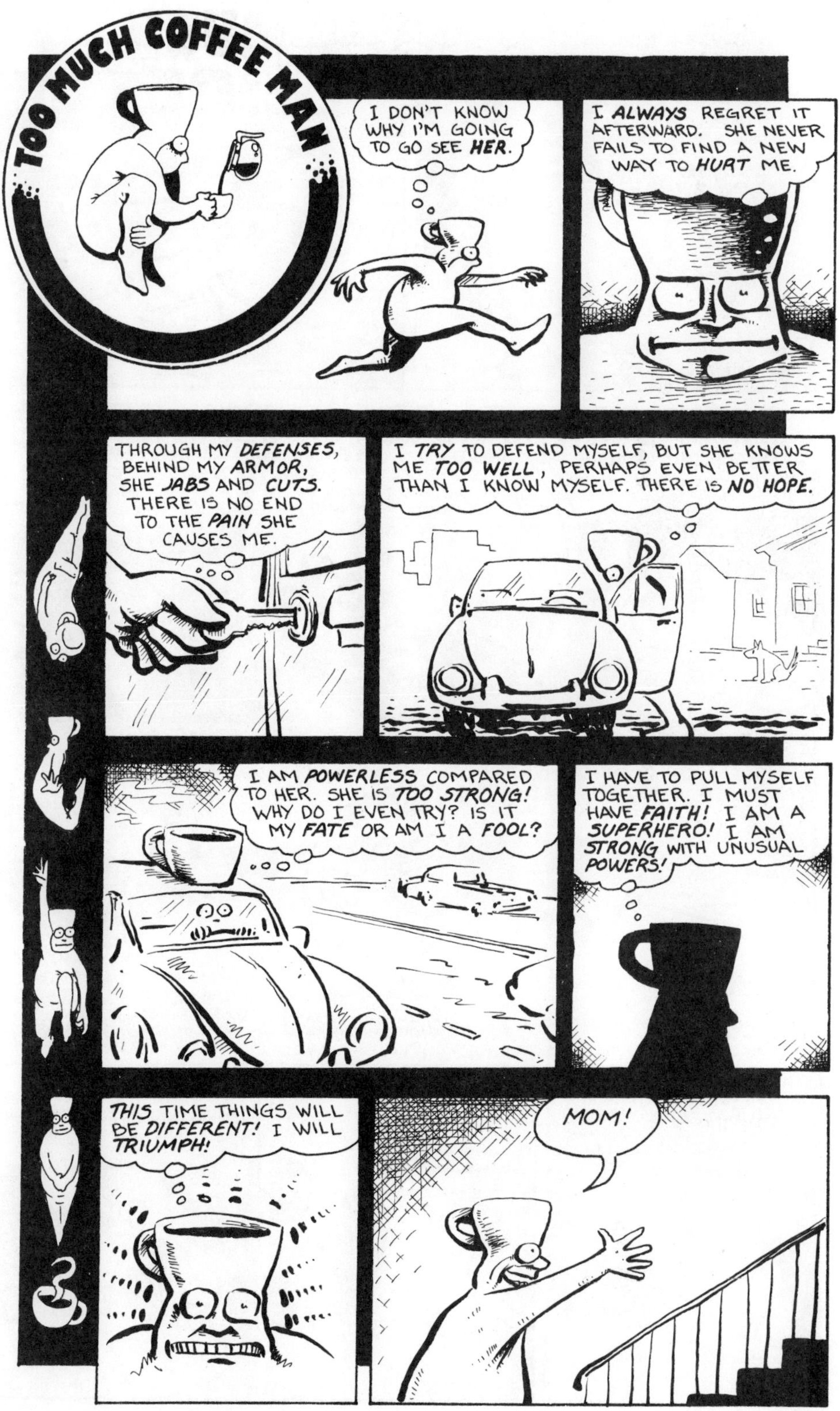
TOO MUCH COFFEE MAN
I DON'T KNOW WHY I'M GOING TO GO SEE HER.
I ALWAYS REGRET IT AFTERWARD. SHE NEVER FAILS TO FIND A NEW WAY TO HURT ME.
THROUGH MY DEFENSES, BEHIND MY ARMOR, SHE JABS AND CUTS. THERE IS NO END TO THE PAIN SHE CAUSES ME.
I TRY TO DEFEND MYSELF, BUT SHE KNOWS ME TOO WELL, PERHAPS EVEN BETTER THAN I KNOW MYSELF. THERE IS NO HOPE.
I AM POWERLESS COMPARED TO HER. SHE IS TOO STRONG! WHY DO I EVEN TRY? IS IT MY FATE OR AM I A FOOL?
I HAVE TO PULL MYSELF TOGETHER. I MUST HAVE FAITH! I AM A SUPERHERO! I AM STRONG WITH UNUSUAL POWERS!
THIS TIME THINGS WILL BE DIFFERENT! I WILL TRIUMPH!
MOM!

THIS CARTOON IS *TERRIBLE!*

IT'S REALLY *AWFUL.*

I CAN'T *BELIEVE* SOMEONE TOOK THE *TIME* TO WRITE AND DRAW THIS *THING.*

I DON'T KNOW WHICH WOULD BE WORSE-- IF IT *SUCKS* BECAUSE THEY DIDN'T WORK ON IT, OR IF THEY WORKED ON IT AND IT *STILL SUCKS!*

THE *CREATION* OF THIS CARTOON IS BUT THE *CENTER* OF A GIANT *MAELSTROM* OF TRAVESTY.

THINK ABOUT THE *COUNTLESS TREES* CUT DOWN IN THEIR *PRIME* FOR *CHEAP PAPER,* THE SMALL RIVER OF *TOXIC INK* NEEDED FOR PRINTING, AND THE TRUCKS CONSTANTLY DRIVING EVERYTHING *TO* AND *FRO.* ALL THE WHILE, *YESTERDAY'S* PAPERS CONTINUE TO PILE UP.

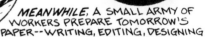

MEANWHILE, A SMALL ARMY OF WORKERS PREPARE TOMORROW'S PAPER--WRITING, EDITING, DESIGNING AND SELLING. THEN THE PRINTERS RUSH TO PRINT WORTHLESS WORDS ON EXPENSIVE PAPER SO MORE PEOPLE CAN *WASTE* THEIR TIME READING IT.

WHAT A PROFOUND *WASTE* OF HUMAN ENERGY AND NATURAL RESOURCES.

THIS *OTHER* CARTOON IS SORT OF FUNNY...

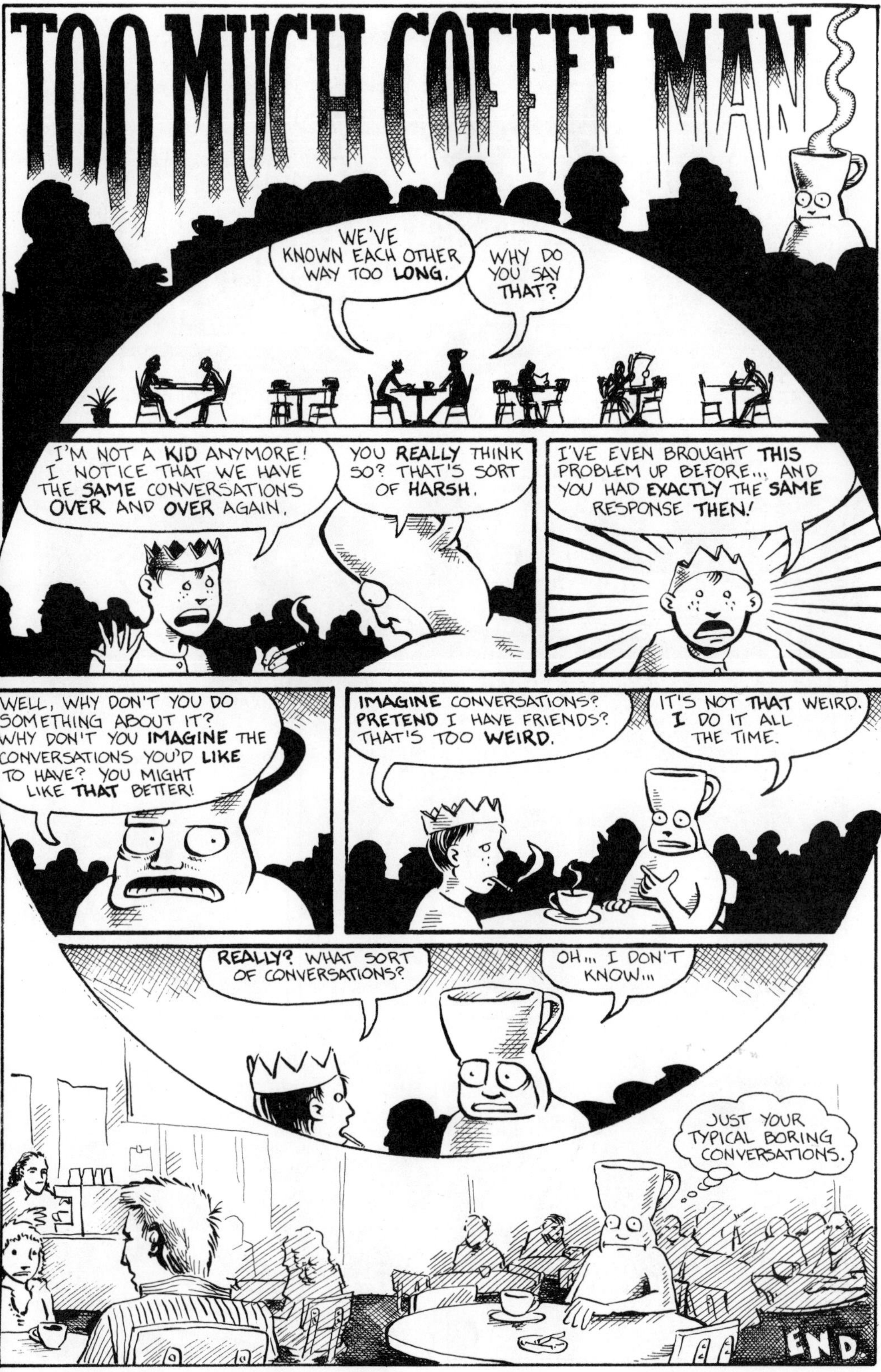
TOO MUCH COFFEE MAN
WE'VE KNOWN EACH OTHER WAY TOO LONG.
WHY DO YOU SAY THAT?
I'M NOT A KID ANYMORE! I NOTICE THAT WE HAVE THE SAME CONVERSATIONS OVER AND OVER AGAIN.
YOU REALLY THINK SO? THAT'S SORT OF HARSH.
I'VE EVEN BROUGHT THIS PROBLEM UP BEFORE... AND YOU HAD EXACTLY THE SAME RESPONSE THEN!
WELL, WHY DON'T YOU DO SOMETHING ABOUT IT? WHY DON'T YOU IMAGINE THE CONVERSATIONS YOU'D LIKE TO HAVE? YOU MIGHT LIKE THAT BETTER!
IMAGINE CONVERSATIONS? PRETEND I HAVE FRIENDS? THAT'S TOO WEIRD.
IT'S NOT THAT WEIRD. I DO IT ALL THE TIME.
REALLY? WHAT SORT OF CONVERSATIONS?
OH... I DON'T KNOW...
JUST YOUR TYPICAL BORING CONVERSATIONS.
END.

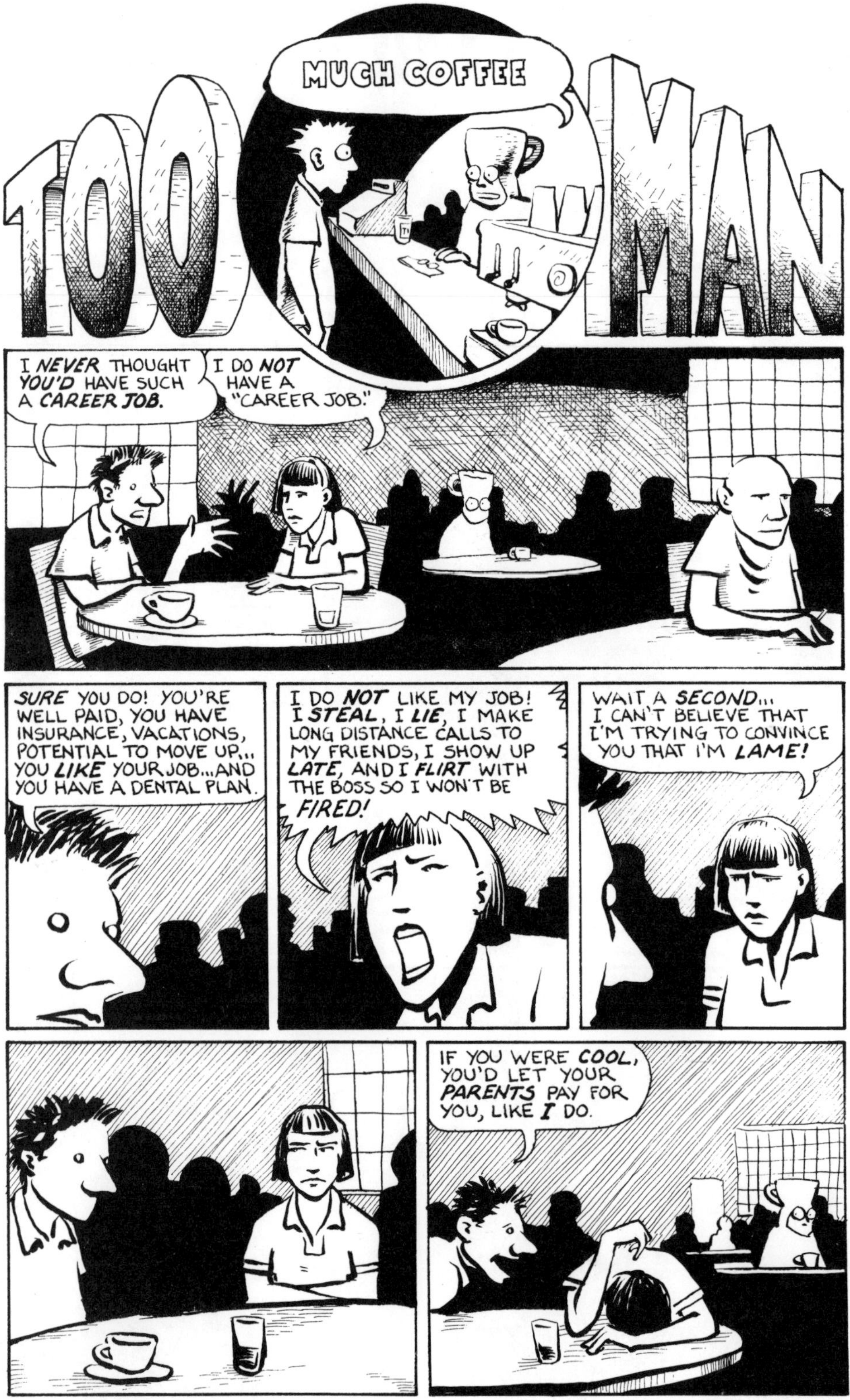
MUCH COFFEE
100
MAN
I NEVER THOUGHT YOU'D HAVE SUCH A CAREER JOB.
I DO NOT HAVE A "CAREER JOB."
SURE YOU DO! YOU'RE WELL PAID, YOU HAVE INSURANCE, VACATIONS, POTENTIAL TO MOVE UP... YOU LIKE YOUR JOB...AND YOU HAVE A DENTAL PLAN.
I DO NOT LIKE MY JOB! I STEAL, I LIE, I MAKE LONG DISTANCE CALLS TO MY FRIENDS, I SHOW UP LATE, AND I FLIRT WITH THE BOSS SO I WON'T BE FIRED!
WAIT A SECOND... I CAN'T BELIEVE THAT I'M TRYING TO CONVINCE YOU THAT I'M LAME!
IF YOU WERE COOL, YOU'D LET YOUR PARENTS PAY FOR YOU, LIKE I DO.

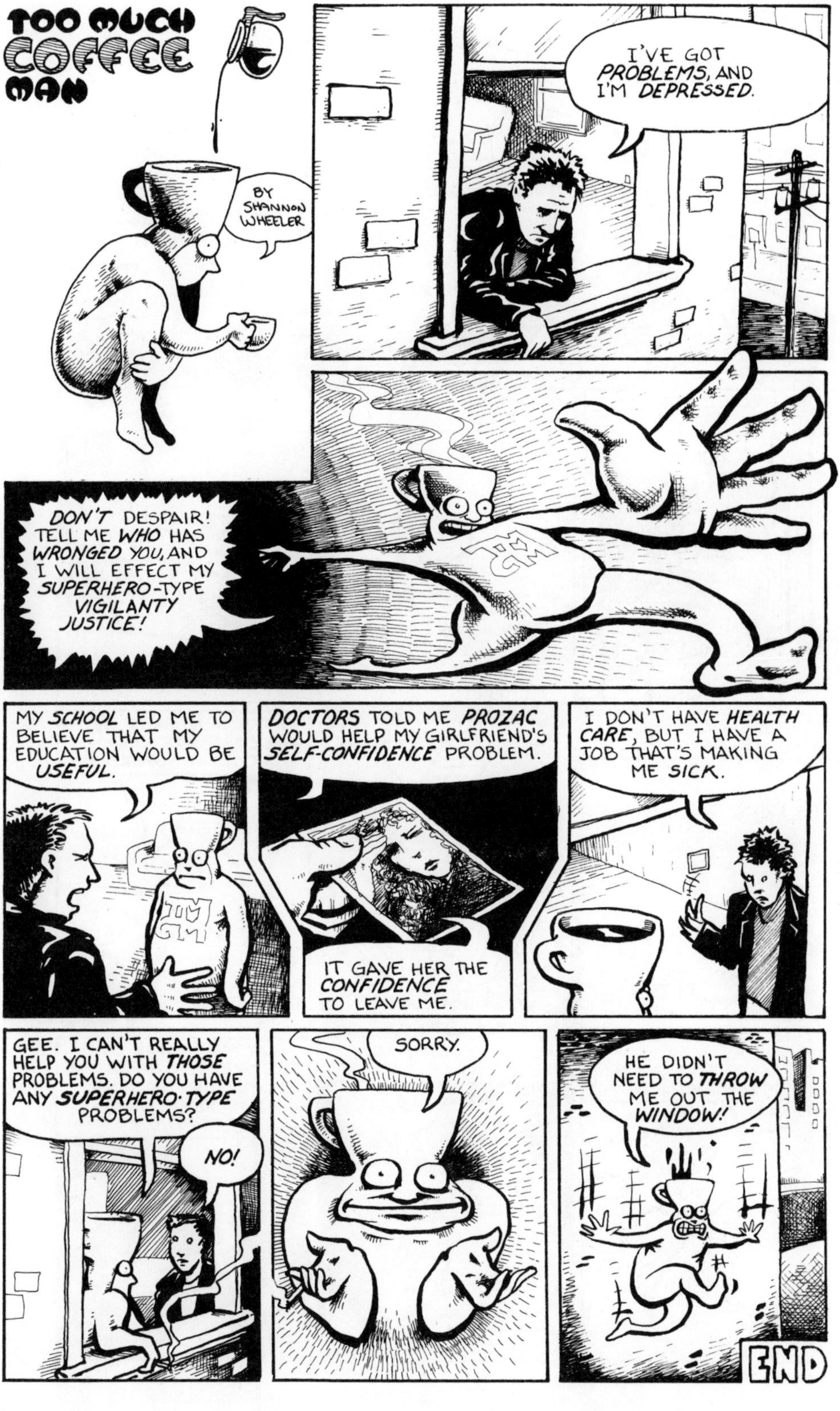
TOO MUCH COFFEE MAN
BY SHANNON WHEELER
I'VE GOT PROBLEMS, AND I'M DEPRESSED.
DON'T DESPAIR! TELL ME WHO HAS WRONGED YOU, AND I WILL EFFECT MY SUPERHERO-TYPE VIGILANTY JUSTICE!
MY SCHOOL LED ME TO BELIEVE THAT MY EDUCATION WOULD BE USEFUL.
DOCTORS TOLD ME PROZAC WOULD HELP MY GIRLFRIEND'S SELF-CONFIDENCE PROBLEM.
IT GAVE HER THE CONFIDENCE TO LEAVE ME.
I DON'T HAVE HEALTH CARE, BUT I HAVE A JOB THAT'S MAKING ME SICK.
GEE. I CAN'T REALLY HELP YOU WITH THOSE PROBLEMS. DO YOU HAVE ANY SUPERHERO-TYPE PROBLEMS?
NO!
SORRY.
HE DIDN'T NEED TO THROW ME OUT THE WINDOW!
END

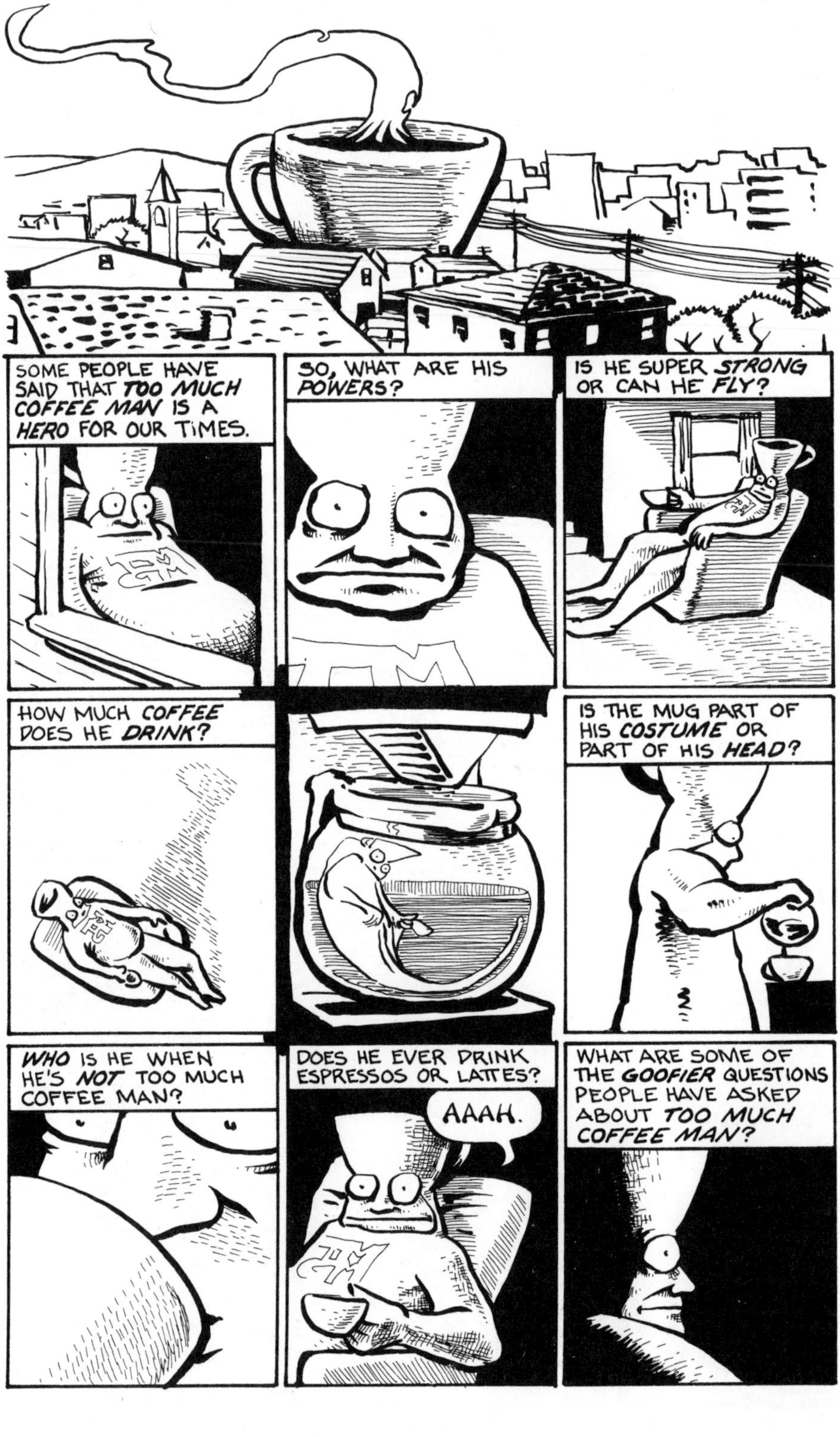
SOME PEOPLE HAVE SAID THAT TOO MUCH COFFEE MAN IS A HERO FOR OUR TIMES.
SO, WHAT ARE HIS POWERS?
IS HE SUPER STRONG OR CAN HE FLY?
HOW MUCH COFFEE DOES HE DRINK?
IS THE MUG PART OF HIS COSTUME OR PART OF HIS HEAD?
WHO IS HE WHEN HE'S NOT TOO MUCH COFFEE MAN?
DOES HE EVER DRINK ESPRESSOS OR LATTES?
AAAH.
WHAT ARE SOME OF THE GOOFIER QUESTIONS PEOPLE HAVE ASKED ABOUT TOO MUCH COFFEE MAN?

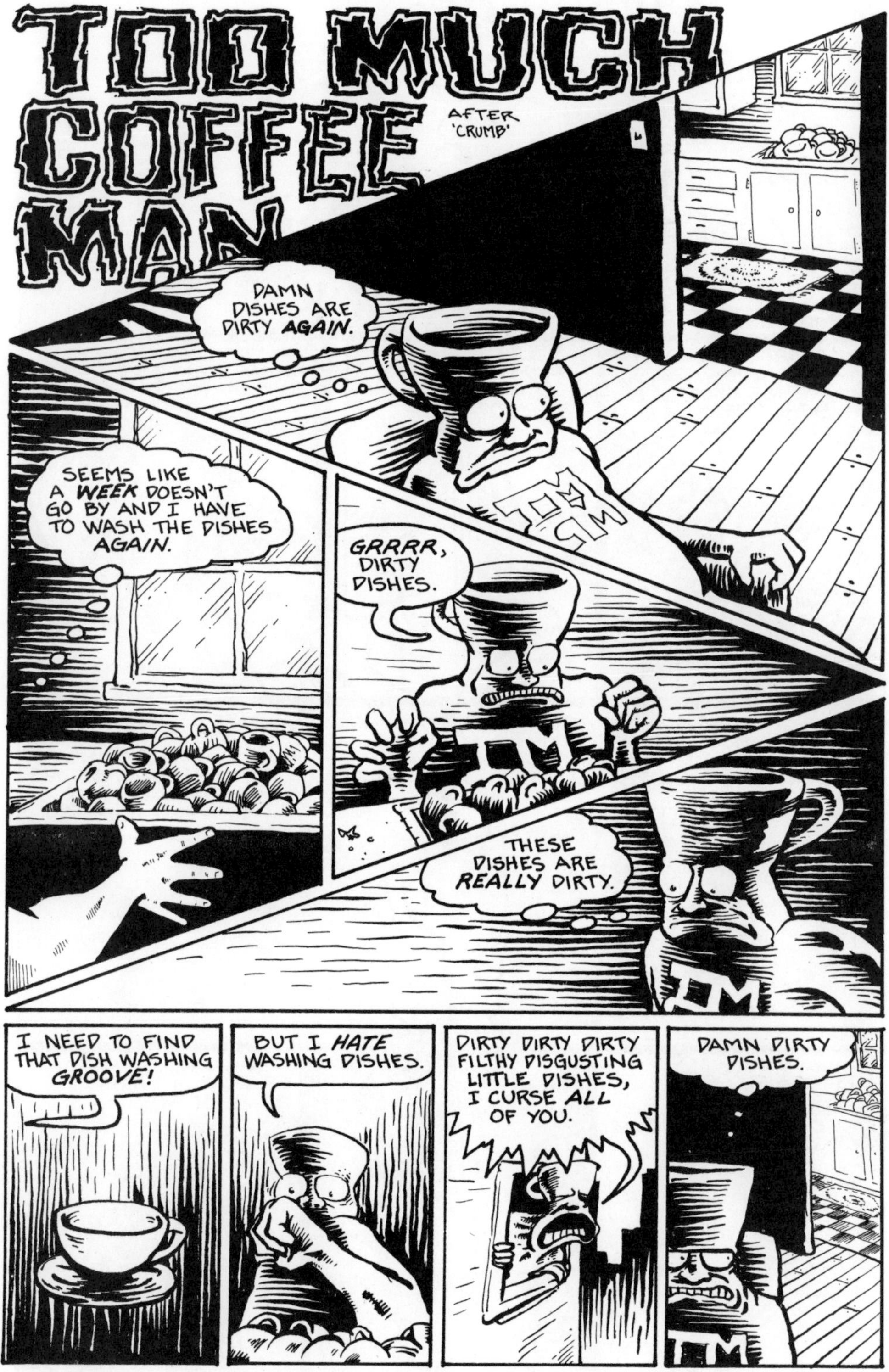
TOO MUCH COFFEE MAN
AFTER 'CRUMB'
DAMN DISHES ARE DIRTY AGAIN.
SEEMS LIKE A WEEK DOESN'T GO BY AND I HAVE TO WASH THE DISHES AGAIN.
GRRRR, DIRTY DISHES.
THESE DISHES ARE REALLY DIRTY.
I NEED TO FIND THAT DISH WASHING GROOVE!
BUT I HATE WASHING DISHES.
DIRTY DIRTY DIRTY FILTHY DISGUSTING LITTLE DISHES, I CURSE ALL OF YOU.
DAMN DIRTY DISHES.

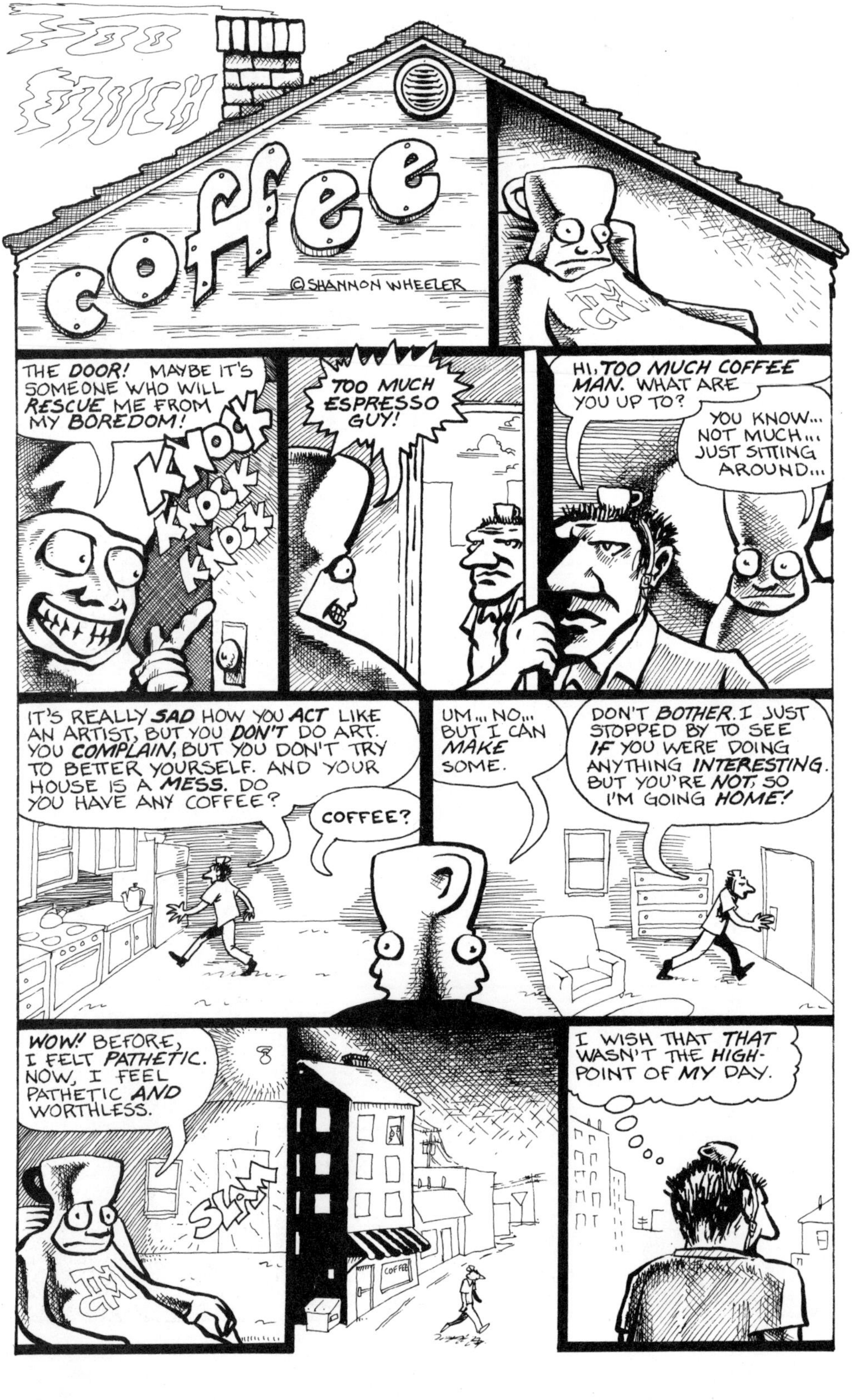TOO MUCH
coffee
©SHANNON WHEELER
THE DOOR! MAYBE IT'S SOMEONE WHO WILL RESCUE ME FROM MY BOREDOM!
KNOCK KNOCK KNOCK
TOO MUCH ESPRESSO GUY!
HI, TOO MUCH COFFEE MAN. WHAT ARE YOU UP TO?
YOU KNOW... NOT MUCH... JUST SITTING AROUND...
IT'S REALLY SAD HOW YOU ACT LIKE AN ARTIST, BUT YOU DON'T DO ART. YOU COMPLAIN, BUT YOU DON'T TRY TO BETTER YOURSELF. AND YOUR HOUSE IS A MESS. DO YOU HAVE ANY COFFEE?
COFFEE?
UM... NO... BUT I CAN MAKE SOME.
DON'T BOTHER. I JUST STOPPED BY TO SEE IF YOU WERE DOING ANYTHING INTERESTING. BUT YOU'RE NOT, SO I'M GOING HOME!
WOW! BEFORE, I FELT PATHETIC. NOW, I FEEL PATHETIC AND WORTHLESS.
SLAM
COFFEE
I WISH THAT THAT WASN'T THE HIGH-POINT OF MY DAY.

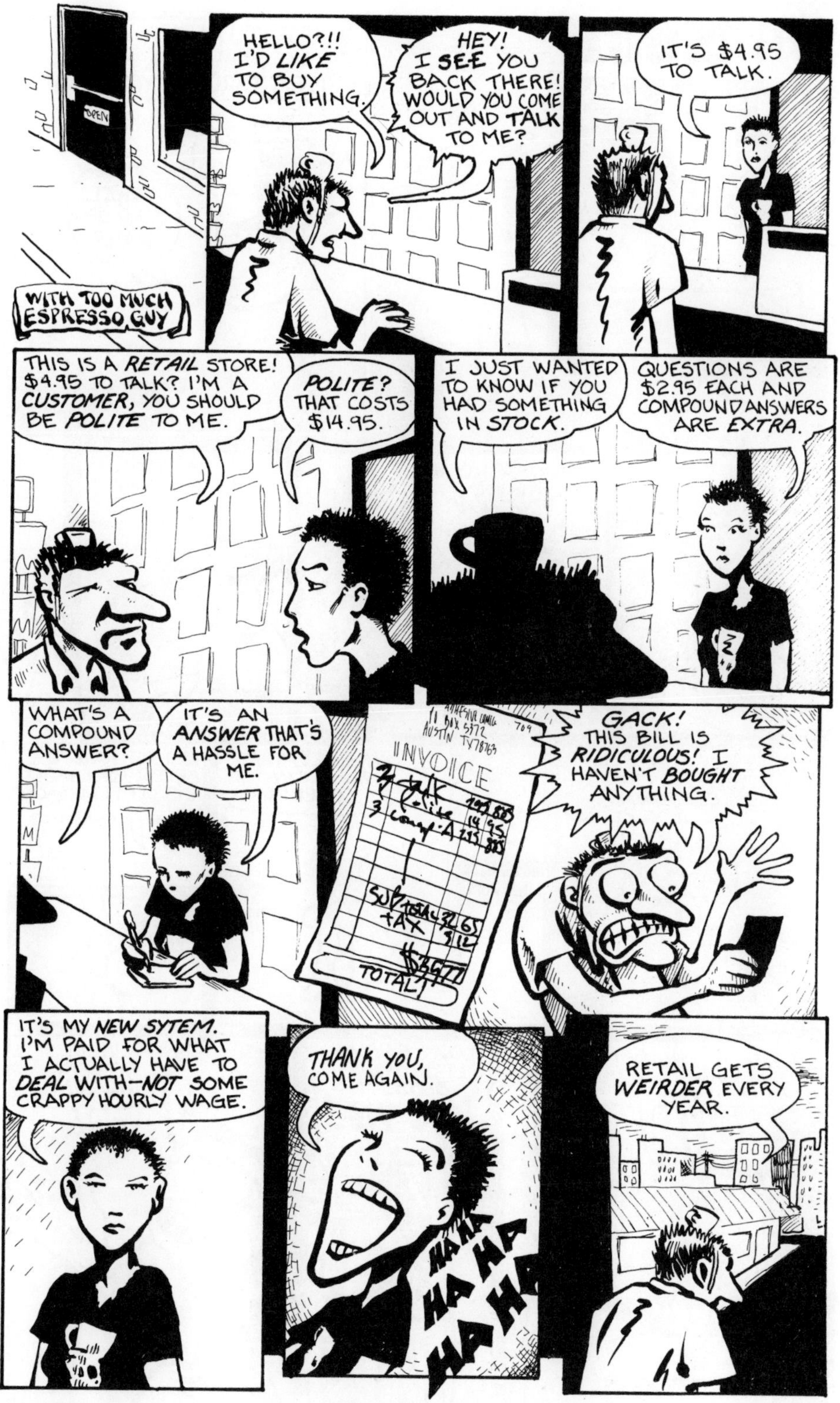
WITH TOO MUCH ESPRESSO GUY
HELLO?!! I'D LIKE TO BUY SOMETHING.
HEY! I SEE YOU BACK THERE! WOULD YOU COME OUT AND TALK TO ME?
IT'S $4.95 TO TALK.
THIS IS A RETAIL STORE! $4.95 TO TALK? I'M A CUSTOMER, YOU SHOULD BE POLITE TO ME.
POLITE? THAT COSTS $14.95.
I JUST WANTED TO KNOW IF YOU HAD SOMETHING IN STOCK.
QUESTIONS ARE $2.95 EACH AND COMPOUND ANSWERS ARE EXTRA.
WHAT'S A COMPOUND ANSWER?
IT'S AN ANSWER THAT'S A HASSLE FOR ME.
INVOICE
TOTAL
GACK! THIS BILL IS RIDICULOUS! I HAVEN'T BOUGHT ANYTHING.
IT'S MY NEW SYTEM. I'M PAID FOR WHAT I ACTUALLY HAVE TO DEAL WITH—NOT SOME CRAPPY HOURLY WAGE.
THANK YOU, COME AGAIN.
HA HA HA HA HA HA
RETAIL GETS WEIRDER EVERY YEAR.

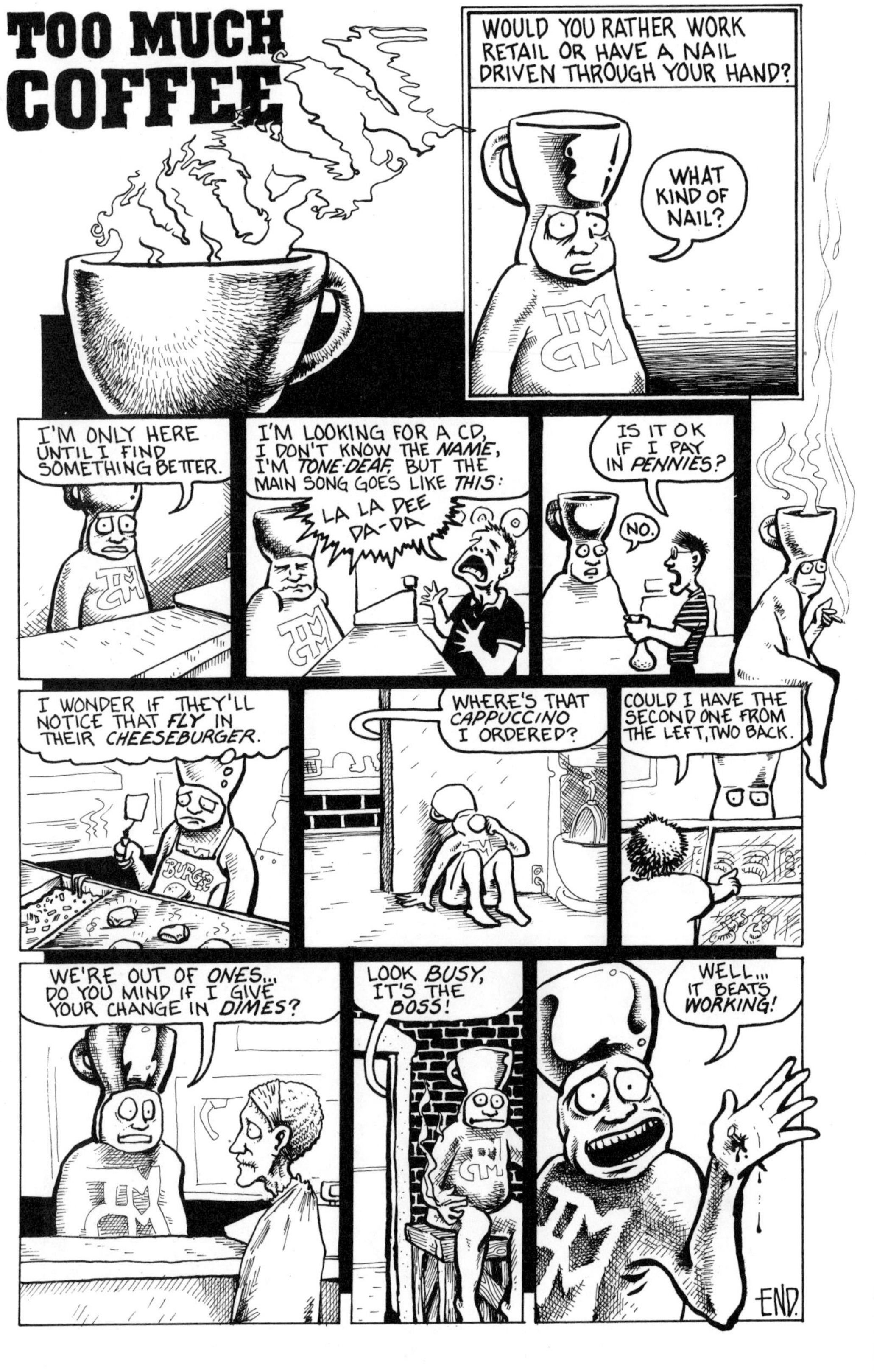
TOO MUCH COFFEE
WOULD YOU RATHER WORK RETAIL OR HAVE A NAIL DRIVEN THROUGH YOUR HAND?
WHAT KIND OF NAIL?
I'M ONLY HERE UNTIL I FIND SOMETHING BETTER.
I'M LOOKING FOR A CD, I DON'T KNOW THE NAME, I'M TONE-DEAF, BUT THE MAIN SONG GOES LIKE THIS:
LA LA DEE DA-DA
IS IT OK IF I PAY IN PENNIES?
NO.
I WONDER IF THEY'LL NOTICE THAT FLY IN THEIR CHEESEBURGER.
BURGER
WHERE'S THAT CAPPUCCINO I ORDERED?
COULD I HAVE THE SECOND ONE FROM THE LEFT, TWO BACK.
WE'RE OUT OF ONES... DO YOU MIND IF I GIVE YOUR CHANGE IN DIMES?
LOOK BUSY, IT'S THE BOSS!
WELL... IT BEATS WORKING!
END.

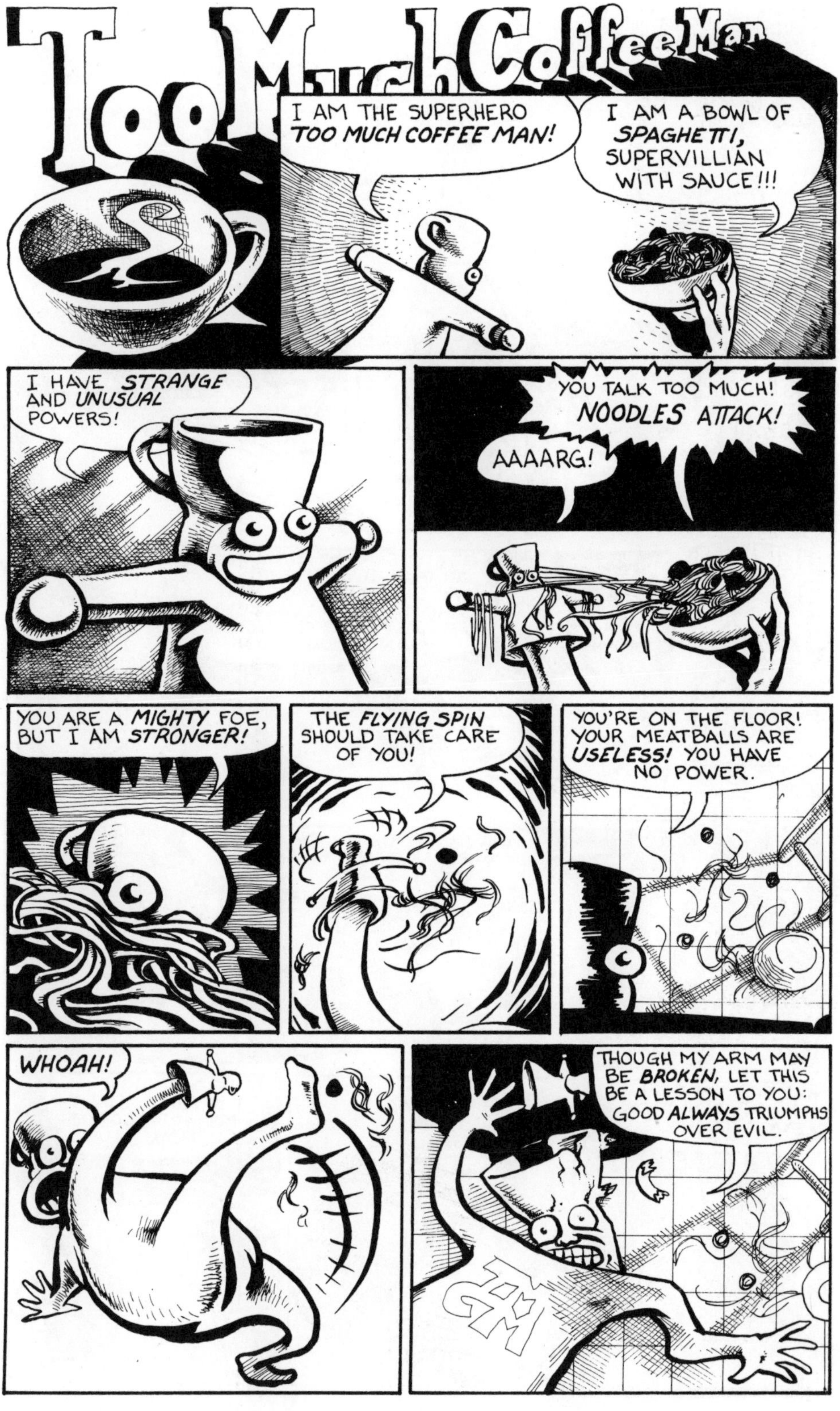
Too Much Coffee Man
I AM THE SUPERHERO TOO MUCH COFFEE MAN!
I AM A BOWL OF SPAGHETTI, SUPERVILLIAN WITH SAUCE!!!
I HAVE STRANGE AND UNUSUAL POWERS!
YOU TALK TOO MUCH! NOODLES ATTACK!
AAAARG!
YOU ARE A MIGHTY FOE, BUT I AM STRONGER!
THE FLYING SPIN SHOULD TAKE CARE OF YOU!
YOU'RE ON THE FLOOR! YOUR MEATBALLS ARE USELESS! YOU HAVE NO POWER.
WHOAH!
THOUGH MY ARM MAY BE BROKEN, LET THIS BE A LESSON TO YOU: GOOD ALWAYS TRIUMPHS OVER EVIL.
TCM

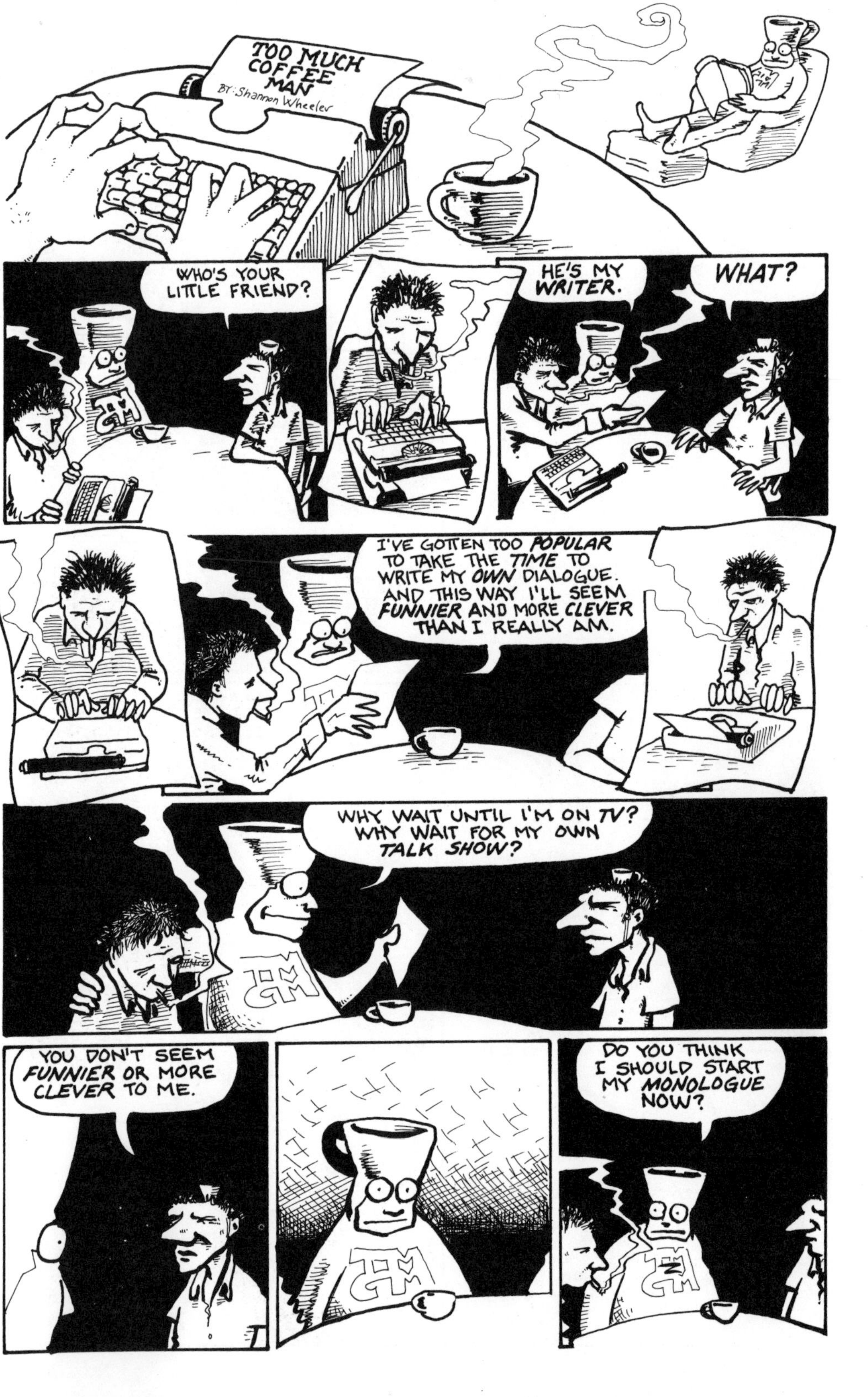
TOO MUCH COFFEE MAN
BY: Shannon Wheeler
WHO'S YOUR LITTLE FRIEND?
HE'S MY WRITER.
WHAT?
I'VE GOTTEN TOO POPULAR TO TAKE THE TIME TO WRITE MY OWN DIALOGUE. AND THIS WAY I'LL SEEM FUNNIER AND MORE CLEVER THAN I REALLY AM.
WHY WAIT UNTIL I'M ON TV? WHY WAIT FOR MY OWN TALK SHOW?
YOU DON'T SEEM FUNNIER OR MORE CLEVER TO ME.
DO YOU THINK I SHOULD START MY MONOLOGUE NOW?

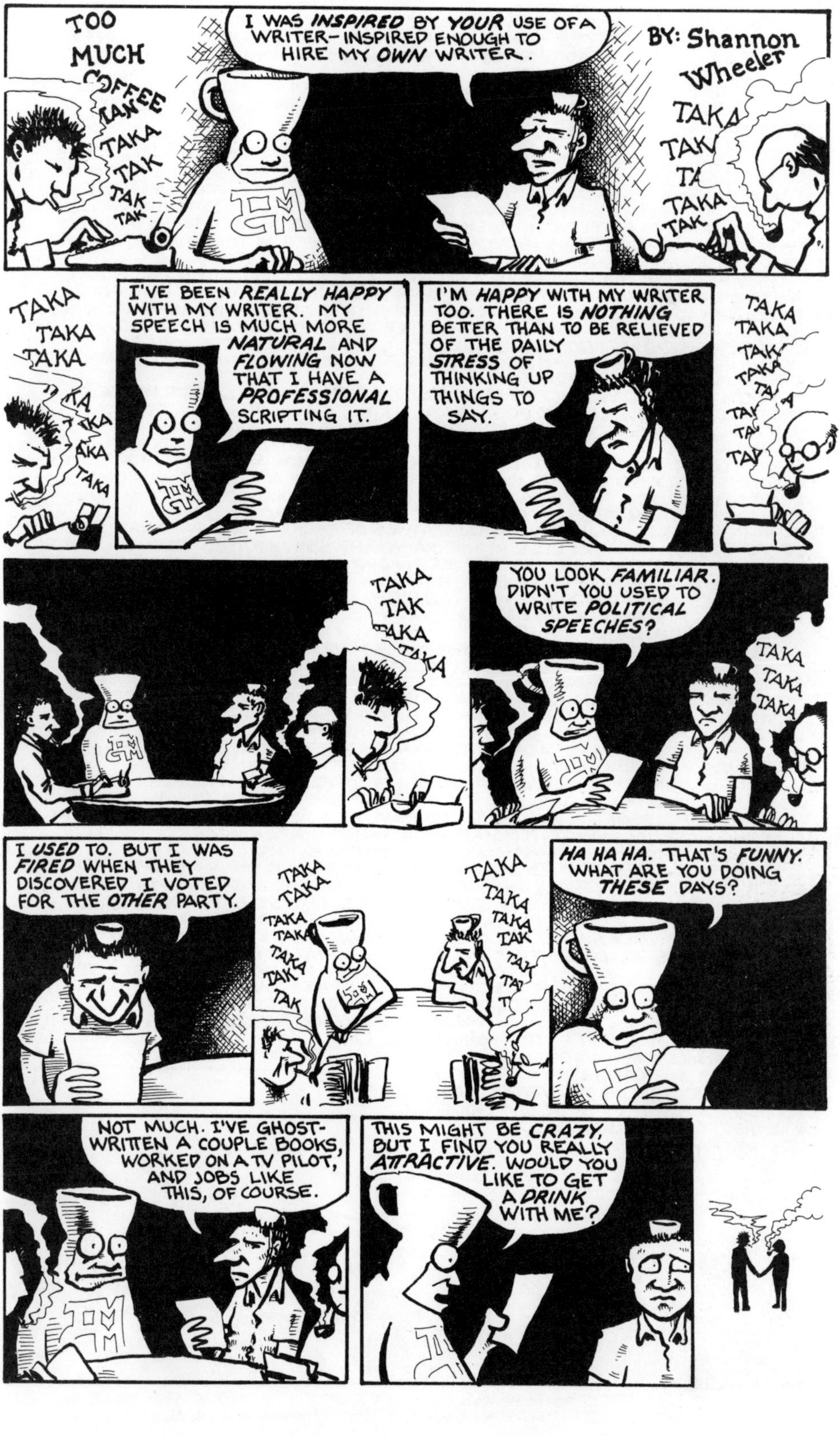
TOO MUCH COFFEE MAN
BY: Shannon Wheeler
I WAS INSPIRED BY YOUR USE OF A WRITER– INSPIRED ENOUGH TO HIRE MY OWN WRITER.
TAKA TAK TAK TAK
I'VE BEEN REALLY HAPPY WITH MY WRITER. MY SPEECH IS MUCH MORE NATURAL AND FLOWING NOW THAT I HAVE A PROFESSIONAL SCRIPTING IT.
I'M HAPPY WITH MY WRITER TOO. THERE IS NOTHING BETTER THAN TO BE RELIEVED OF THE DAILY STRESS OF THINKING UP THINGS TO SAY.
TAKA TAK
YOU LOOK FAMILIAR. DIDN'T YOU USED TO WRITE POLITICAL SPEECHES?
I USED TO. BUT I WAS FIRED WHEN THEY DISCOVERED I VOTED FOR THE OTHER PARTY.
HA HA HA. THAT'S FUNNY. WHAT ARE YOU DOING THESE DAYS?
NOT MUCH. I'VE GHOST-WRITTEN A COUPLE BOOKS, WORKED ON A TV PILOT, AND JOBS LIKE THIS, OF COURSE.
THIS MIGHT BE CRAZY, BUT I FIND YOU REALLY ATTRACTIVE. WOULD YOU LIKE TO GET A DRINK WITH ME?

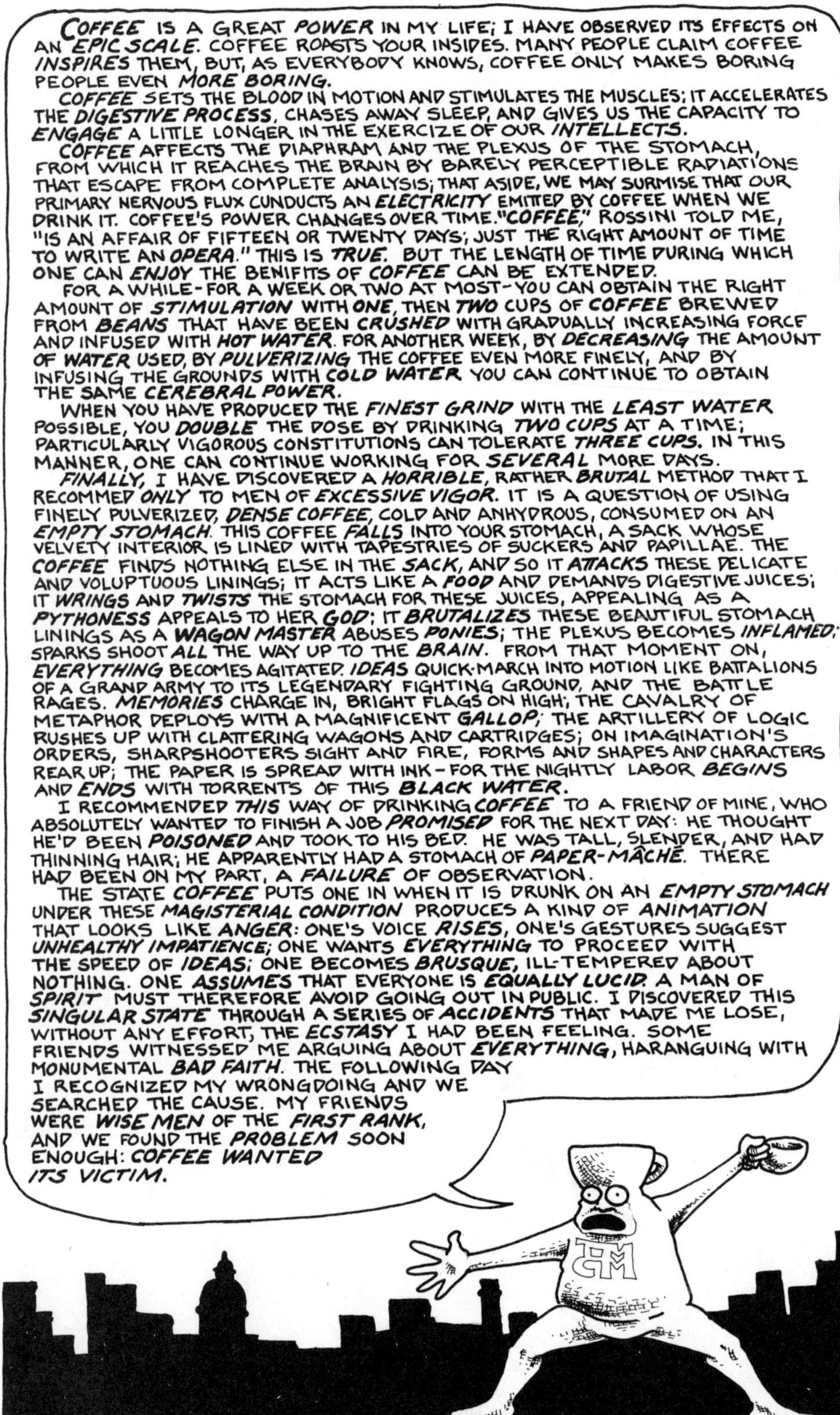
COFFEE IS A GREAT POWER IN MY LIFE; I HAVE OBSERVED ITS EFFECTS ON AN EPIC SCALE. COFFEE ROASTS YOUR INSIDES. MANY PEOPLE CLAIM COFFEE INSPIRES THEM, BUT, AS EVERYBODY KNOWS, COFFEE ONLY MAKES BORING PEOPLE EVEN MORE BORING.
COFFEE SETS THE BLOOD IN MOTION AND STIMULATES THE MUSCLES; IT ACCELERATES THE DIGESTIVE PROCESS, CHASES AWAY SLEEP, AND GIVES US THE CAPACITY TO ENGAGE A LITTLE LONGER IN THE EXERCIZE OF OUR INTELLECTS.
COFFEE AFFECTS THE DIAPHRAM AND THE PLEXUS OF THE STOMACH, FROM WHICH IT REACHES THE BRAIN BY BARELY PERCEPTIBLE RADIATIONS THAT ESCAPE FROM COMPLETE ANALYSIS; THAT ASIDE, WE MAY SURMISE THAT OUR PRIMARY NERVOUS FLUX CUNDUCTS AN ELECTRICITY EMITTED BY COFFEE WHEN WE DRINK IT. COFFEE'S POWER CHANGES OVER TIME. "COFFEE," ROSSINI TOLD ME, "IS AN AFFAIR OF FIFTEEN OR TWENTY DAYS; JUST THE RIGHT AMOUNT OF TIME TO WRITE AN OPERA." THIS IS TRUE. BUT THE LENGTH OF TIME DURING WHICH ONE CAN ENJOY THE BENIFITS OF COFFEE CAN BE EXTENDED.
FOR A WHILE - FOR A WEEK OR TWO AT MOST - YOU CAN OBTAIN THE RIGHT AMOUNT OF STIMULATION WITH ONE, THEN TWO CUPS OF COFFEE BREWED FROM BEANS THAT HAVE BEEN CRUSHED WITH GRADUALLY INCREASING FORCE AND INFUSED WITH HOT WATER. FOR ANOTHER WEEK, BY DECREASING THE AMOUNT OF WATER USED, BY PULVERIZING THE COFFEE EVEN MORE FINELY, AND BY INFUSING THE GROUNDS WITH COLD WATER YOU CAN CONTINUE TO OBTAIN THE SAME CEREBRAL POWER.
WHEN YOU HAVE PRODUCED THE FINEST GRIND WITH THE LEAST WATER POSSIBLE, YOU DOUBLE THE DOSE BY DRINKING TWO CUPS AT A TIME; PARTICULARLY VIGOROUS CONSTITUTIONS CAN TOLERATE THREE CUPS. IN THIS MANNER, ONE CAN CONTINUE WORKING FOR SEVERAL MORE DAYS.
FINALLY, I HAVE DISCOVERED A HORRIBLE, RATHER BRUTAL METHOD THAT I RECOMMED ONLY TO MEN OF EXCESSIVE VIGOR. IT IS A QUESTION OF USING FINELY PULVERIZED, DENSE COFFEE, COLD AND ANHYDROUS, CONSUMED ON AN EMPTY STOMACH. THIS COFFEE FALLS INTO YOUR STOMACH, A SACK WHOSE VELVETY INTERIOR IS LINED WITH TAPESTRIES OF SUCKERS AND PAPILLAE. THE COFFEE FINDS NOTHING ELSE IN THE SACK, AND SO IT ATTACKS THESE DELICATE AND VOLUPTUOUS LININGS; IT ACTS LIKE A FOOD AND DEMANDS DIGESTIVE JUICES; IT WRINGS AND TWISTS THE STOMACH FOR THESE JUICES, APPEALING AS A PYTHONESS APPEALS TO HER GOD; IT BRUTALIZES THESE BEAUTIFUL STOMACH LININGS AS A WAGON MASTER ABUSES PONIES; THE PLEXUS BECOMES INFLAMED; SPARKS SHOOT ALL THE WAY UP TO THE BRAIN. FROM THAT MOMENT ON, EVERYTHING BECOMES AGITATED. IDEAS QUICK-MARCH INTO MOTION LIKE BATTALIONS OF A GRAND ARMY TO ITS LEGENDARY FIGHTING GROUND, AND THE BATTLE RAGES. MEMORIES CHARGE IN, BRIGHT FLAGS ON HIGH; THE CAVALRY OF METAPHOR DEPLOYS WITH A MAGNIFICENT GALLOP; THE ARTILLERY OF LOGIC RUSHES UP WITH CLATTERING WAGONS AND CARTRIDGES; ON IMAGINATION'S ORDERS, SHARPSHOOTERS SIGHT AND FIRE, FORMS AND SHAPES AND CHARACTERS REAR UP; THE PAPER IS SPREAD WITH INK - FOR THE NIGHTLY LABOR BEGINS AND ENDS WITH TORRENTS OF THIS BLACK WATER.
I RECOMMENDED THIS WAY OF DRINKING COFFEE TO A FRIEND OF MINE, WHO ABSOLUTELY WANTED TO FINISH A JOB PROMISED FOR THE NEXT DAY: HE THOUGHT HE'D BEEN POISONED AND TOOK TO HIS BED. HE WAS TALL, SLENDER, AND HAD THINNING HAIR; HE APPARENTLY HAD A STOMACH OF PAPER-MÂCHÉ. THERE HAD BEEN ON MY PART, A FAILURE OF OBSERVATION.
THE STATE COFFEE PUTS ONE IN WHEN IT IS DRUNK ON AN EMPTY STOMACH UNDER THESE MAGISTERIAL CONDITION PRODUCES A KIND OF ANIMATION THAT LOOKS LIKE ANGER: ONE'S VOICE RISES, ONE'S GESTURES SUGGEST UNHEALTHY IMPATIENCE; ONE WANTS EVERYTHING TO PROCEED WITH THE SPEED OF IDEAS; ONE BECOMES BRUSQUE, ILL-TEMPERED ABOUT NOTHING. ONE ASSUMES THAT EVERYONE IS EQUALLY LUCID. A MAN OF SPIRIT MUST THEREFORE AVOID GOING OUT IN PUBLIC. I DISCOVERED THIS SINGULAR STATE THROUGH A SERIES OF ACCIDENTS THAT MADE ME LOSE, WITHOUT ANY EFFORT, THE ECSTASY I HAD BEEN FEELING. SOME FRIENDS WITNESSED ME ARGUING ABOUT EVERYTHING, HARANGUING WITH MONUMENTAL BAD FAITH. THE FOLLOWING DAY I RECOGNIZED MY WRONGDOING AND WE SEARCHED THE CAUSE. MY FRIENDS WERE WISE MEN OF THE FIRST RANK, AND WE FOUND THE PROBLEM SOON ENOUGH: COFFEE WANTED ITS VICTIM.

FROM "THE PLEASURES AND PAINS OF COFFEE" BY HONORÉ DE BALZAC
TRANSLATED BY ROBERT ONOPA DRAWN BY SHANNON WHEELER

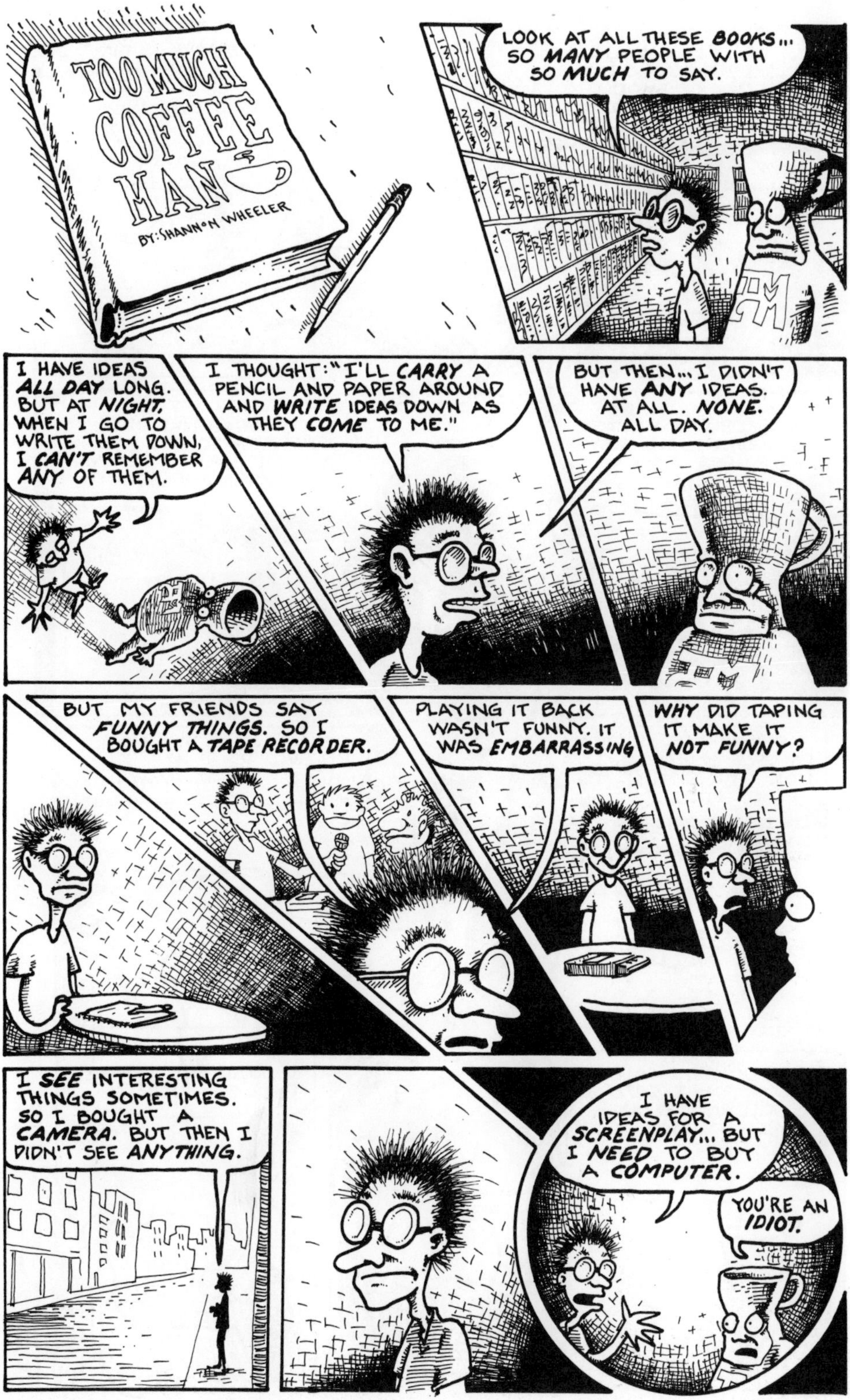
TOO MUCH COFFEE MAN
BY: SHANNON WHEELER
TOO MUCH COFFEE MAN'S...
LOOK AT ALL THESE BOOKS... SO MANY PEOPLE WITH SO MUCH TO SAY.
I HAVE IDEAS ALL DAY LONG. BUT AT NIGHT, WHEN I GO TO WRITE THEM DOWN, I CAN'T REMEMBER ANY OF THEM.
I THOUGHT: "I'LL CARRY A PENCIL AND PAPER AROUND AND WRITE IDEAS DOWN AS THEY COME TO ME."
BUT THEN... I DIDN'T HAVE ANY IDEAS. AT ALL. NONE. ALL DAY.
BUT MY FRIENDS SAY FUNNY THINGS. SO I BOUGHT A TAPE RECORDER.
PLAYING IT BACK WASN'T FUNNY. IT WAS EMBARRASSING
WHY DID TAPING IT MAKE IT NOT FUNNY?
I SEE INTERESTING THINGS SOMETIMES. SO I BOUGHT A CAMERA. BUT THEN I DIDN'T SEE ANYTHING.
I HAVE IDEAS FOR A SCREENPLAY... BUT I NEED TO BUY A COMPUTER.
YOU'RE AN IDIOT.

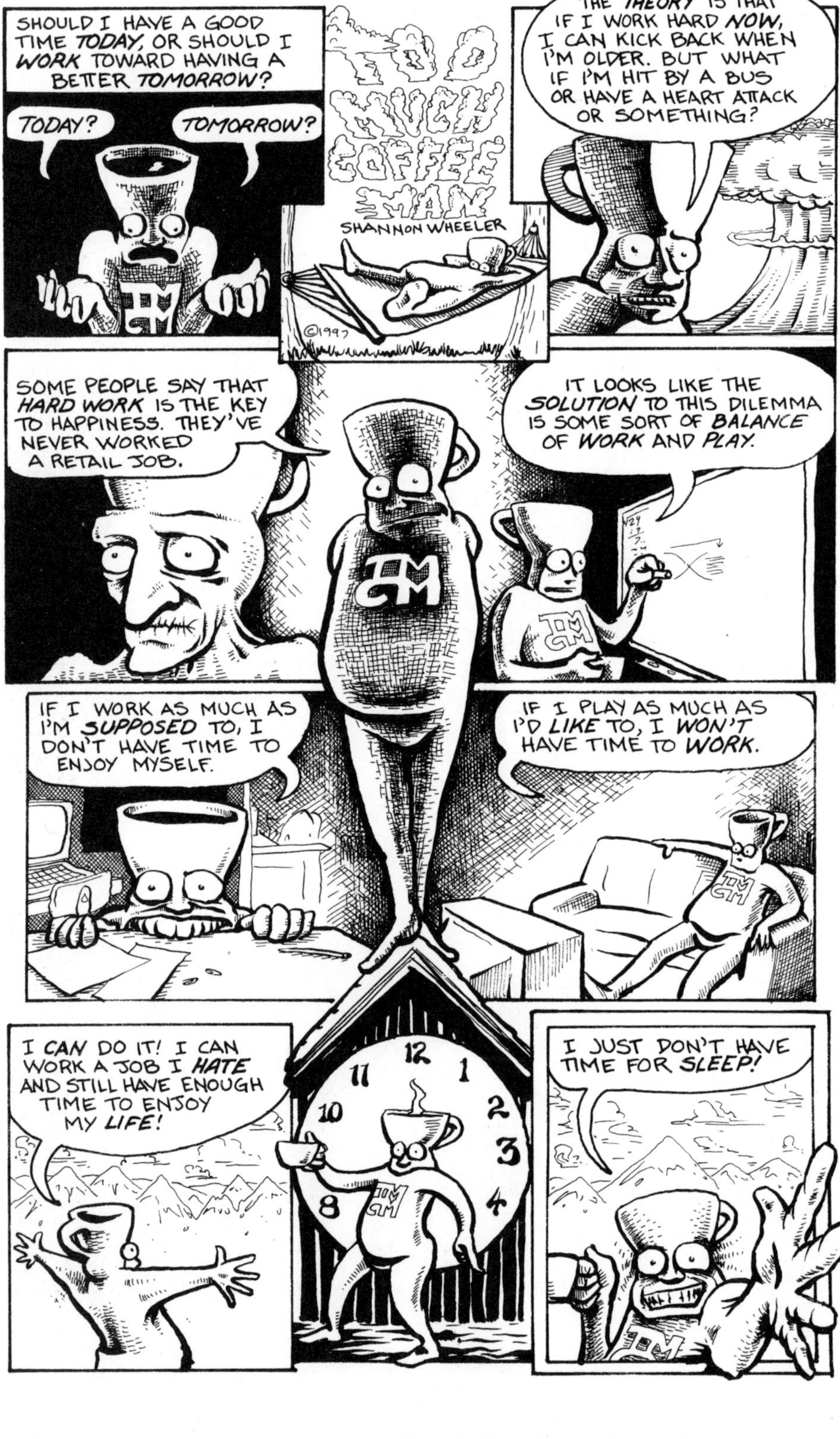
SHOULD I HAVE A GOOD TIME TODAY, OR SHOULD I WORK TOWARD HAVING A BETTER TOMORROW?
TODAY?
TOMORROW?
TOO MUCH COFFEE MAN
SHANNON WHEELER
©1997
THE THEORY IS THAT IF I WORK HARD NOW, I CAN KICK BACK WHEN I'M OLDER. BUT WHAT IF I'M HIT BY A BUS OR HAVE A HEART ATTACK OR SOMETHING?
SOME PEOPLE SAY THAT HARD WORK IS THE KEY TO HAPPINESS. THEY'VE NEVER WORKED A RETAIL JOB.
IT LOOKS LIKE THE SOLUTION TO THIS DILEMMA IS SOME SORT OF BALANCE OF WORK AND PLAY.
IF I WORK AS MUCH AS I'M SUPPOSED TO, I DON'T HAVE TIME TO ENJOY MYSELF.
IF I PLAY AS MUCH AS I'D LIKE TO, I WON'T HAVE TIME TO WORK.
I CAN DO IT! I CAN WORK A JOB I HATE AND STILL HAVE ENOUGH TIME TO ENJOY MY LIFE!
I JUST DON'T HAVE TIME FOR SLEEP!

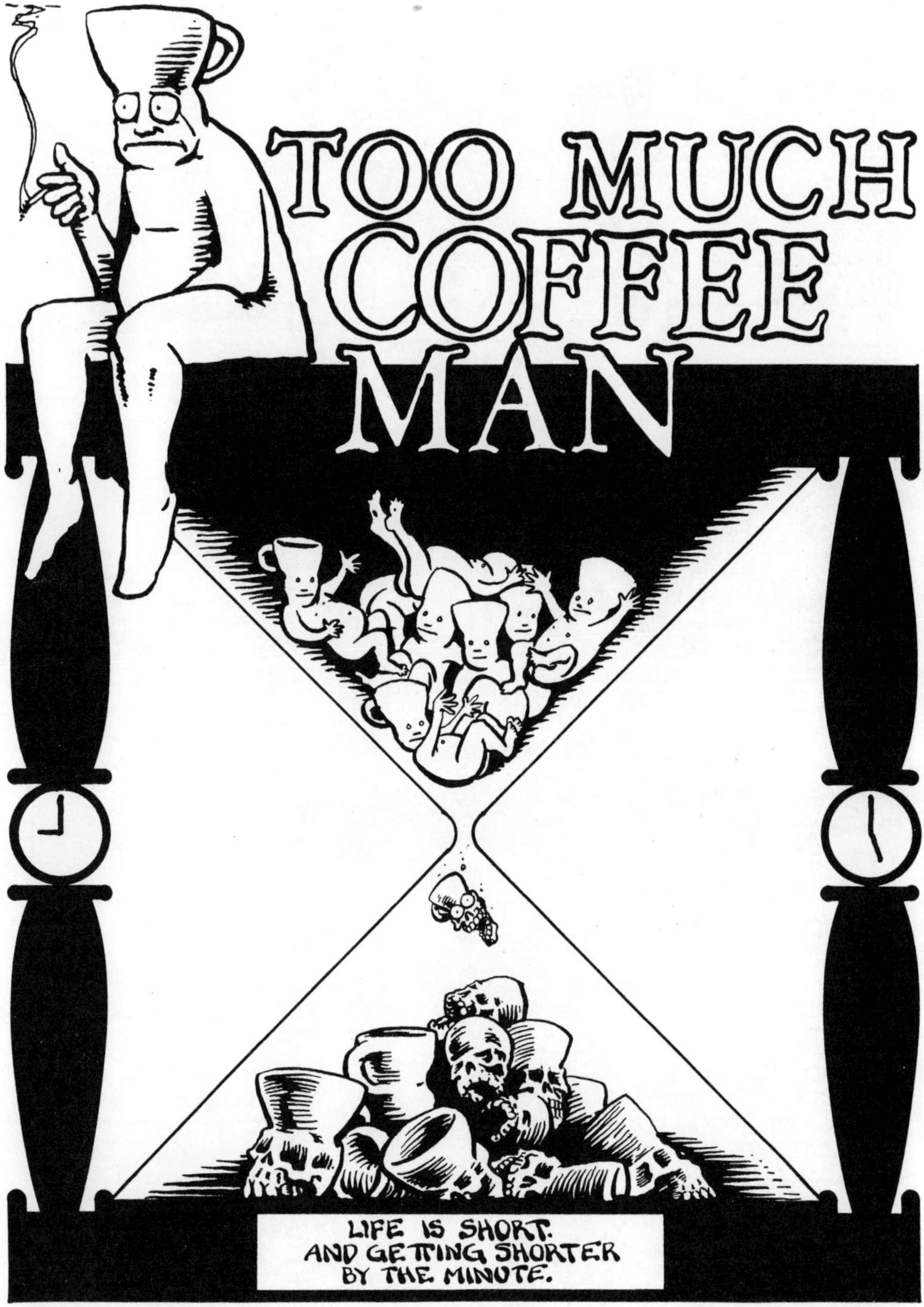
TOO MUCH COFFEE MAN
LIFE IS SHORT. AND GETTING SHORTER BY THE MINUTE.

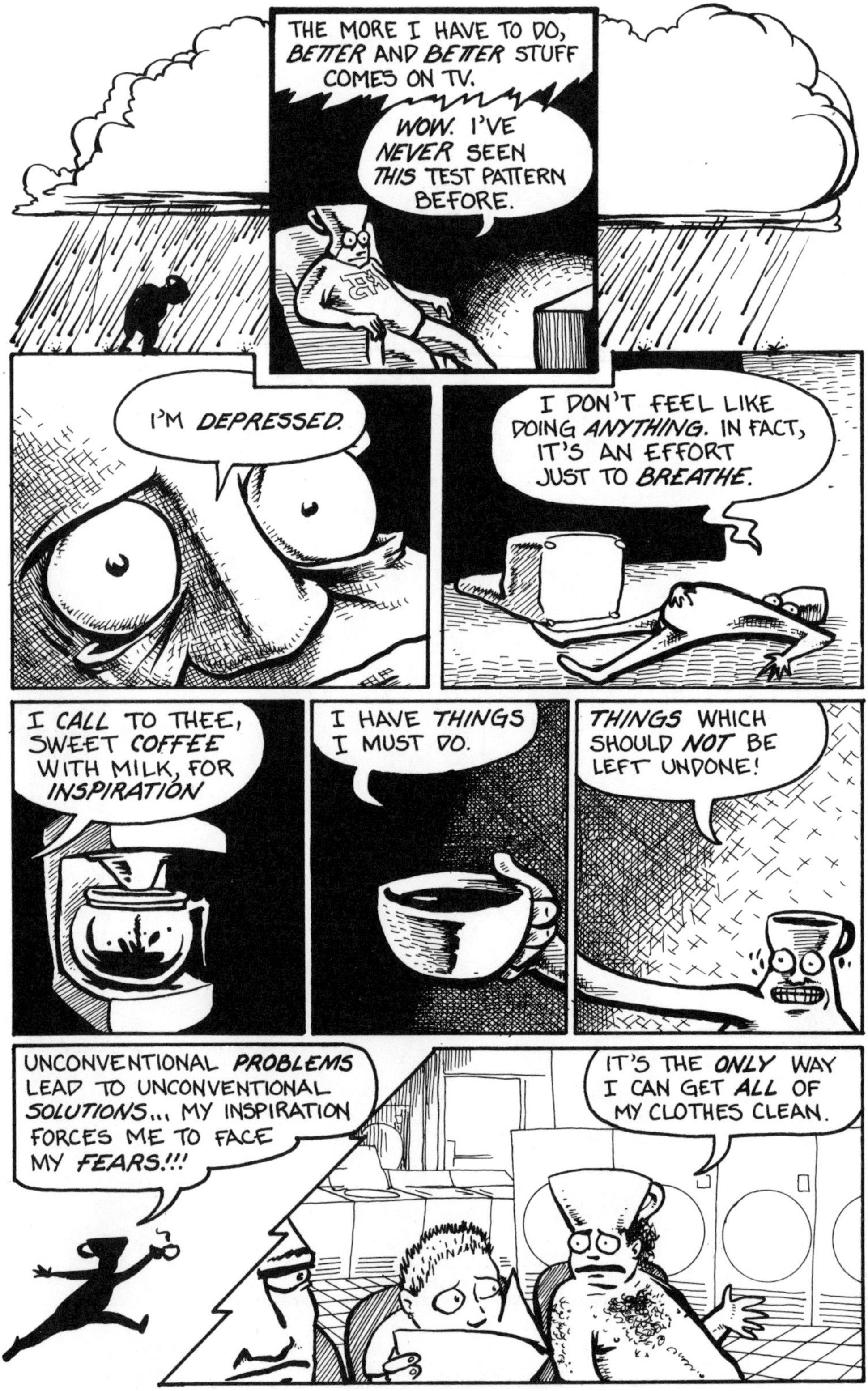
THE MORE I HAVE TO DO, BETTER AND BETTER STUFF COMES ON TV.
WOW. I'VE NEVER SEEN THIS TEST PATTERN BEFORE.
I'M DEPRESSED.
I DON'T FEEL LIKE DOING ANYTHING. IN FACT, IT'S AN EFFORT JUST TO BREATHE.
I CALL TO THEE, SWEET COFFEE WITH MILK, FOR INSPIRATION
I HAVE THINGS I MUST DO.
THINGS WHICH SHOULD NOT BE LEFT UNDONE!
UNCONVENTIONAL PROBLEMS LEAD TO UNCONVENTIONAL SOLUTIONS... MY INSPIRATION FORCES ME TO FACE MY FEARS!!!
IT'S THE ONLY WAY I CAN GET ALL OF MY CLOTHES CLEAN.

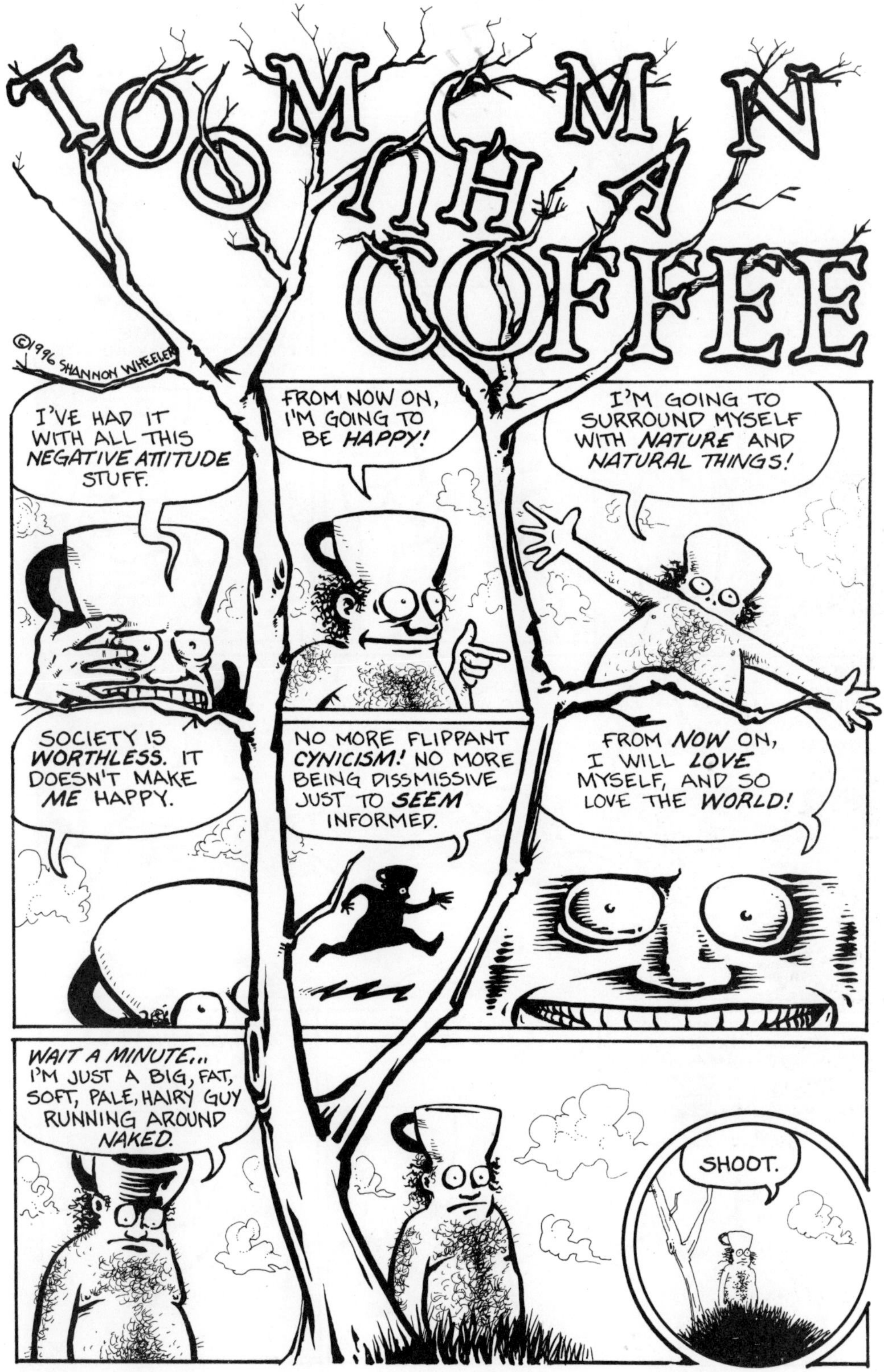

100% MOCHA MAN COFFEE
©1996 SHANNON WHEELER
I'VE HAD IT WITH ALL THIS NEGATIVE ATTITUDE STUFF.
FROM NOW ON, I'M GOING TO BE HAPPY!
I'M GOING TO SURROUND MYSELF WITH NATURE AND NATURAL THINGS!
SOCIETY IS WORTHLESS. IT DOESN'T MAKE ME HAPPY.
NO MORE FLIPPANT CYNICISM! NO MORE BEING DISSMISSIVE JUST TO SEEM INFORMED.
FROM NOW ON, I WILL LOVE MYSELF, AND SO LOVE THE WORLD!
WAIT A MINUTE... I'M JUST A BIG, FAT, SOFT, PALE, HAIRY GUY RUNNING AROUND NAKED.
SHOOT.

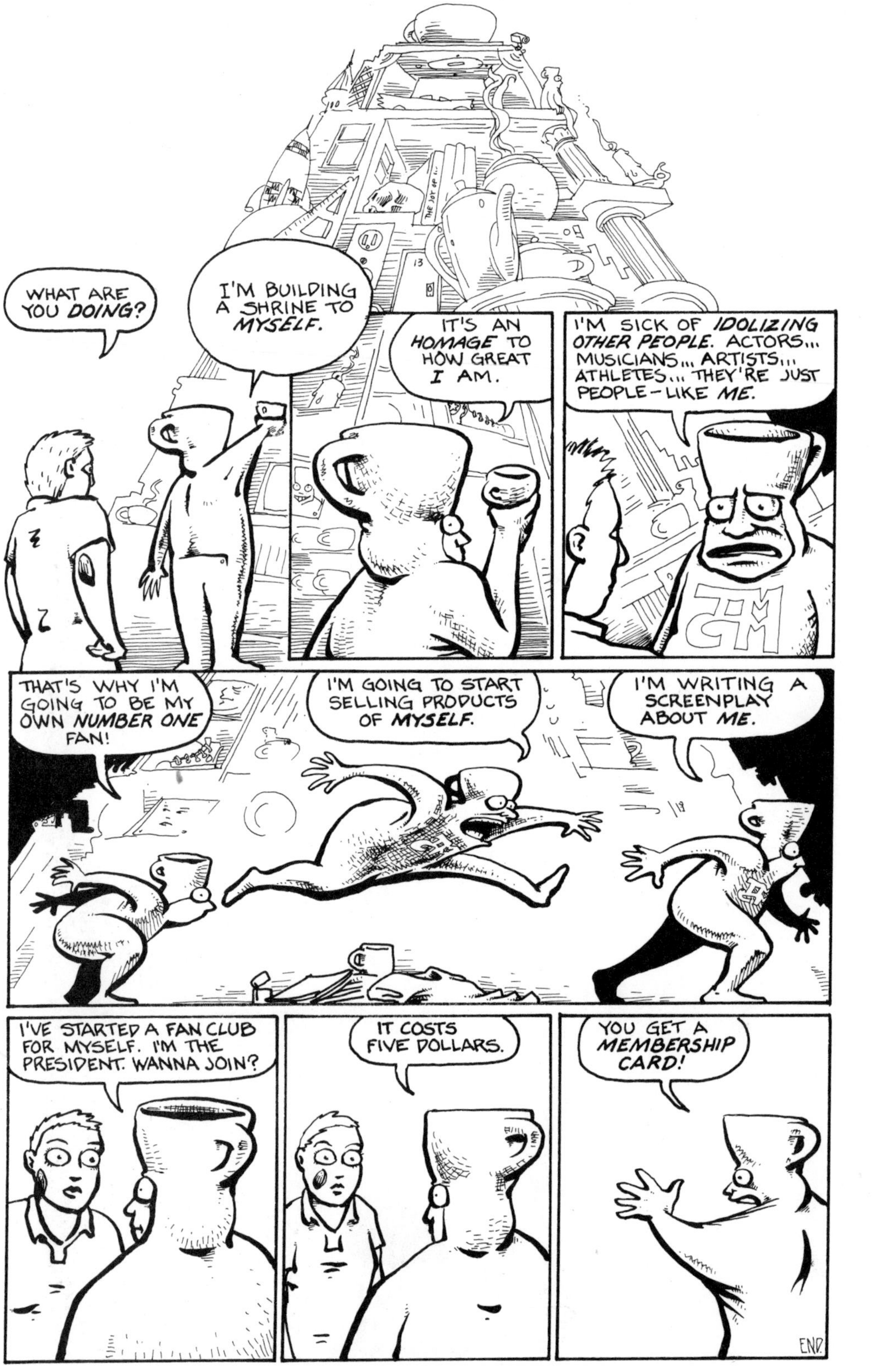
WHAT ARE YOU DOING?
I'M BUILDING A SHRINE TO MYSELF.
IT'S AN HOMAGE TO HOW GREAT I AM.
I'M SICK OF IDOLIZING OTHER PEOPLE. ACTORS... MUSICIANS... ARTISTS... ATHLETES... THEY'RE JUST PEOPLE-LIKE ME.
THAT'S WHY I'M GOING TO BE MY OWN NUMBER ONE FAN!
I'M GOING TO START SELLING PRODUCTS OF MYSELF.
I'M WRITING A SCREENPLAY ABOUT ME.
I'VE STARTED A FAN CLUB FOR MYSELF. I'M THE PRESIDENT. WANNA JOIN?
IT COSTS FIVE DOLLARS.
YOU GET A MEMBERSHIP CARD!
END.

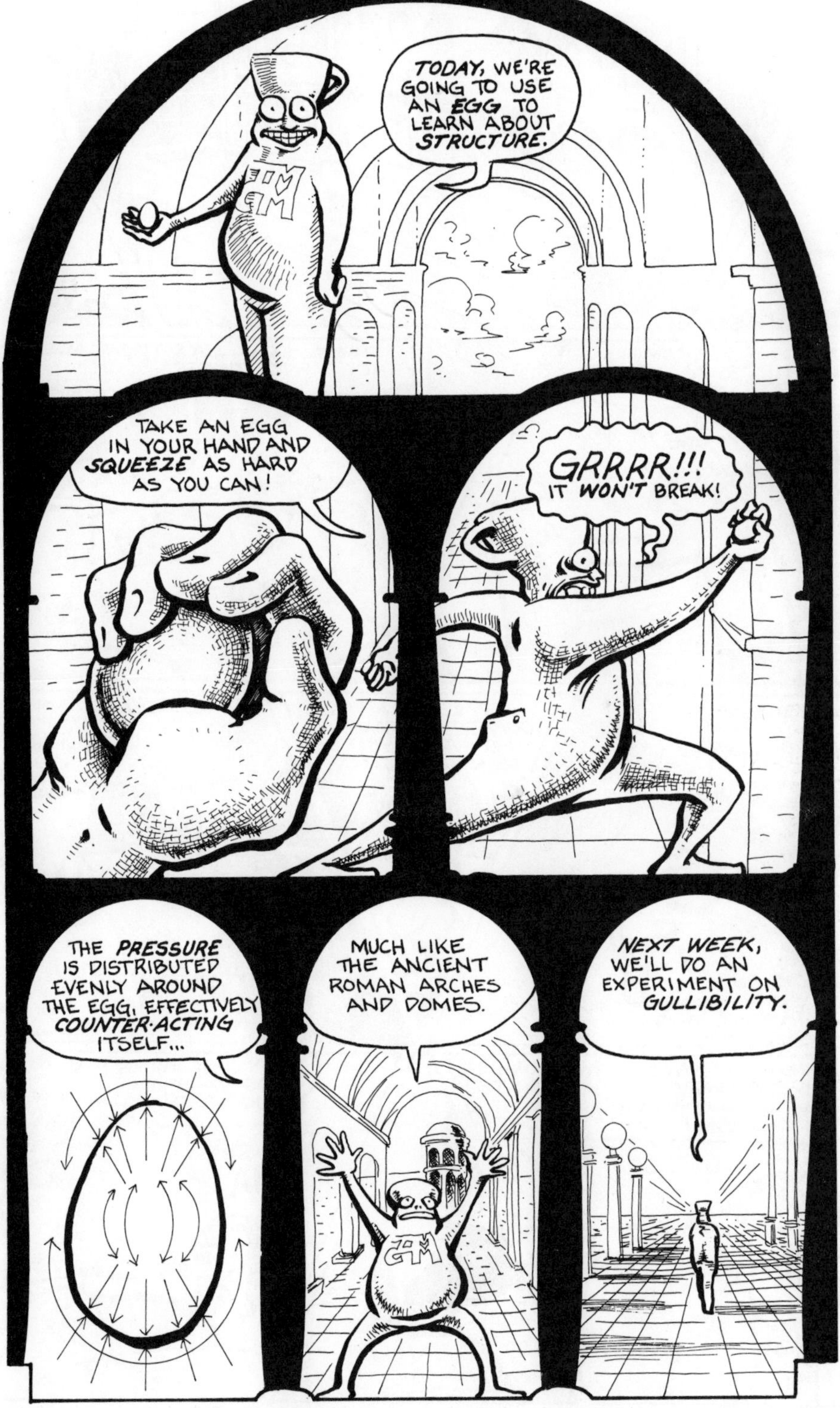
TODAY, WE'RE GOING TO USE AN EGG TO LEARN ABOUT STRUCTURE.
TAKE AN EGG IN YOUR HAND AND SQUEEZE AS HARD AS YOU CAN!
GRRRR!!! IT WON'T BREAK!
THE PRESSURE IS DISTRIBUTED EVENLY AROUND THE EGG, EFFECTIVELY COUNTER-ACTING ITSELF...
MUCH LIKE THE ANCIENT ROMAN ARCHES AND DOMES.
NEXT WEEK, WE'LL DO AN EXPERIMENT ON GULLIBILITY.

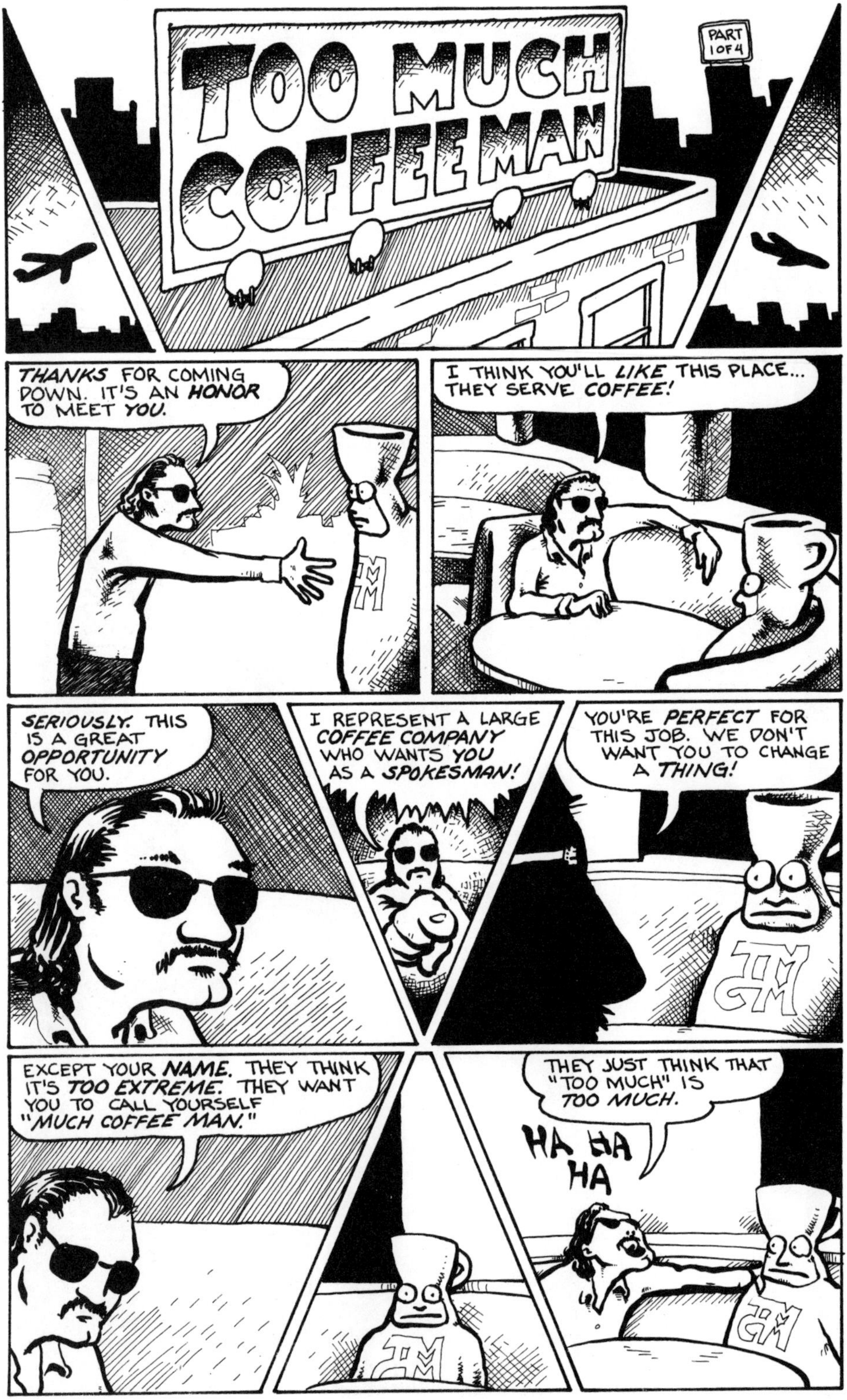
TOO MUCH COFFEE MAN
PART 1 OF 4
THANKS FOR COMING DOWN. IT'S AN HONOR TO MEET YOU.
I THINK YOU'LL LIKE THIS PLACE... THEY SERVE COFFEE!
SERIOUSLY. THIS IS A GREAT OPPORTUNITY FOR YOU.
I REPRESENT A LARGE COFFEE COMPANY WHO WANTS YOU AS A SPOKESMAN!
YOU'RE PERFECT FOR THIS JOB. WE DON'T WANT YOU TO CHANGE A THING!
EXCEPT YOUR NAME. THEY THINK IT'S TOO EXTREME. THEY WANT YOU TO CALL YOURSELF "MUCH COFFEE MAN."
THEY JUST THINK THAT "TOO MUCH" IS TOO MUCH.
HA HA HA

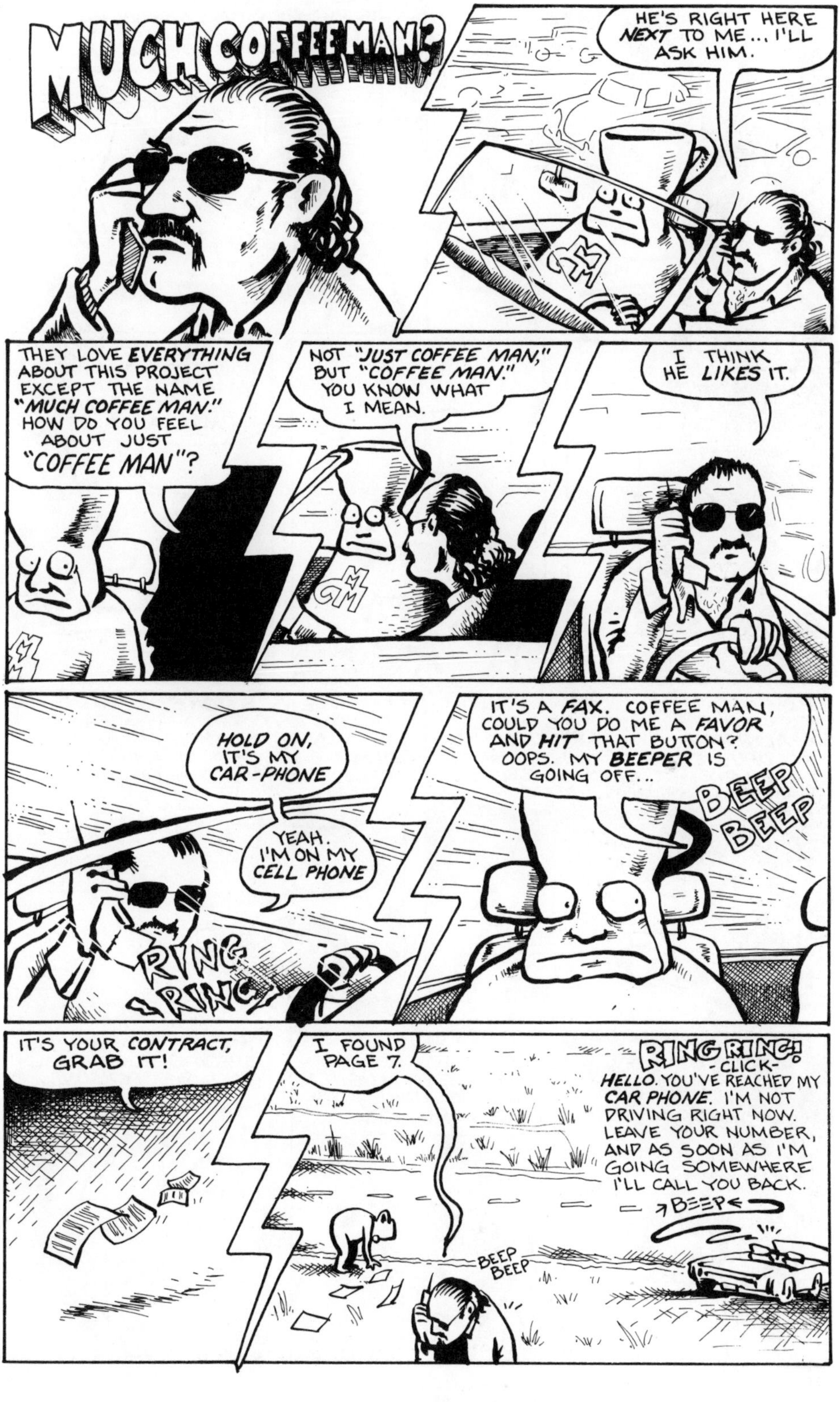
MUCH COFFEE MAN?
HE'S RIGHT HERE NEXT TO ME... I'LL ASK HIM.
THEY LOVE EVERYTHING ABOUT THIS PROJECT EXCEPT THE NAME "MUCH COFFEE MAN." HOW DO YOU FEEL ABOUT JUST "COFFEE MAN"?
NOT "JUST COFFEE MAN," BUT "COFFEE MAN." YOU KNOW WHAT I MEAN.
I THINK HE LIKES IT.
HOLD ON, IT'S MY CAR-PHONE
YEAH. I'M ON MY CELL PHONE
RING RING!
IT'S A FAX. COFFEE MAN, COULD YOU DO ME A FAVOR AND HIT THAT BUTTON? OOPS. MY BEEPER IS GOING OFF...
BEEP BEEP
IT'S YOUR CONTRACT, GRAB IT!
I FOUND PAGE 7.
RING RING! -CLICK- HELLO. YOU'VE REACHED MY CAR PHONE. I'M NOT DRIVING RIGHT NOW. LEAVE YOUR NUMBER, AND AS SOON AS I'M GOING SOMEWHERE I'LL CALL YOU BACK.
BEEP
BEEP BEEP

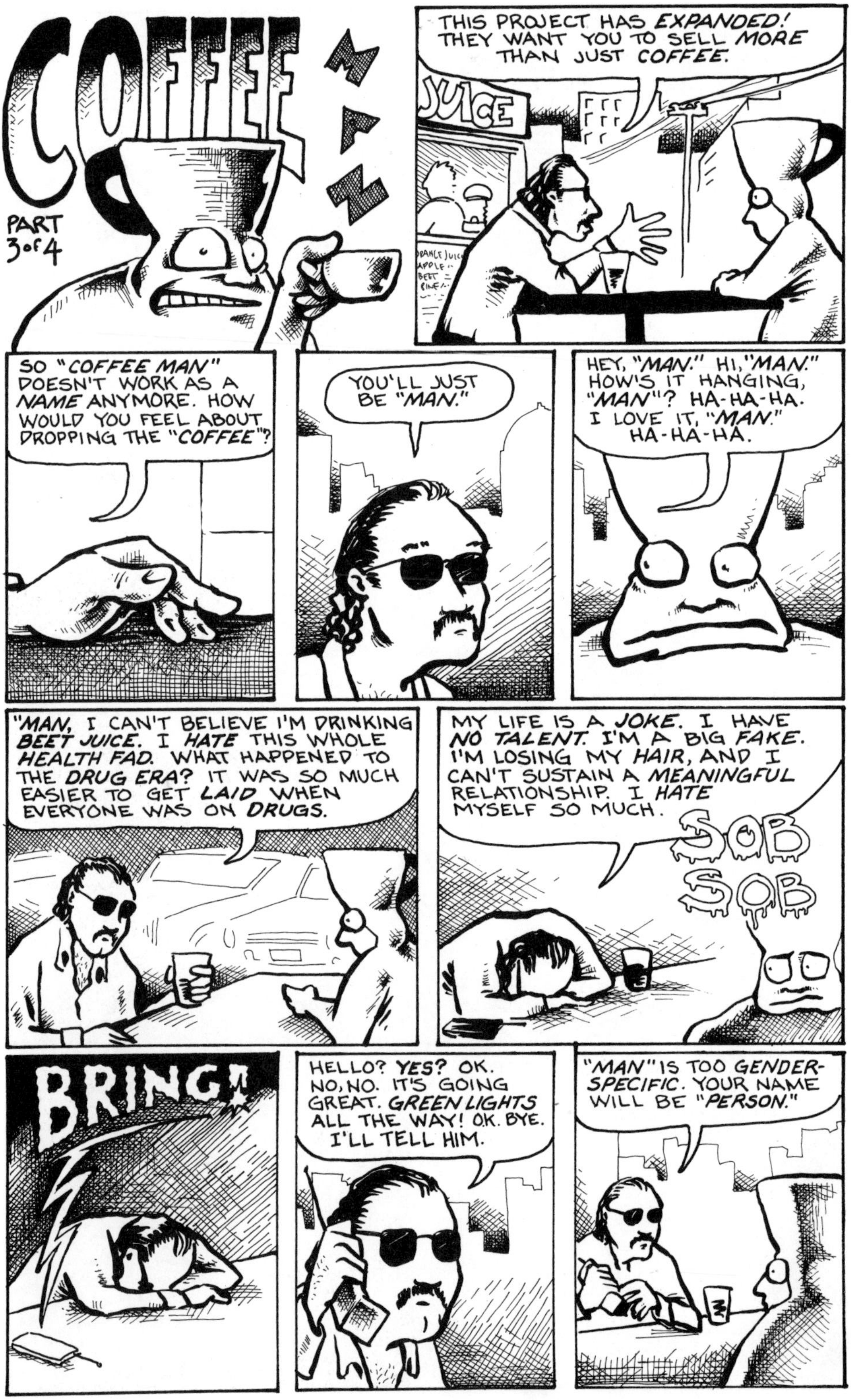
COFFEE MAN
PART 3 of 4
THIS PROJECT HAS EXPANDED! THEY WANT YOU TO SELL MORE THAN JUST COFFEE.
JUICE
SO "COFFEE MAN" DOESN'T WORK AS A NAME ANYMORE. HOW WOULD YOU FEEL ABOUT DROPPING THE "COFFEE"?
YOU'LL JUST BE "MAN."
HEY, "MAN." HI, "MAN." HOW'S IT HANGING, "MAN"? HA-HA-HA. I LOVE IT, "MAN." HA-HA-HA.
"MAN, I CAN'T BELIEVE I'M DRINKING BEET JUICE. I HATE THIS WHOLE HEALTH FAD. WHAT HAPPENED TO THE DRUG ERA? IT WAS SO MUCH EASIER TO GET LAID WHEN EVERYONE WAS ON DRUGS.
MY LIFE IS A JOKE. I HAVE NO TALENT. I'M A BIG FAKE. I'M LOSING MY HAIR, AND I CAN'T SUSTAIN A MEANINGFUL RELATIONSHIP. I HATE MYSELF SO MUCH.
SOB SOB
BRING!
HELLO? YES? OK. NO, NO. IT'S GOING GREAT. GREEN LIGHTS ALL THE WAY! O.K. BYE. I'LL TELL HIM.
"MAN" IS TOO GENDER-SPECIFIC. YOUR NAME WILL BE "PERSON."

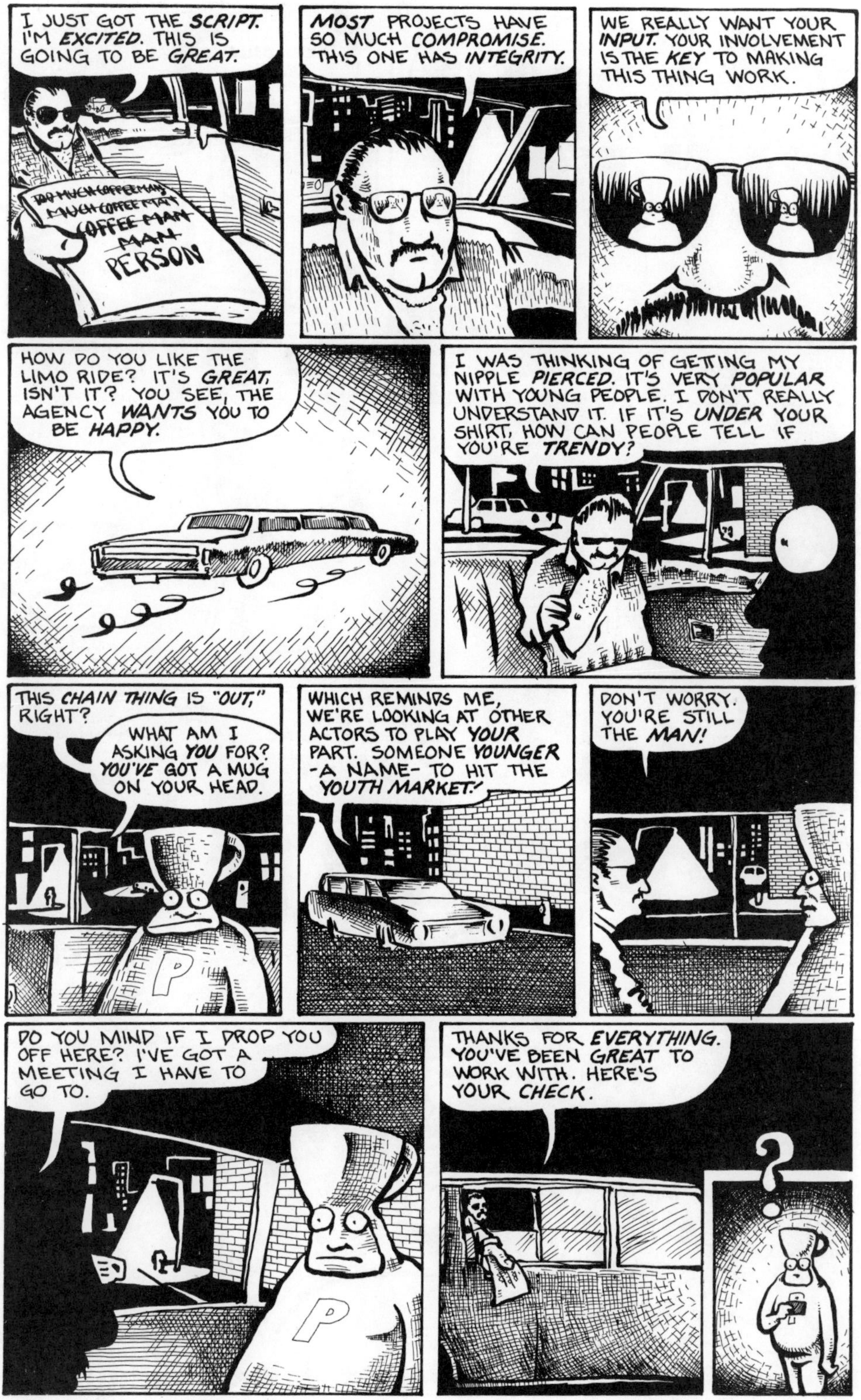
I JUST GOT THE SCRIPT. I'M EXCITED. THIS IS GOING TO BE GREAT.
TOO MUCH COFFEE MAN
MUCH COFFEE MAN
COFFEE MAN
MAN
PERSON
MOST PROJECTS HAVE SO MUCH COMPROMISE. THIS ONE HAS INTEGRITY.
WE REALLY WANT YOUR INPUT. YOUR INVOLVEMENT IS THE KEY TO MAKING THIS THING WORK.
HOW DO YOU LIKE THE LIMO RIDE? IT'S GREAT, ISN'T IT? YOU SEE, THE AGENCY WANTS YOU TO BE HAPPY.
I WAS THINKING OF GETTING MY NIPPLE PIERCED. IT'S VERY POPULAR WITH YOUNG PEOPLE. I DON'T REALLY UNDERSTAND IT. IF IT'S UNDER YOUR SHIRT, HOW CAN PEOPLE TELL IF YOU'RE TRENDY?
THIS CHAIN THING IS "OUT," RIGHT?
WHAT AM I ASKING YOU FOR? YOU'VE GOT A MUG ON YOUR HEAD.
WHICH REMINDS ME, WE'RE LOOKING AT OTHER ACTORS TO PLAY YOUR PART. SOMEONE YOUNGER -A NAME- TO HIT THE YOUTH MARKET!
DON'T WORRY. YOU'RE STILL THE MAN!
DO YOU MIND IF I DROP YOU OFF HERE? I'VE GOT A MEETING I HAVE TO GO TO.
THANKS FOR EVERYTHING. YOU'VE BEEN GREAT TO WORK WITH. HERE'S YOUR CHECK.
?

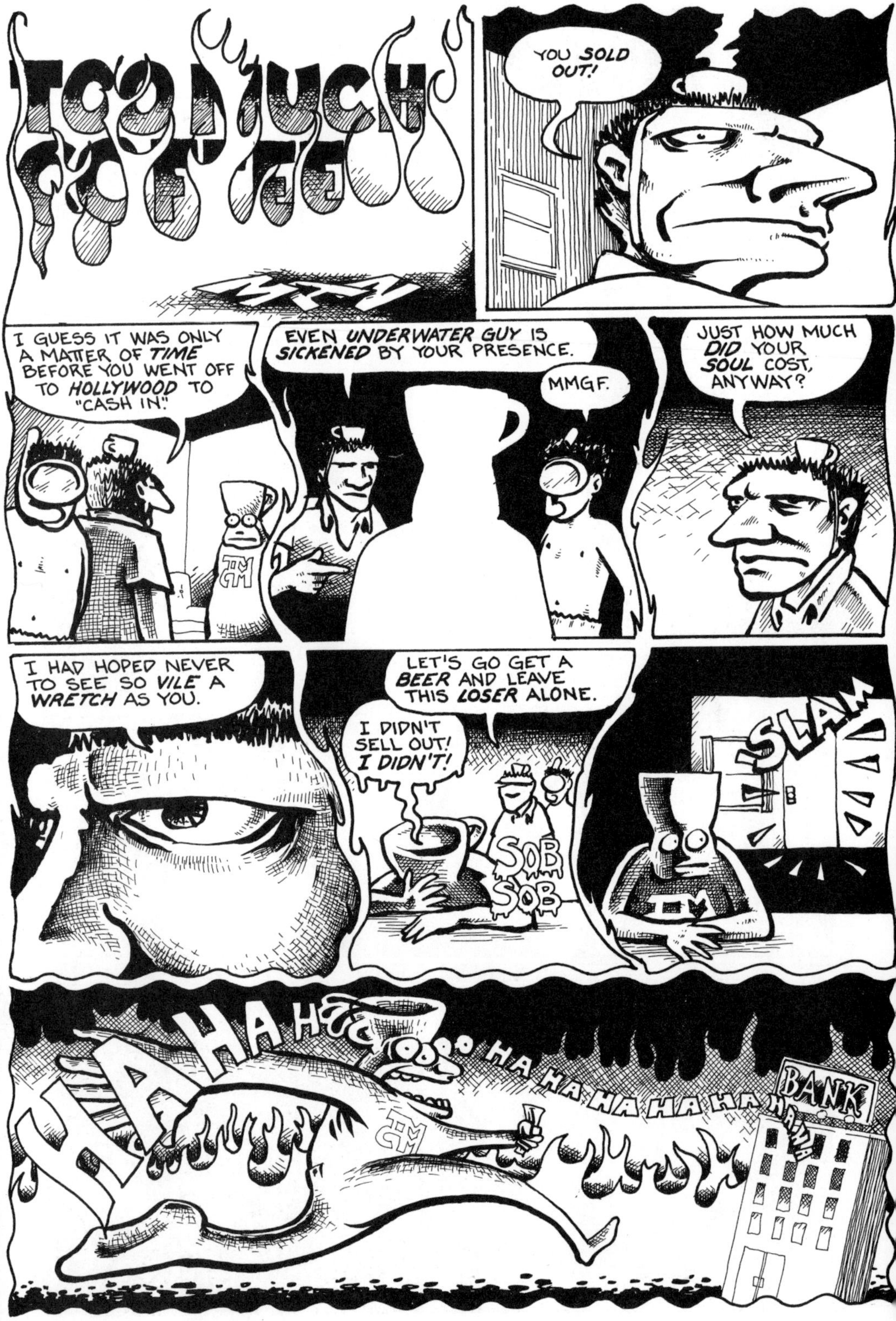
TOO MUCH COFFEE MAN
YOU SOLD OUT!
I GUESS IT WAS ONLY A MATTER OF TIME BEFORE YOU WENT OFF TO HOLLYWOOD TO "CASH IN."
EVEN UNDERWATER GUY IS SICKENED BY YOUR PRESENCE.
MMGF.
JUST HOW MUCH DID YOUR SOUL COST, ANYWAY?
I HAD HOPED NEVER TO SEE SO VILE A WRETCH AS YOU.
LET'S GO GET A BEER AND LEAVE THIS LOSER ALONE.
I DIDN'T SELL OUT! I DIDN'T!
SOB SOB
SLAM
HA HA HA
HA HA HA HA HA HA
BANK

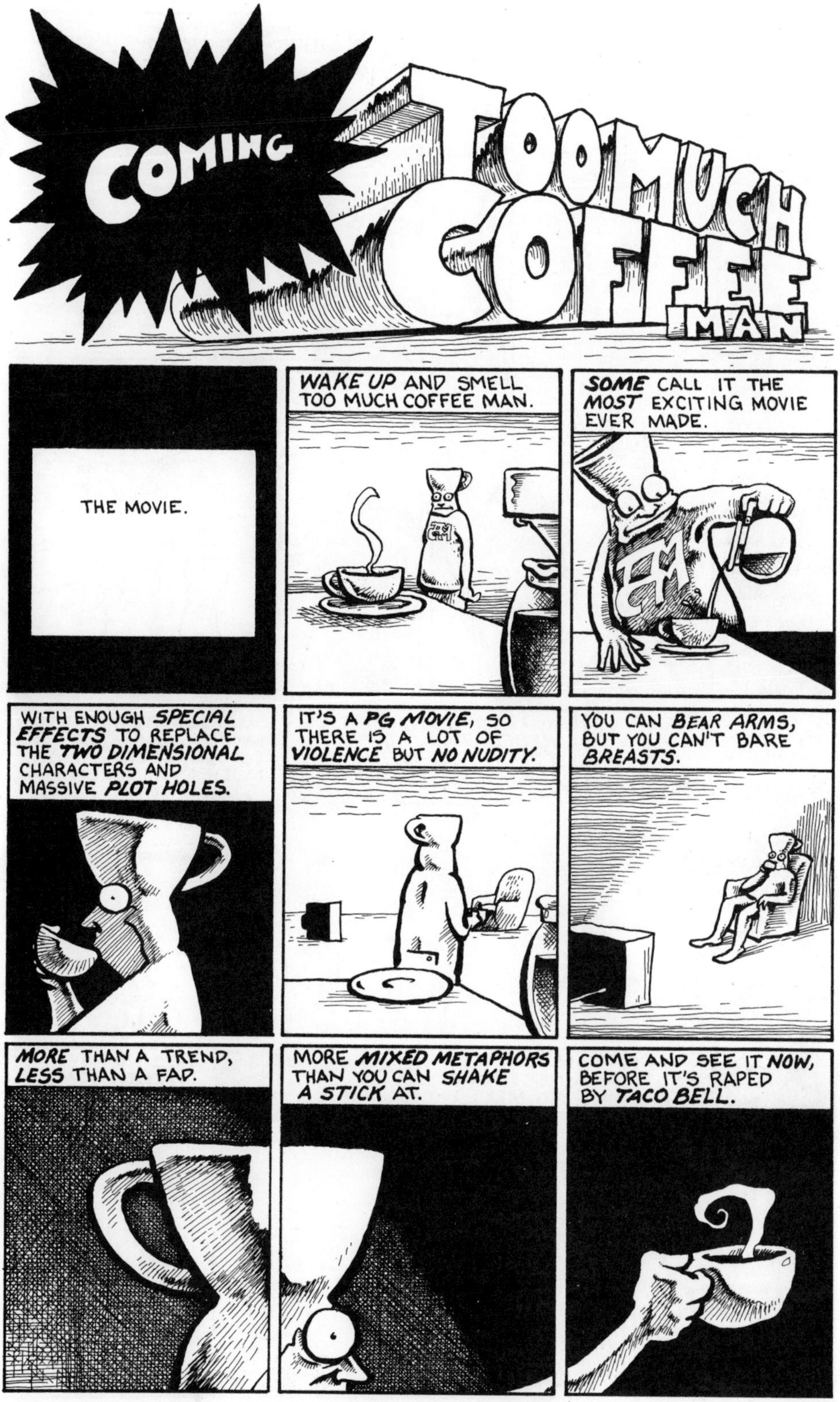
COMING
TOO MUCH COFFEE MAN
THE MOVIE.
WAKE UP AND SMELL TOO MUCH COFFEE MAN.
SOME CALL IT THE MOST EXCITING MOVIE EVER MADE.
WITH ENOUGH SPECIAL EFFECTS TO REPLACE THE TWO DIMENSIONAL CHARACTERS AND MASSIVE PLOT HOLES.
IT'S A PG MOVIE, SO THERE IS A LOT OF VIOLENCE BUT NO NUDITY.
YOU CAN BEAR ARMS, BUT YOU CAN'T BARE BREASTS.
MORE THAN A TREND, LESS THAN A FAD.
MORE MIXED METAPHORS THAN YOU CAN SHAKE A STICK AT.
COME AND SEE IT NOW, BEFORE IT'S RAPED BY TACO BELL.

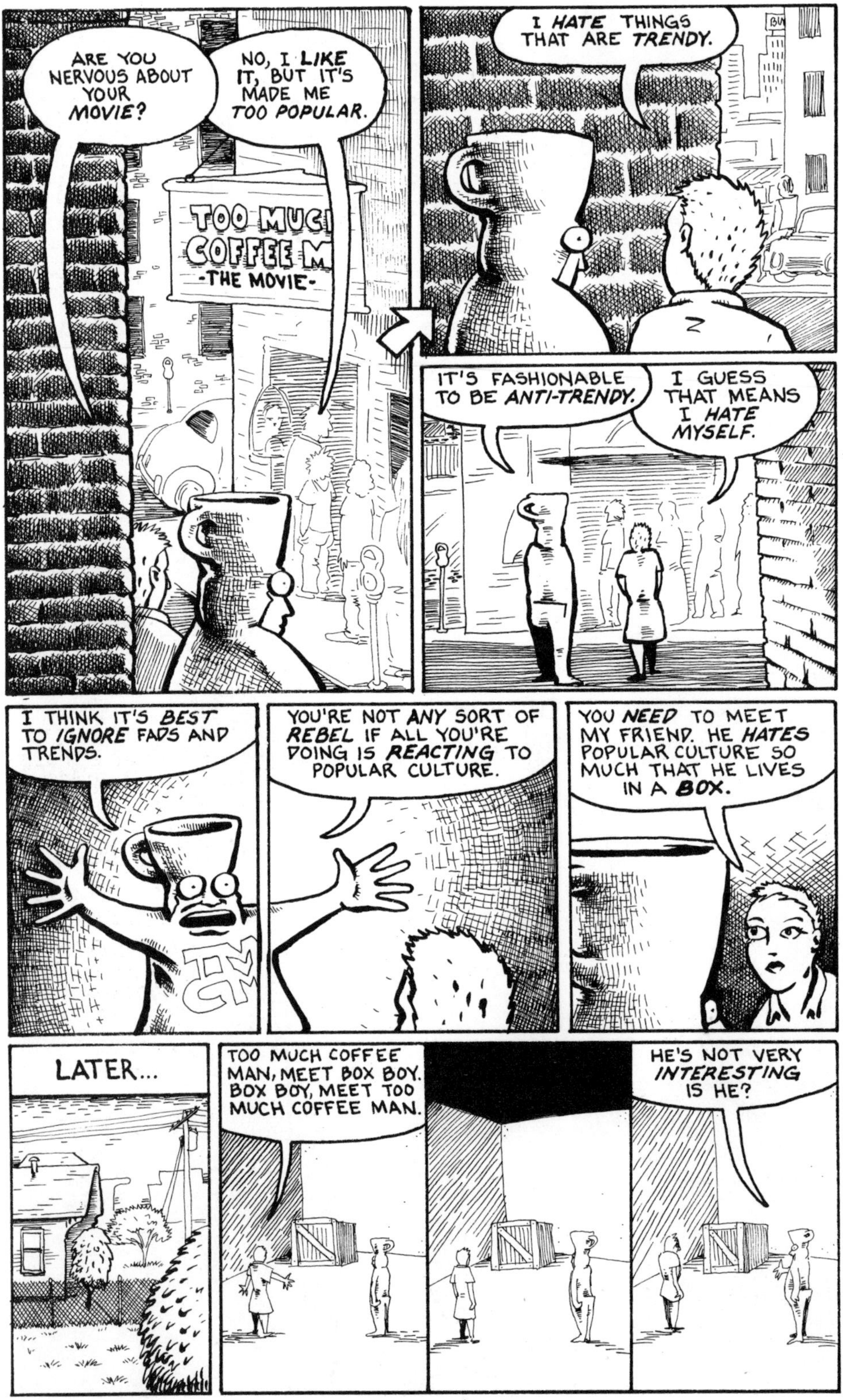
ARE YOU NERVOUS ABOUT YOUR MOVIE?
NO, I LIKE IT, BUT IT'S MADE ME TOO POPULAR.
TOO MUCH COFFEE M -THE MOVIE-
I HATE THINGS THAT ARE TRENDY.
IT'S FASHIONABLE TO BE ANTI-TRENDY.
I GUESS THAT MEANS I HATE MYSELF.
I THINK IT'S BEST TO IGNORE FADS AND TRENDS.
YOU'RE NOT ANY SORT OF REBEL IF ALL YOU'RE DOING IS REACTING TO POPULAR CULTURE.
YOU NEED TO MEET MY FRIEND. HE HATES POPULAR CULTURE SO MUCH THAT HE LIVES IN A BOX.
LATER...
TOO MUCH COFFEE MAN, MEET BOX BOY. BOX BOY, MEET TOO MUCH COFFEE MAN.
HE'S NOT VERY INTERESTING IS HE?

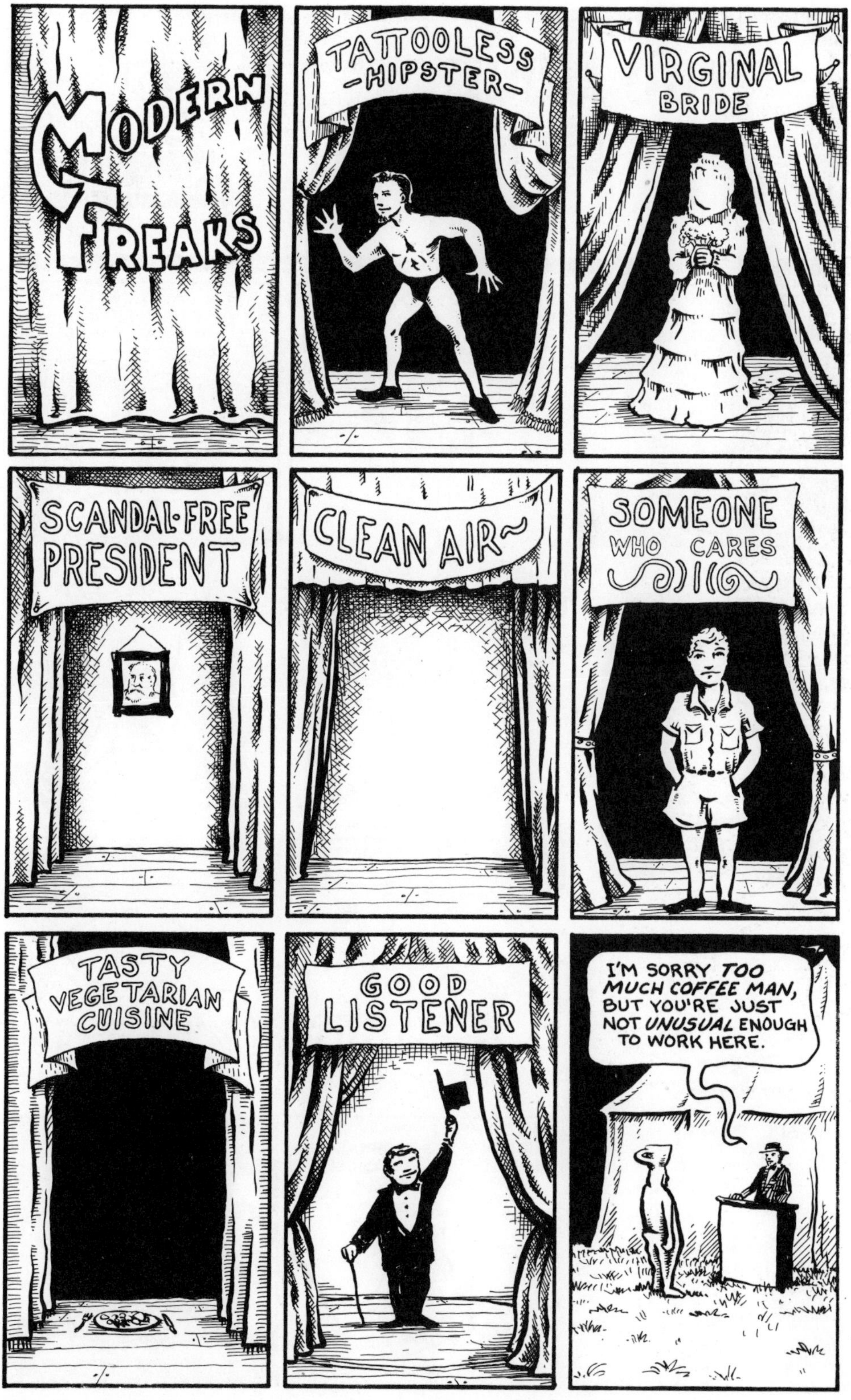
MODERN FREAKS
TATTOOLESS HIPSTER
VIRGINAL BRIDE
SCANDAL-FREE PRESIDENT
CLEAN AIR
SOMEONE WHO CARES
TASTY VEGETARIAN CUISINE
GOOD LISTENER
I'M SORRY TOO MUCH COFFEE MAN, BUT YOU'RE JUST NOT UNUSUAL ENOUGH TO WORK HERE.

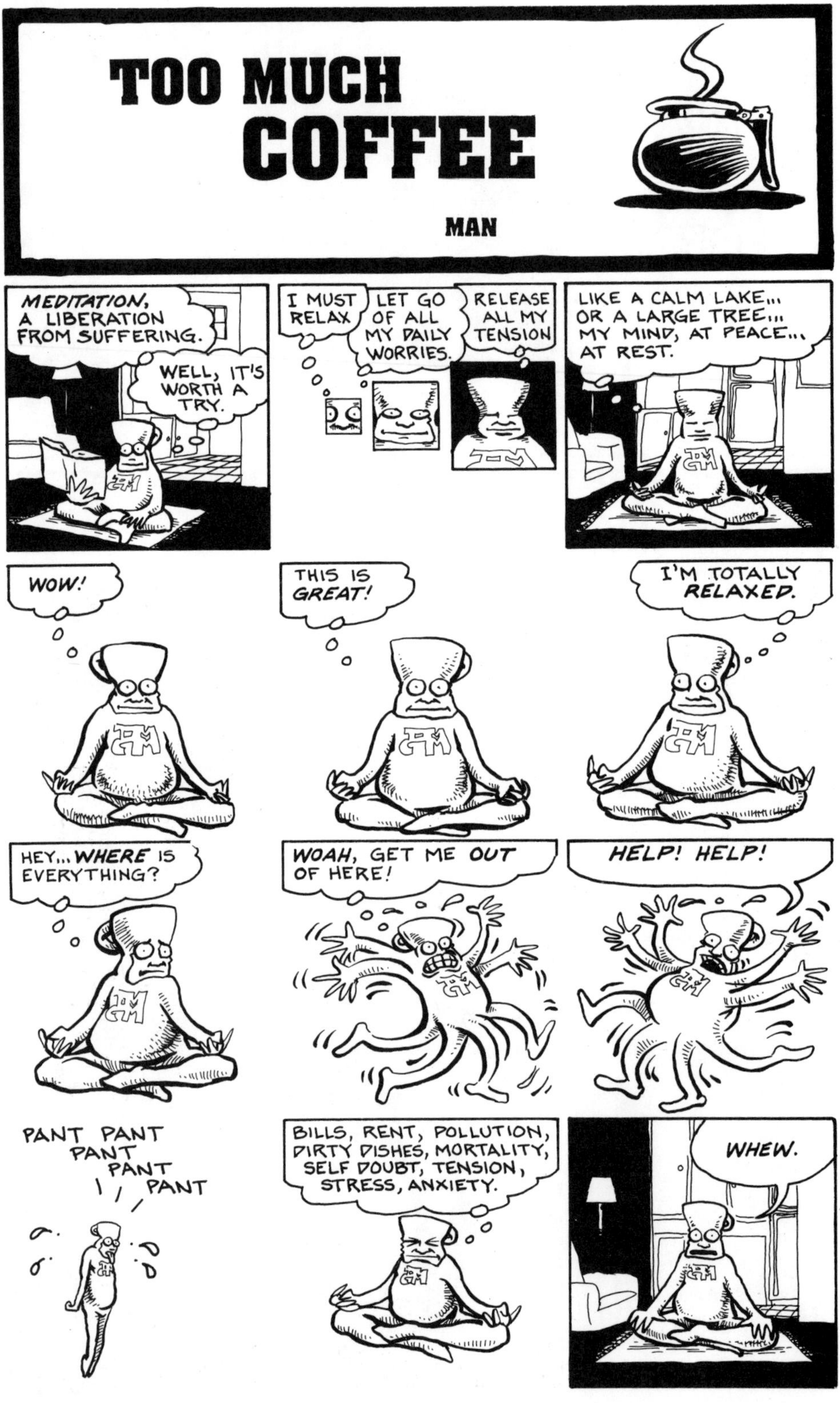

TOO MUCH COFFEE MAN
MEDITATION, A LIBERATION FROM SUFFERING.
WELL, IT'S WORTH A TRY.
I MUST RELAX
LET GO OF ALL MY DAILY WORRIES.
RELEASE ALL MY TENSION
LIKE A CALM LAKE... OR A LARGE TREE... MY MIND, AT PEACE... AT REST.
WOW!
THIS IS GREAT!
I'M TOTALLY RELAXED.
HEY... WHERE IS EVERYTHING?
WOAH, GET ME OUT OF HERE!
HELP! HELP!
PANT PANT PANT PANT PANT
BILLS, RENT, POLLUTION, DIRTY DISHES, MORTALITY, SELF DOUBT, TENSION, STRESS, ANXIETY.
WHEW.

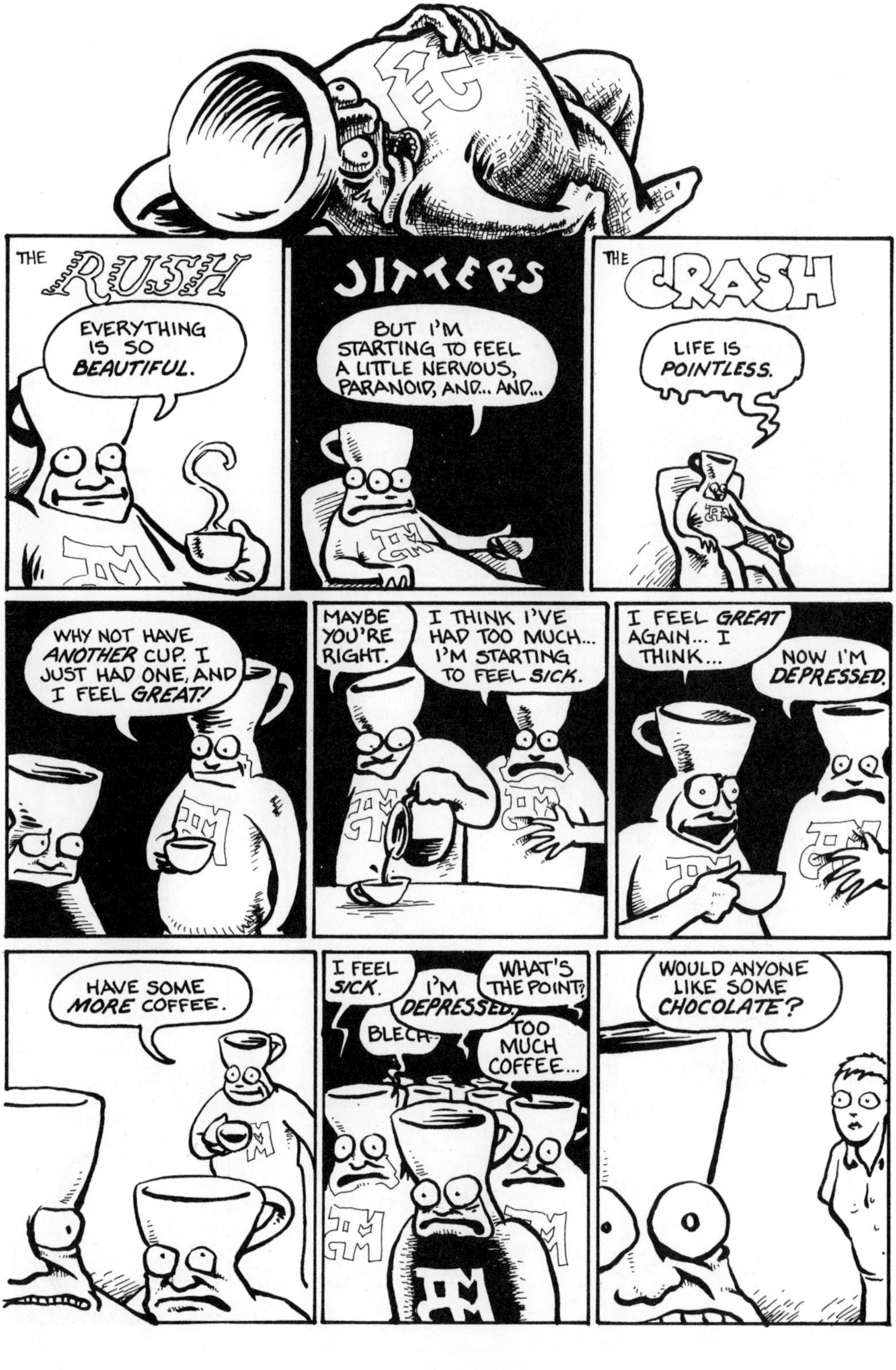
THE RUSH
EVERYTHING IS SO BEAUTIFUL.
JITTERS
BUT I'M STARTING TO FEEL A LITTLE NERVOUS, PARANOID, AND... AND...
THE CRASH
LIFE IS POINTLESS.
WHY NOT HAVE ANOTHER CUP. I JUST HAD ONE, AND I FEEL GREAT!
MAYBE YOU'RE RIGHT.
I THINK I'VE HAD TOO MUCH... I'M STARTING TO FEEL SICK.
I FEEL GREAT AGAIN... I THINK...
NOW I'M DEPRESSED.
HAVE SOME MORE COFFEE.
I FEEL SICK.
I'M DEPRESSED.
WHAT'S THE POINT?
BLECH-
TOO MUCH COFFEE...
WOULD ANYONE LIKE SOME CHOCOLATE?

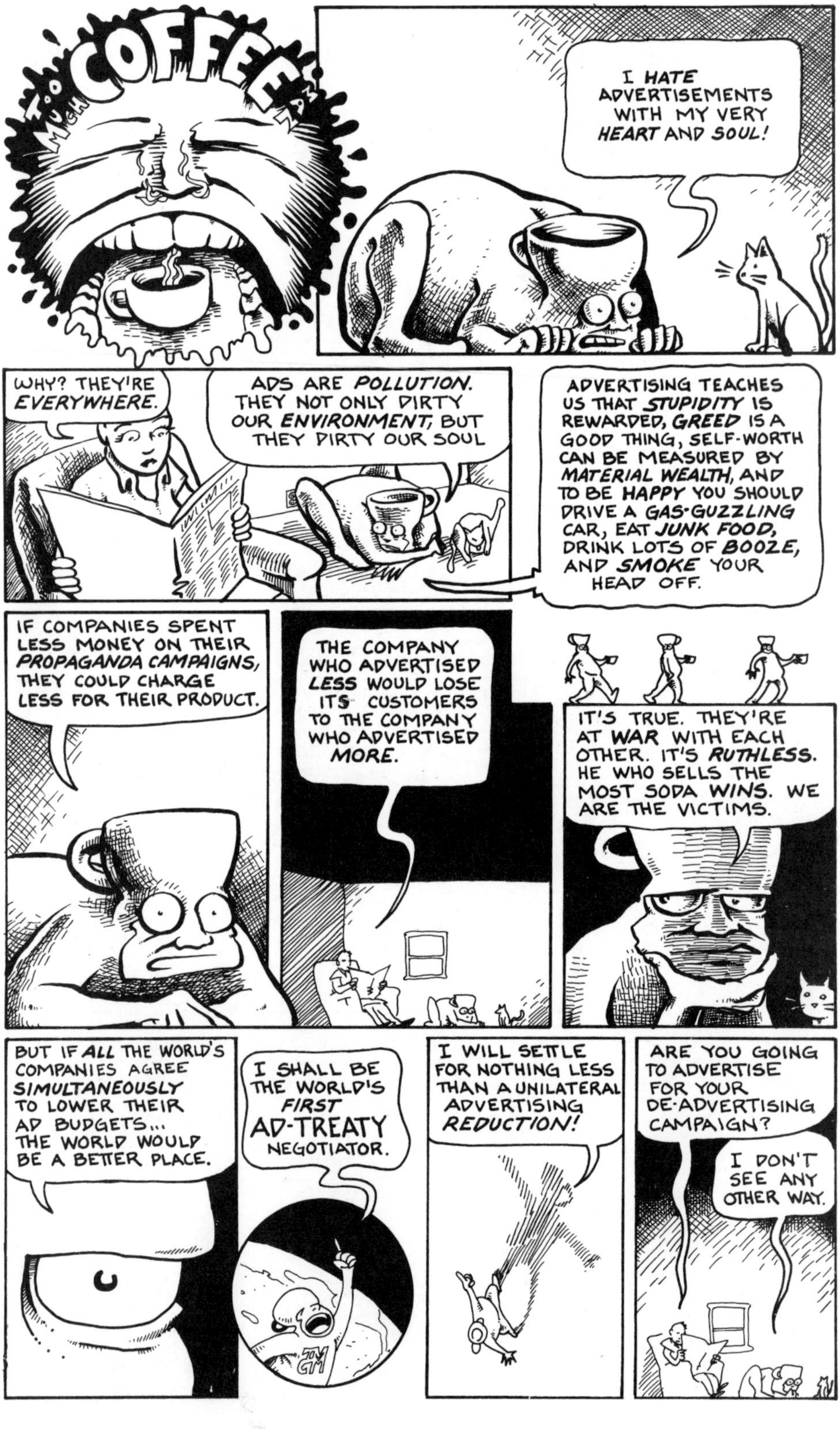
TOO MUCH COFFEE MAN
I HATE ADVERTISEMENTS WITH MY VERY HEART AND SOUL!
WHY? THEY'RE EVERYWHERE.
ADS ARE POLLUTION. THEY NOT ONLY DIRTY OUR ENVIRONMENT, BUT THEY DIRTY OUR SOUL
ADVERTISING TEACHES US THAT STUPIDITY IS REWARDED, GREED IS A GOOD THING, SELF-WORTH CAN BE MEASURED BY MATERIAL WEALTH, AND TO BE HAPPY YOU SHOULD DRIVE A GAS-GUZZLING CAR, EAT JUNK FOOD, DRINK LOTS OF BOOZE, AND SMOKE YOUR HEAD OFF.
IF COMPANIES SPENT LESS MONEY ON THEIR PROPAGANDA CAMPAIGNS, THEY COULD CHARGE LESS FOR THEIR PRODUCT.
THE COMPANY WHO ADVERTISED LESS WOULD LOSE ITS CUSTOMERS TO THE COMPANY WHO ADVERTISED MORE.
IT'S TRUE. THEY'RE AT WAR WITH EACH OTHER. IT'S RUTHLESS. HE WHO SELLS THE MOST SODA WINS. WE ARE THE VICTIMS.
BUT IF ALL THE WORLD'S COMPANIES AGREE SIMULTANEOUSLY TO LOWER THEIR AD BUDGETS... THE WORLD WOULD BE A BETTER PLACE.
I SHALL BE THE WORLD'S FIRST AD-TREATY NEGOTIATOR.
I WILL SETTLE FOR NOTHING LESS THAN A UNILATERAL ADVERTISING REDUCTION!
ARE YOU GOING TO ADVERTISE FOR YOUR DE-ADVERTISING CAMPAIGN?
I DON'T SEE ANY OTHER WAY.

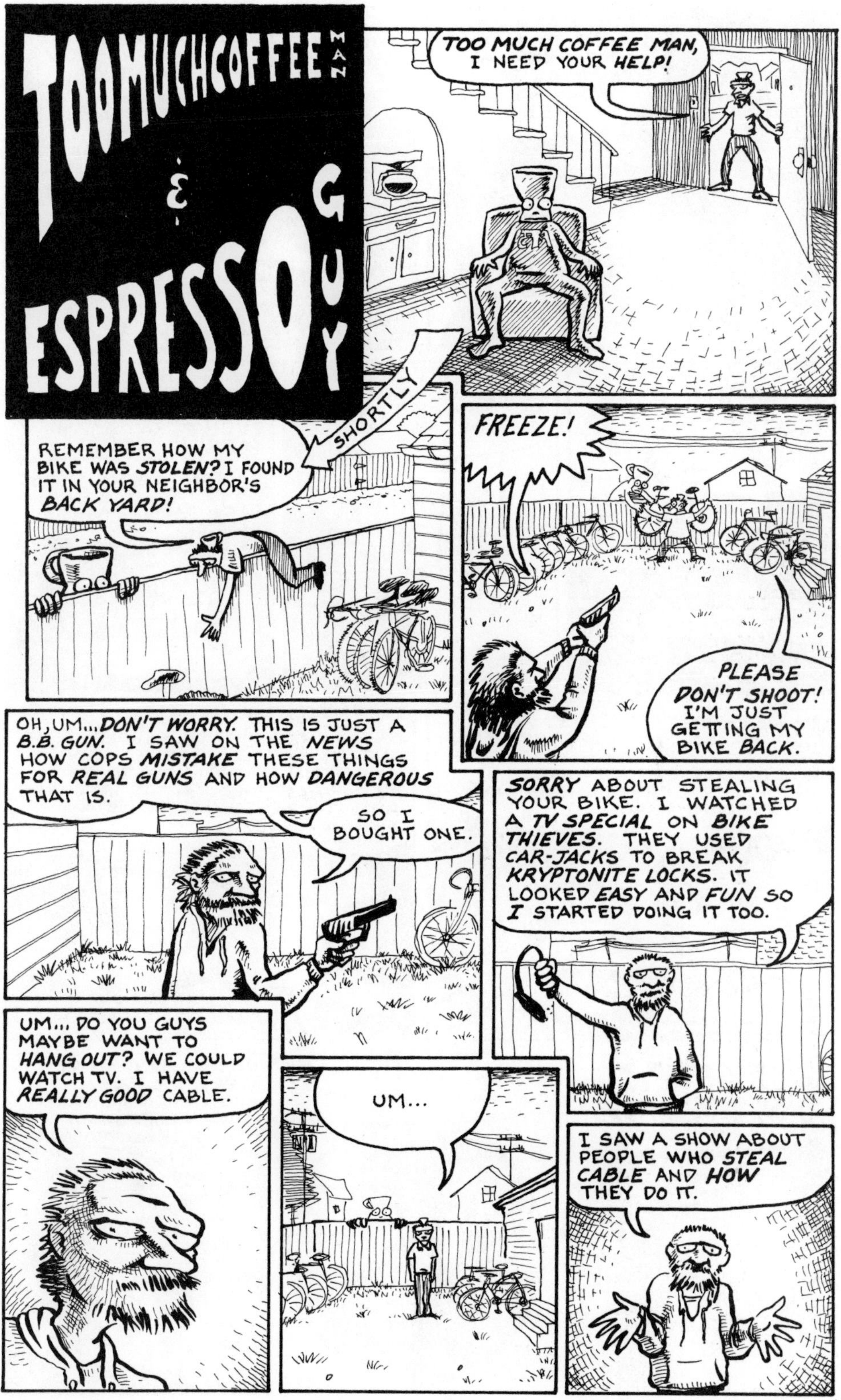
TOO MUCH COFFEE MAN
&
ESPRESSO GUY
TOO MUCH COFFEE MAN, I NEED YOUR HELP!
SHORTLY
REMEMBER HOW MY BIKE WAS STOLEN? I FOUND IT IN YOUR NEIGHBOR'S BACK YARD!
FREEZE!
PLEASE DON'T SHOOT! I'M JUST GETTING MY BIKE BACK.
OH, UM... DON'T WORRY. THIS IS JUST A B.B. GUN. I SAW ON THE NEWS HOW COPS MISTAKE THESE THINGS FOR REAL GUNS AND HOW DANGEROUS THAT IS.
SO I BOUGHT ONE.
SORRY ABOUT STEALING YOUR BIKE. I WATCHED A TV SPECIAL ON BIKE THIEVES. THEY USED CAR-JACKS TO BREAK KRYPTONITE LOCKS. IT LOOKED EASY AND FUN SO I STARTED DOING IT TOO.
UM... DO YOU GUYS MAYBE WANT TO HANG OUT? WE COULD WATCH TV. I HAVE REALLY GOOD CABLE.
UM...
I SAW A SHOW ABOUT PEOPLE WHO STEAL CABLE AND HOW THEY DO IT.

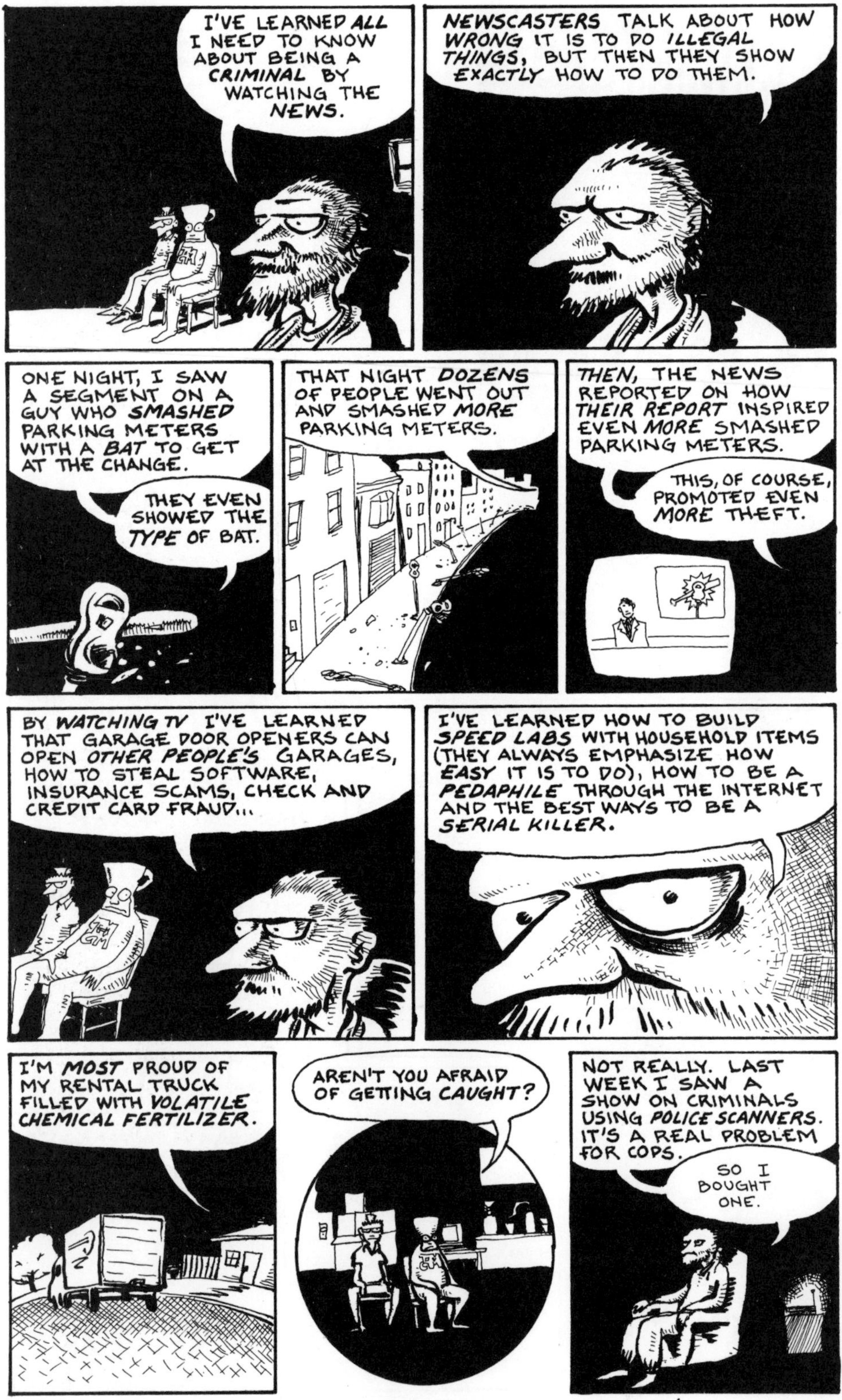
I'VE LEARNED ALL I NEED TO KNOW ABOUT BEING A CRIMINAL BY WATCHING THE NEWS.
NEWSCASTERS TALK ABOUT HOW WRONG IT IS TO DO ILLEGAL THINGS, BUT THEN THEY SHOW EXACTLY HOW TO DO THEM.
ONE NIGHT, I SAW A SEGMENT ON A GUY WHO SMASHED PARKING METERS WITH A BAT TO GET AT THE CHANGE.
THEY EVEN SHOWED THE TYPE OF BAT.
THAT NIGHT DOZENS OF PEOPLE WENT OUT AND SMASHED MORE PARKING METERS.
THEN, THE NEWS REPORTED ON HOW THEIR REPORT INSPIRED EVEN MORE SMASHED PARKING METERS.
THIS, OF COURSE, PROMOTED EVEN MORE THEFT.
BY WATCHING TV I'VE LEARNED THAT GARAGE DOOR OPENERS CAN OPEN OTHER PEOPLE'S GARAGES, HOW TO STEAL SOFTWARE, INSURANCE SCAMS, CHECK AND CREDIT CARD FRAUD...
I'VE LEARNED HOW TO BUILD SPEED LABS WITH HOUSEHOLD ITEMS (THEY ALWAYS EMPHASIZE HOW EASY IT IS TO DO), HOW TO BE A PEDAPHILE THROUGH THE INTERNET AND THE BEST WAYS TO BE A SERIAL KILLER.
I'M MOST PROUD OF MY RENTAL TRUCK FILLED WITH VOLATILE CHEMICAL FERTILIZER.
AREN'T YOU AFRAID OF GETTING CAUGHT?
NOT REALLY. LAST WEEK I SAW A SHOW ON CRIMINALS USING POLICE SCANNERS. IT'S A REAL PROBLEM FOR COPS.
SO I BOUGHT ONE.

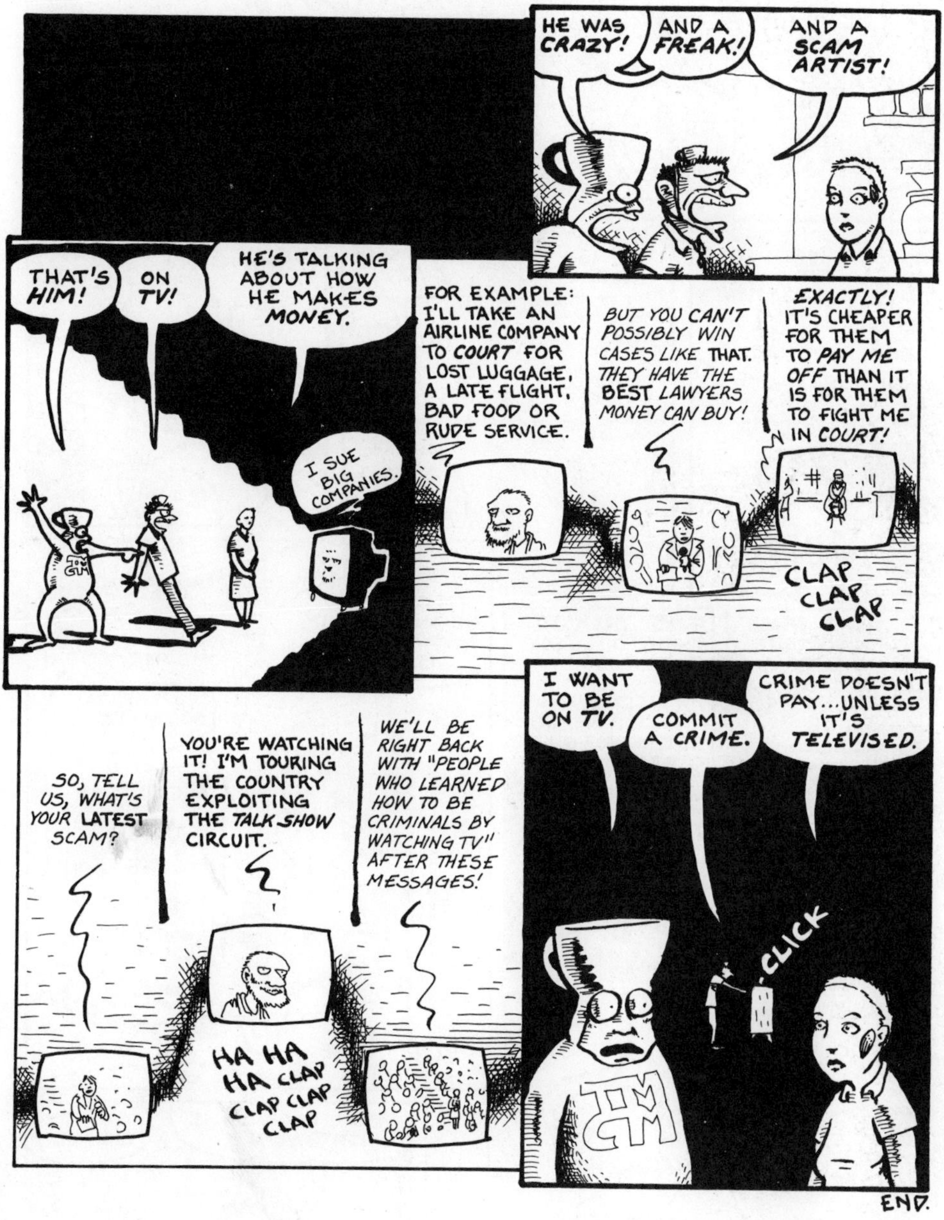

HE WAS CRAZY!
AND A FREAK!
AND A SCAM ARTIST!
THAT'S HIM!
ON TV!
HE'S TALKING ABOUT HOW HE MAKES MONEY.
I SUE BIG COMPANIES.
FOR EXAMPLE: I'LL TAKE AN AIRLINE COMPANY TO COURT FOR LOST LUGGAGE, A LATE FLIGHT, BAD FOOD OR RUDE SERVICE.
BUT YOU CAN'T POSSIBLY WIN CASES LIKE THAT. THEY HAVE THE BEST LAWYERS MONEY CAN BUY!
EXACTLY! IT'S CHEAPER FOR THEM TO PAY ME OFF THAN IT IS FOR THEM TO FIGHT ME IN COURT!
CLAP CLAP CLAP
SO, TELL US, WHAT'S YOUR LATEST SCAM?
YOU'RE WATCHING IT! I'M TOURING THE COUNTRY EXPLOITING THE TALK SHOW CIRCUIT.
WE'LL BE RIGHT BACK WITH "PEOPLE WHO LEARNED HOW TO BE CRIMINALS BY WATCHING TV" AFTER THESE MESSAGES!
HA HA HA CLAP CLAP CLAP CLAP
I WANT TO BE ON TV.
COMMIT A CRIME.
CRIME DOESN'T PAY...UNLESS IT'S TELEVISED.
CLICK
END.

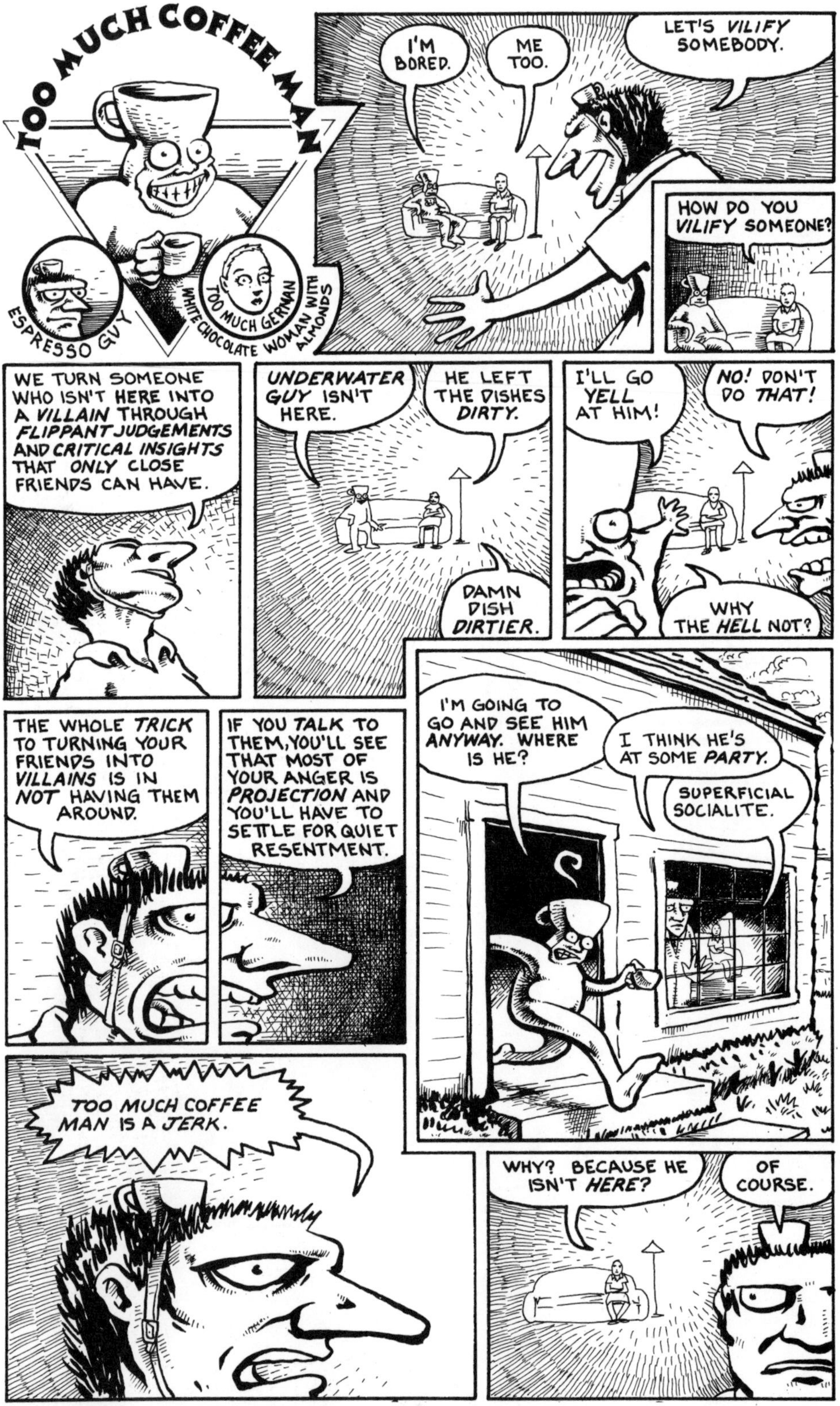
TOO MUCH COFFEE MAN
ESPRESSO GUY
TOO MUCH GERMAN
WHITE CHOCOLATE WOMAN WITH ALMONDS
I'M BORED.
ME TOO.
LET'S VILIFY SOMEBODY.
HOW DO YOU VILIFY SOMEONE?
WE TURN SOMEONE WHO ISN'T HERE INTO A VILLAIN THROUGH FLIPPANT JUDGEMENTS AND CRITICAL INSIGHTS THAT ONLY CLOSE FRIENDS CAN HAVE.
UNDERWATER GUY ISN'T HERE.
HE LEFT THE DISHES DIRTY.
DAMN DISH DIRTIER.
I'LL GO YELL AT HIM!
NO! DON'T DO THAT!
WHY THE HELL NOT?
THE WHOLE TRICK TO TURNING YOUR FRIENDS INTO VILLAINS IS IN NOT HAVING THEM AROUND.
IF YOU TALK TO THEM, YOU'LL SEE THAT MOST OF YOUR ANGER IS PROJECTION AND YOU'LL HAVE TO SETTLE FOR QUIET RESENTMENT.
I'M GOING TO GO AND SEE HIM ANYWAY. WHERE IS HE?
I THINK HE'S AT SOME PARTY.
SUPERFICIAL SOCIALITE.
TOO MUCH COFFEE MAN IS A JERK.
WHY? BECAUSE HE ISN'T HERE?
OF COURSE.

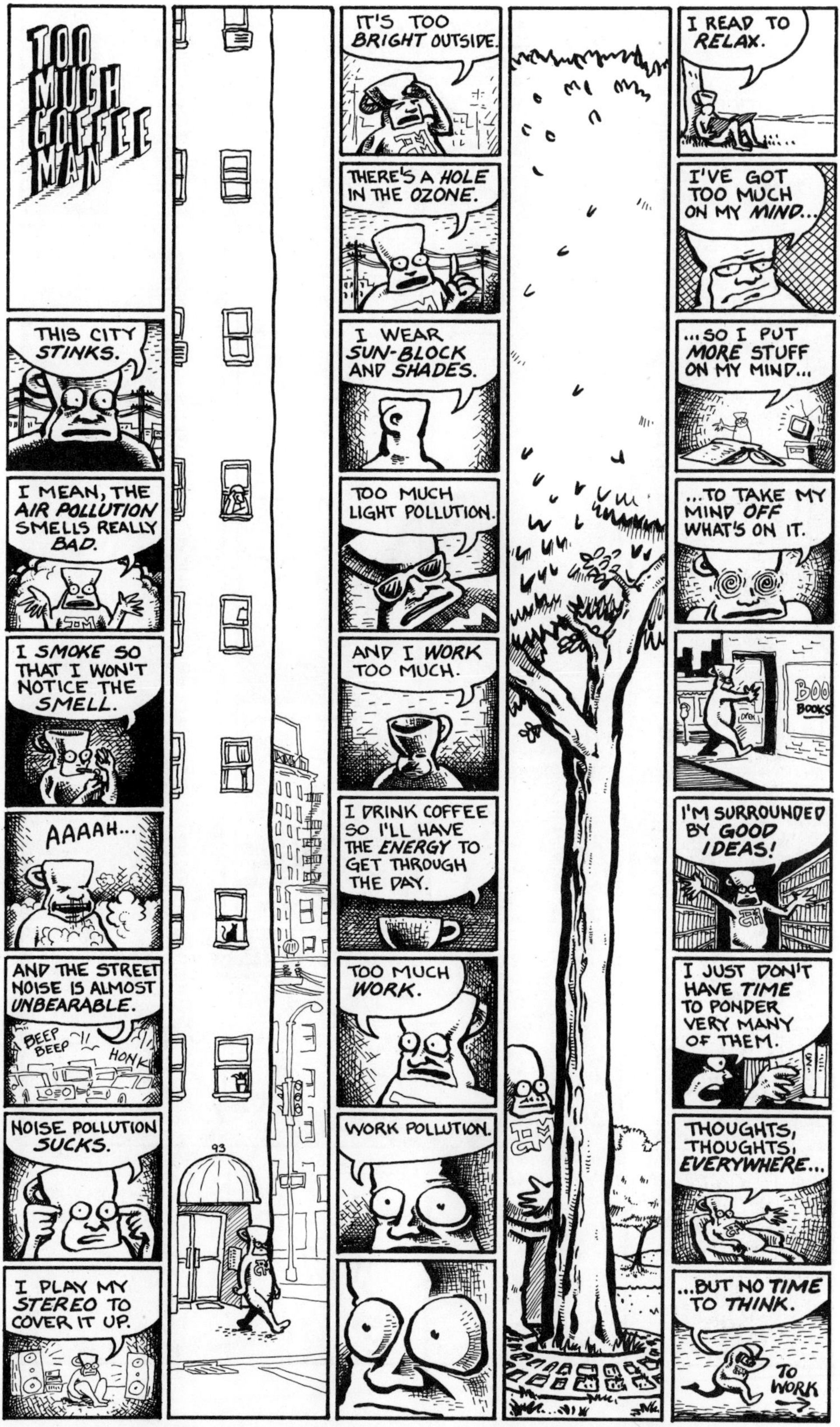
TOO MUCH COFFEE MAN
THIS CITY STINKS.
I MEAN, THE AIR POLLUTION SMELLS REALLY BAD.
I SMOKE SO THAT I WON'T NOTICE THE SMELL.
AAAAH...
AND THE STREET NOISE IS ALMOST UNBEARABLE.
BEEP BEEP
HONK
NOISE POLLUTION SUCKS.
I PLAY MY STEREO TO COVER IT UP.
93
IT'S TOO BRIGHT OUTSIDE.
THERE'S A HOLE IN THE OZONE.
I WEAR SUN-BLOCK AND SHADES.
TOO MUCH LIGHT POLLUTION.
AND I WORK TOO MUCH.
I DRINK COFFEE SO I'LL HAVE THE ENERGY TO GET THROUGH THE DAY.
TOO MUCH WORK.
WORK POLLUTION.
I READ TO RELAX.
I'VE GOT TOO MUCH ON MY MIND...
...SO I PUT MORE STUFF ON MY MIND...
...TO TAKE MY MIND OFF WHAT'S ON IT.
BOOKS
I'M SURROUNDED BY GOOD IDEAS!
I JUST DON'T HAVE TIME TO PONDER VERY MANY OF THEM.
THOUGHTS, THOUGHTS, EVERYWHERE...
...BUT NO TIME TO THINK.
TO WORK

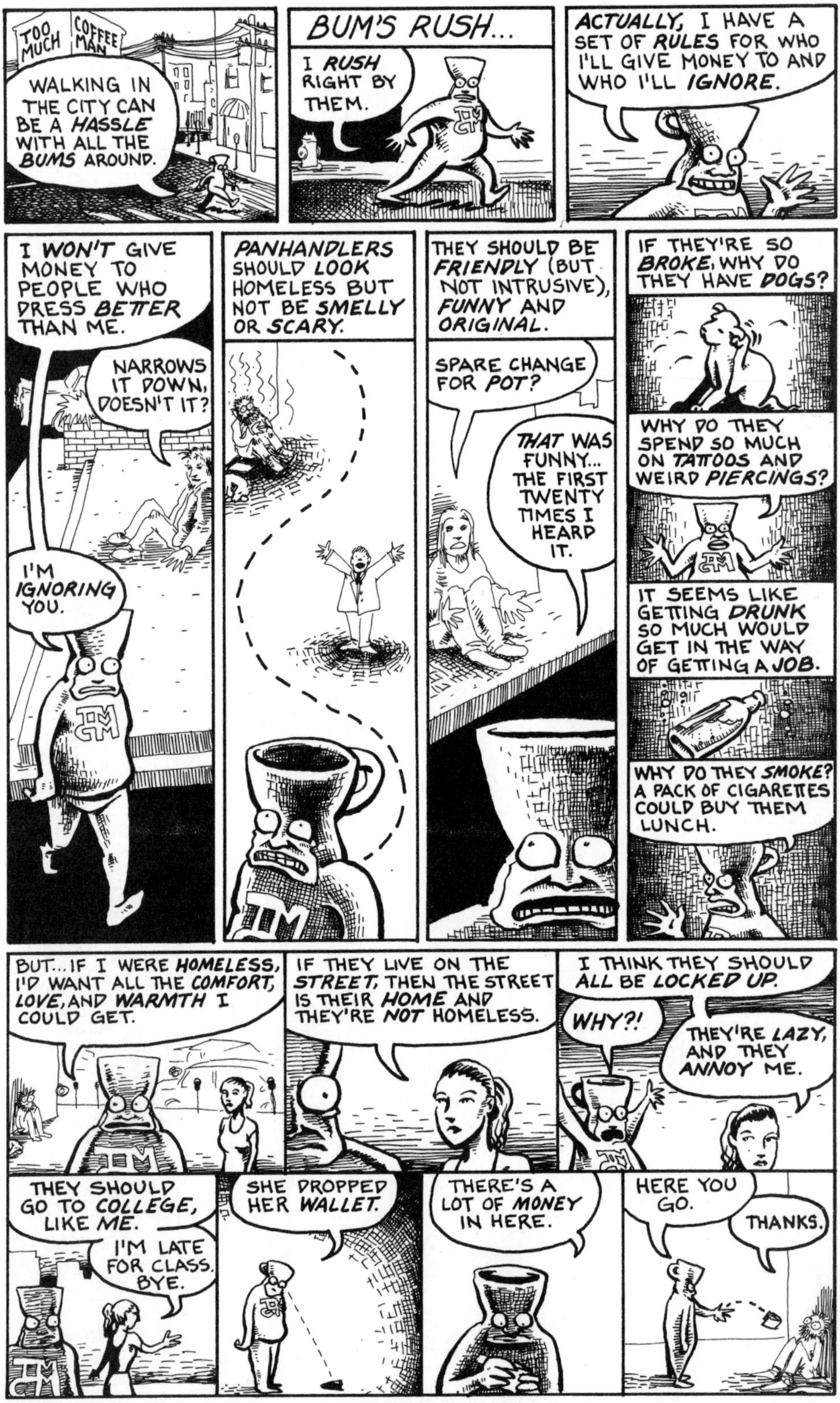
TOO MUCH COFFEE MAN
WALKING IN THE CITY CAN BE A HASSLE WITH ALL THE BUMS AROUND.
BUM'S RUSH...
I RUSH RIGHT BY THEM.
ACTUALLY, I HAVE A SET OF RULES FOR WHO I'LL GIVE MONEY TO AND WHO I'LL IGNORE.
I WON'T GIVE MONEY TO PEOPLE WHO DRESS BETTER THAN ME.
NARROWS IT DOWN, DOESN'T IT?
I'M IGNORING YOU.
PANHANDLERS SHOULD LOOK HOMELESS BUT NOT BE SMELLY OR SCARY.
THEY SHOULD BE FRIENDLY (BUT NOT INTRUSIVE), FUNNY AND ORIGINAL.
SPARE CHANGE FOR POT?
THAT WAS FUNNY... THE FIRST TWENTY TIMES I HEARD IT.
IF THEY'RE SO BROKE, WHY DO THEY HAVE DOGS?
WHY DO THEY SPEND SO MUCH ON TATTOOS AND WEIRD PIERCINGS?
IT SEEMS LIKE GETTING DRUNK SO MUCH WOULD GET IN THE WAY OF GETTING A JOB.
WHY DO THEY SMOKE? A PACK OF CIGARETTES COULD BUY THEM LUNCH.
BUT... IF I WERE HOMELESS, I'D WANT ALL THE COMFORT, LOVE, AND WARMTH I COULD GET.
IF THEY LIVE ON THE STREET, THEN THE STREET IS THEIR HOME AND THEY'RE NOT HOMELESS.
I THINK THEY SHOULD ALL BE LOCKED UP.
WHY?!
THEY'RE LAZY, AND THEY ANNOY ME.
THEY SHOULD GO TO COLLEGE, LIKE ME.
I'M LATE FOR CLASS. BYE.
SHE DROPPED HER WALLET.
THERE'S A LOT OF MONEY IN HERE.
HERE YOU GO.
THANKS.

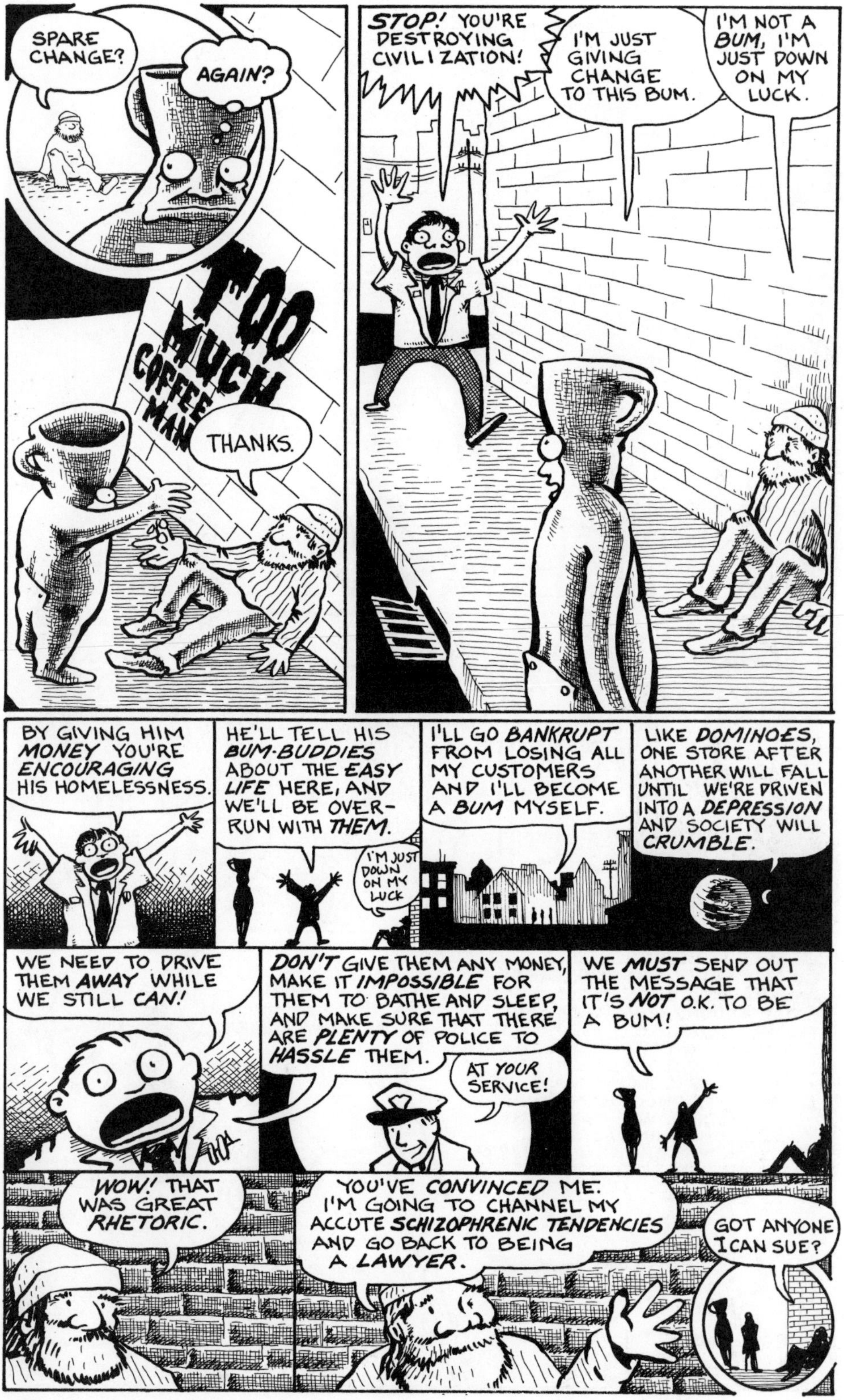
SPARE CHANGE?
AGAIN?
TOO MUCH COFFEE MAN
THANKS.
STOP! YOU'RE DESTROYING CIVILIZATION!
I'M JUST GIVING CHANGE TO THIS BUM.
I'M NOT A BUM, I'M JUST DOWN ON MY LUCK.
BY GIVING HIM MONEY YOU'RE ENCOURAGING HIS HOMELESSNESS.
HE'LL TELL HIS BUM-BUDDIES ABOUT THE EASY LIFE HERE, AND WE'LL BE OVER-RUN WITH THEM.
I'M JUST DOWN ON MY LUCK
I'LL GO BANKRUPT FROM LOSING ALL MY CUSTOMERS AND I'LL BECOME A BUM MYSELF.
LIKE DOMINOES, ONE STORE AFTER ANOTHER WILL FALL UNTIL WE'RE DRIVEN INTO A DEPRESSION AND SOCIETY WILL CRUMBLE.
WE NEED TO DRIVE THEM AWAY WHILE WE STILL CAN!
DON'T GIVE THEM ANY MONEY, MAKE IT IMPOSSIBLE FOR THEM TO BATHE AND SLEEP, AND MAKE SURE THAT THERE ARE PLENTY OF POLICE TO HASSLE THEM.
AT YOUR SERVICE!
WE MUST SEND OUT THE MESSAGE THAT IT'S NOT O.K. TO BE A BUM!
WOW! THAT WAS GREAT RHETORIC.
YOU'VE CONVINCED ME. I'M GOING TO CHANNEL MY ACCUTE SCHIZOPHRENIC TENDENCIES AND GO BACK TO BEING A LAWYER.
GOT ANYONE I CAN SUE?

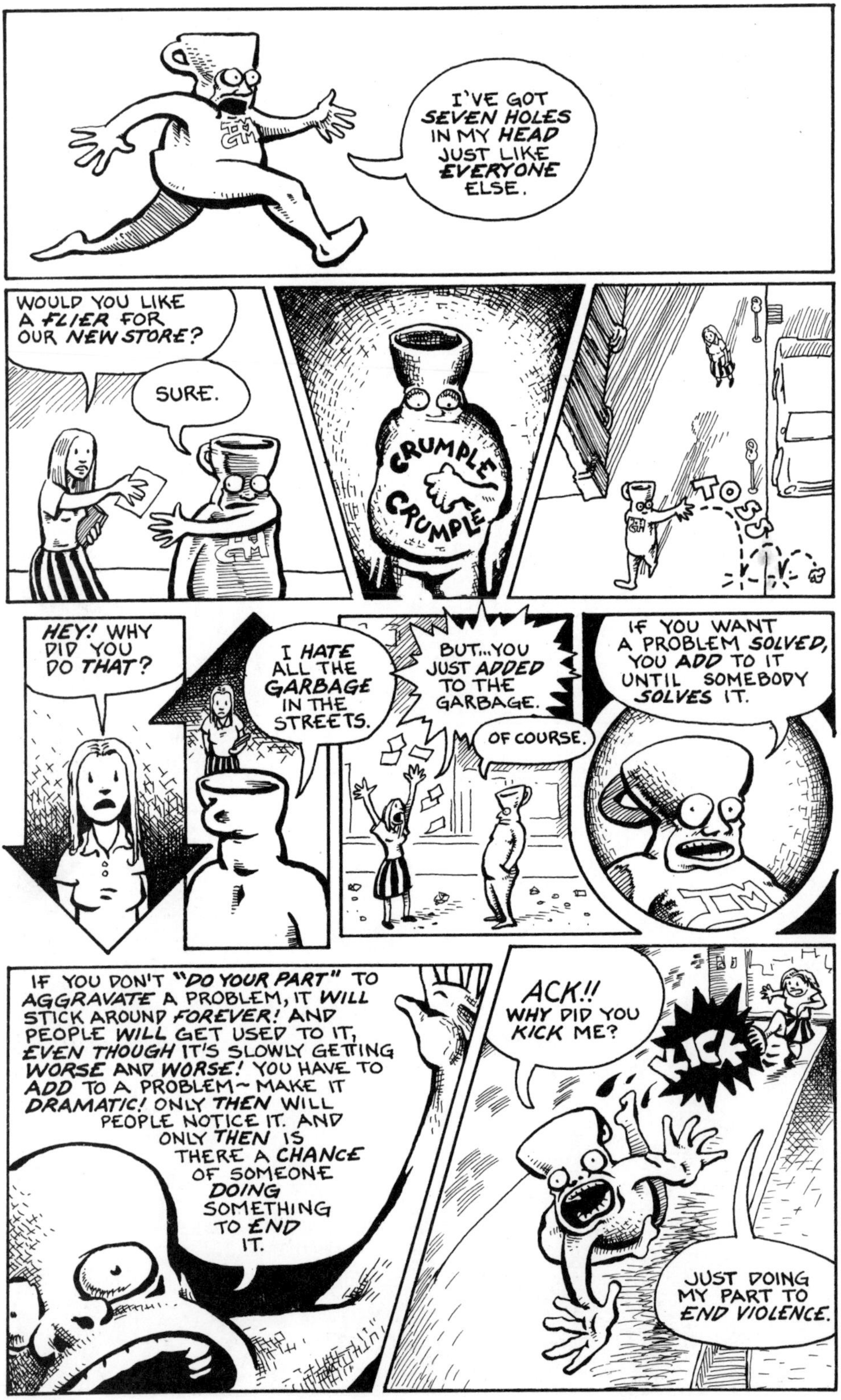
I'VE GOT SEVEN HOLES IN MY HEAD JUST LIKE EVERYONE ELSE.
WOULD YOU LIKE A FLIER FOR OUR NEW STORE?
SURE.
CRUMPLE CRUMPLE
TOSS
HEY! WHY DID YOU DO THAT?
I HATE ALL THE GARBAGE IN THE STREETS.
BUT...YOU JUST ADDED TO THE GARBAGE.
OF COURSE.
IF YOU WANT A PROBLEM SOLVED, YOU ADD TO IT UNTIL SOMEBODY SOLVES IT.
IF YOU DON'T "DO YOUR PART" TO AGGRAVATE A PROBLEM, IT WILL STICK AROUND FOREVER! AND PEOPLE WILL GET USED TO IT, EVEN THOUGH IT'S SLOWLY GETTING WORSE AND WORSE! YOU HAVE TO ADD TO A PROBLEM~ MAKE IT DRAMATIC! ONLY THEN WILL PEOPLE NOTICE IT. AND ONLY THEN IS THERE A CHANCE OF SOMEONE DOING SOMETHING TO END IT.
KICK
ACK!! WHY DID YOU KICK ME?
JUST DOING MY PART TO END VIOLENCE.

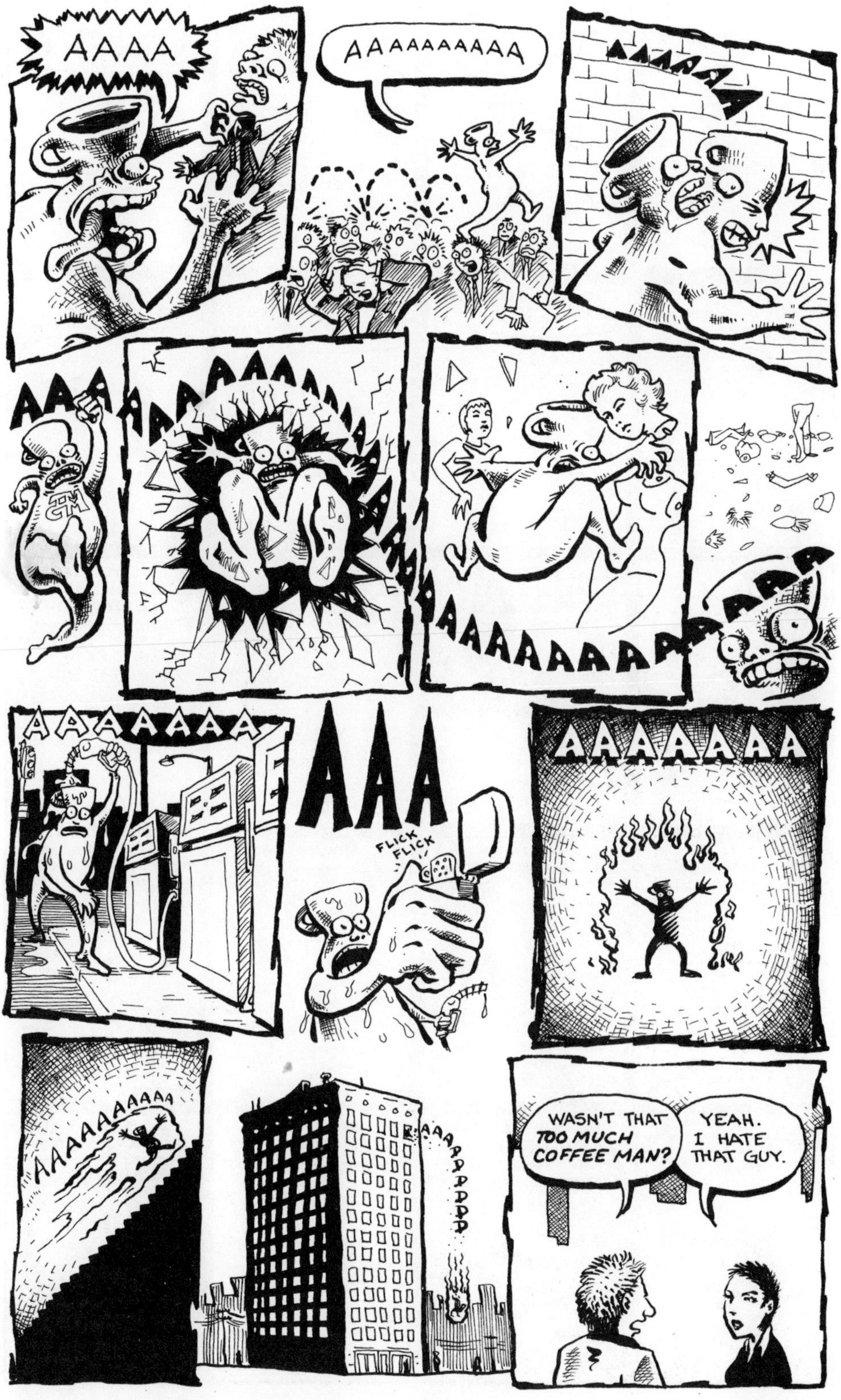
AAAA
AAAAAAAAAA
AAAAAA
AAA
FLICK FLICK
AAAAAAA
AAAAAAAAAA
WASN'T THAT *TOO MUCH COFFEE MAN?*
YEAH. I HATE THAT GUY.

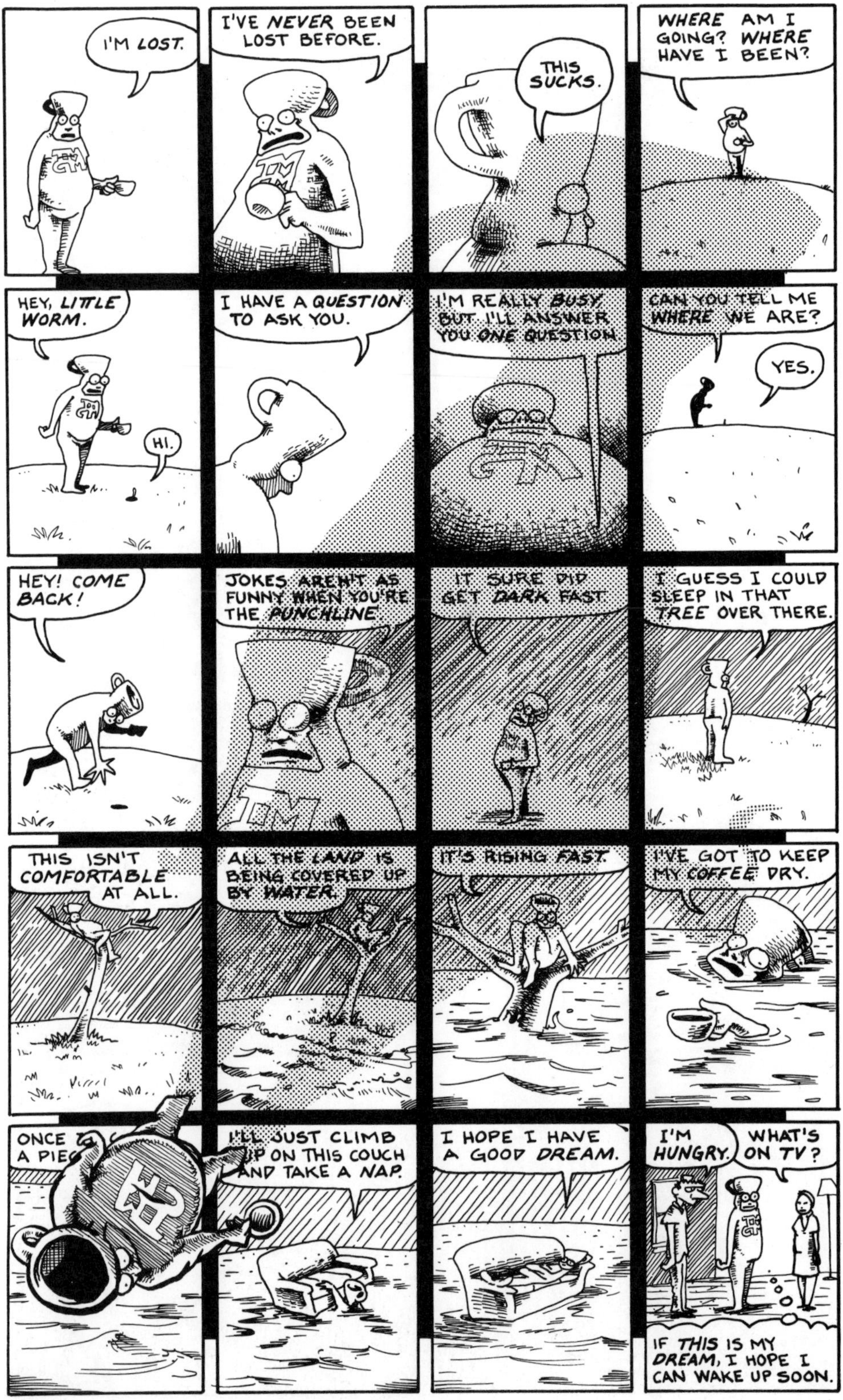
I'M LOST.
I'VE NEVER BEEN LOST BEFORE.
THIS SUCKS.
WHERE AM I GOING? WHERE HAVE I BEEN?
HEY, LITTLE WORM.
HI.
I HAVE A QUESTION TO ASK YOU.
I'M REALLY BUSY BUT I'LL ANSWER YOU ONE QUESTION.
CAN YOU TELL ME WHERE WE ARE?
YES.
HEY! COME BACK!
JOKES AREN'T AS FUNNY WHEN YOU'RE THE PUNCHLINE.
IT SURE DID GET DARK FAST.
I GUESS I COULD SLEEP IN THAT TREE OVER THERE.
THIS ISN'T COMFORTABLE AT ALL.
ALL THE LAND IS BEING COVERED UP BY WATER.
IT'S RISING FAST.
I'VE GOT TO KEEP MY COFFEE DRY.
ONCE
I'LL JUST CLIMB UP ON THIS COUCH AND TAKE A NAP.
I HOPE I HAVE A GOOD DREAM.
I'M HUNGRY.
WHAT'S ON TV?
IF THIS IS MY DREAM, I HOPE I CAN WAKE UP SOON.

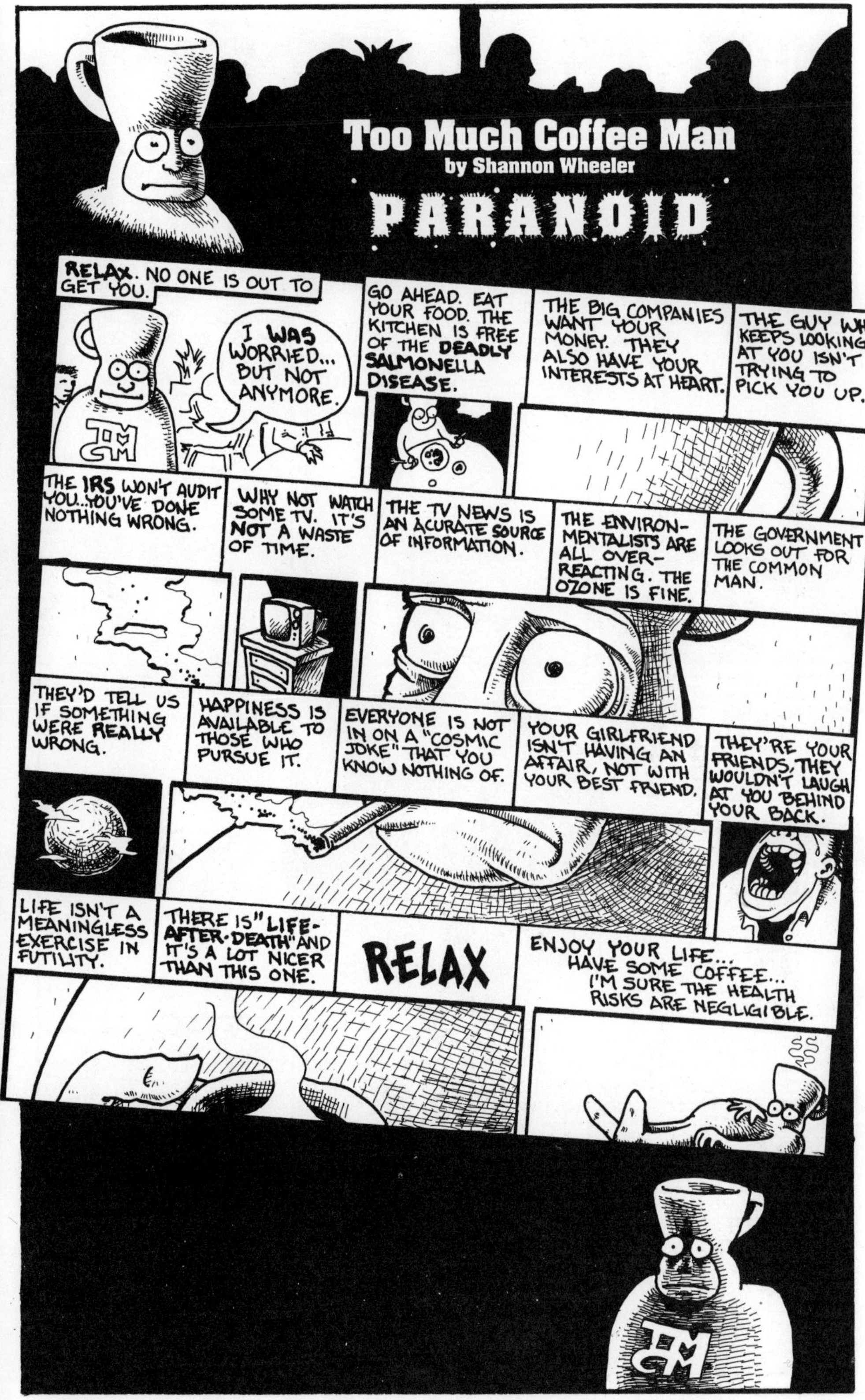
Too Much Coffee Man
by Shannon Wheeler
PARANOID
RELAX. NO ONE IS OUT TO GET YOU.
I WAS WORRIED... BUT NOT ANYMORE.
GO AHEAD. EAT YOUR FOOD. THE KITCHEN IS FREE OF THE DEADLY SALMONELLA DISEASE.
THE BIG COMPANIES WANT YOUR MONEY. THEY ALSO HAVE YOUR INTERESTS AT HEART.
THE GUY WHO KEEPS LOOKING AT YOU ISN'T TRYING TO PICK YOU UP.
THE IRS WON'T AUDIT YOU...YOU'VE DONE NOTHING WRONG.
WHY NOT WATCH SOME TV. IT'S NOT A WASTE OF TIME.
THE TV NEWS IS AN ACURATE SOURCE OF INFORMATION.
THE ENVIRONMENTALISTS ARE ALL OVER-REACTING. THE OZONE IS FINE.
THE GOVERNMENT LOOKS OUT FOR THE COMMON MAN.
THEY'D TELL US IF SOMETHING WERE REALLY WRONG.
HAPPINESS IS AVAILABLE TO THOSE WHO PURSUE IT.
EVERYONE IS NOT IN ON A "COSMIC JOKE" THAT YOU KNOW NOTHING OF.
YOUR GIRLFRIEND ISN'T HAVING AN AFFAIR, NOT WITH YOUR BEST FRIEND.
THEY'RE YOUR FRIENDS, THEY WOULDN'T LAUGH AT YOU BEHIND YOUR BACK.
LIFE ISN'T A MEANINGLESS EXERCISE IN FUTILITY.
THERE IS "LIFE-AFTER-DEATH" AND IT'S A LOT NICER THAN THIS ONE.
RELAX
ENJOY YOUR LIFE... HAVE SOME COFFEE... I'M SURE THE HEALTH RISKS ARE NEGLIGIBLE.
TMCM

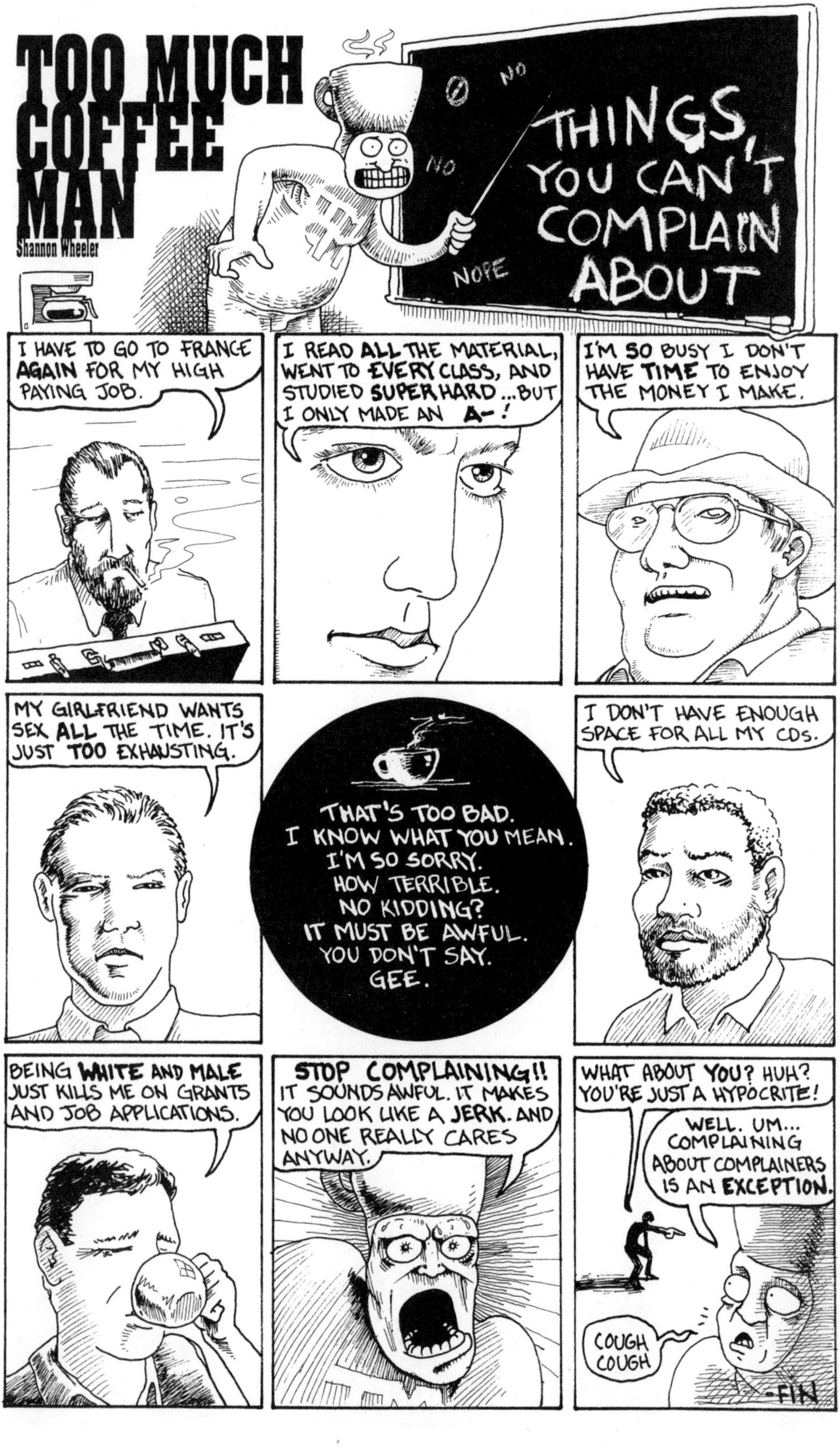

TOO MUCH COFFEE MAN
Shannon Wheeler
NO
NO
NOPE
THINGS YOU CAN'T COMPLAIN ABOUT
I HAVE TO GO TO FRANCE AGAIN FOR MY HIGH PAYING JOB.
I READ ALL THE MATERIAL, WENT TO EVERY CLASS, AND STUDIED SUPER HARD... BUT I ONLY MADE AN A-!
I'M SO BUSY I DON'T HAVE TIME TO ENJOY THE MONEY I MAKE.
MY GIRLFRIEND WANTS SEX ALL THE TIME. IT'S JUST TOO EXHAUSTING.
THAT'S TOO BAD. I KNOW WHAT YOU MEAN. I'M SO SORRY. HOW TERRIBLE. NO KIDDING? IT MUST BE AWFUL. YOU DON'T SAY. GEE.
I DON'T HAVE ENOUGH SPACE FOR ALL MY CDs.
BEING WHITE AND MALE JUST KILLS ME ON GRANTS AND JOB APPLICATIONS.
STOP COMPLAINING!! IT SOUNDS AWFUL. IT MAKES YOU LOOK LIKE A JERK. AND NO ONE REALLY CARES ANYWAY.
WHAT ABOUT YOU? HUH? YOU'RE JUST A HYPOCRITE!
WELL. UM... COMPLAINING ABOUT COMPLAINERS IS AN EXCEPTION.
COUGH COUGH
-FIN

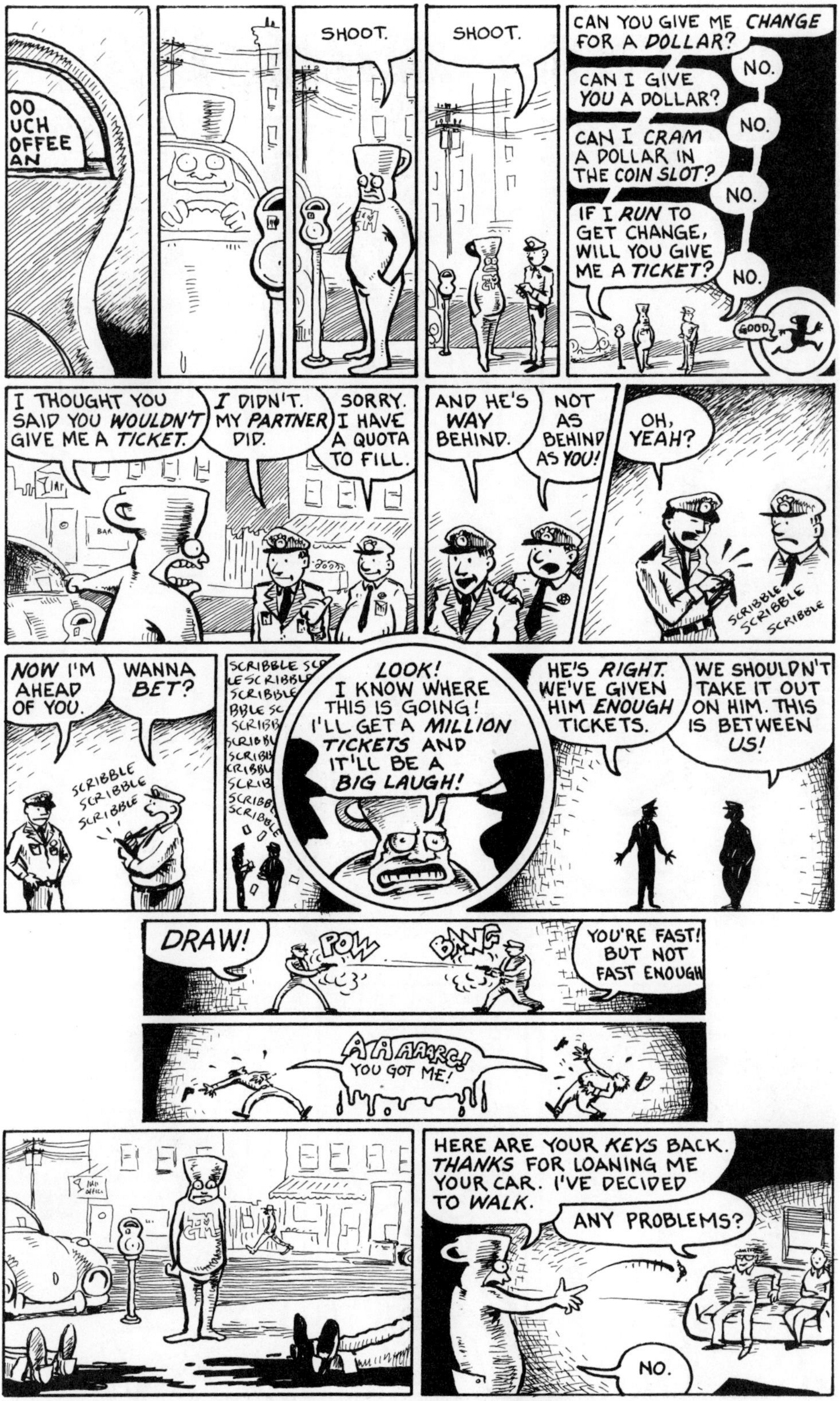
OO
UCH
OFFEE
AN
SHOOT.
SHOOT.
CAN YOU GIVE ME CHANGE FOR A DOLLAR?
NO.
CAN I GIVE YOU A DOLLAR?
NO.
CAN I CRAM A DOLLAR IN THE COIN SLOT?
NO.
IF I RUN TO GET CHANGE, WILL YOU GIVE ME A TICKET?
NO.
GOOD.
I THOUGHT YOU SAID YOU WOULDN'T GIVE ME A TICKET.
I DIDN'T. MY PARTNER DID.
SORRY. I HAVE A QUOTA TO FILL.
AND HE'S WAY BEHIND.
NOT AS BEHIND AS YOU!
OH, YEAH?
SCRIBBLE SCRIBBLE SCRIBBLE
NOW I'M AHEAD OF YOU.
WANNA BET?
SCRIBBLE SCRIBBLE SCRIBBLE
LOOK! I KNOW WHERE THIS IS GOING! I'LL GET A MILLION TICKETS AND IT'LL BE A BIG LAUGH!
HE'S RIGHT. WE'VE GIVEN HIM ENOUGH TICKETS.
WE SHOULDN'T TAKE IT OUT ON HIM. THIS IS BETWEEN US!
DRAW!
POW
BANG
YOU'RE FAST! BUT NOT FAST ENOUGH
AAAARG! YOU GOT ME!
HERE ARE YOUR KEYS BACK. THANKS FOR LOANING ME YOUR CAR. I'VE DECIDED TO WALK.
ANY PROBLEMS?
NO.

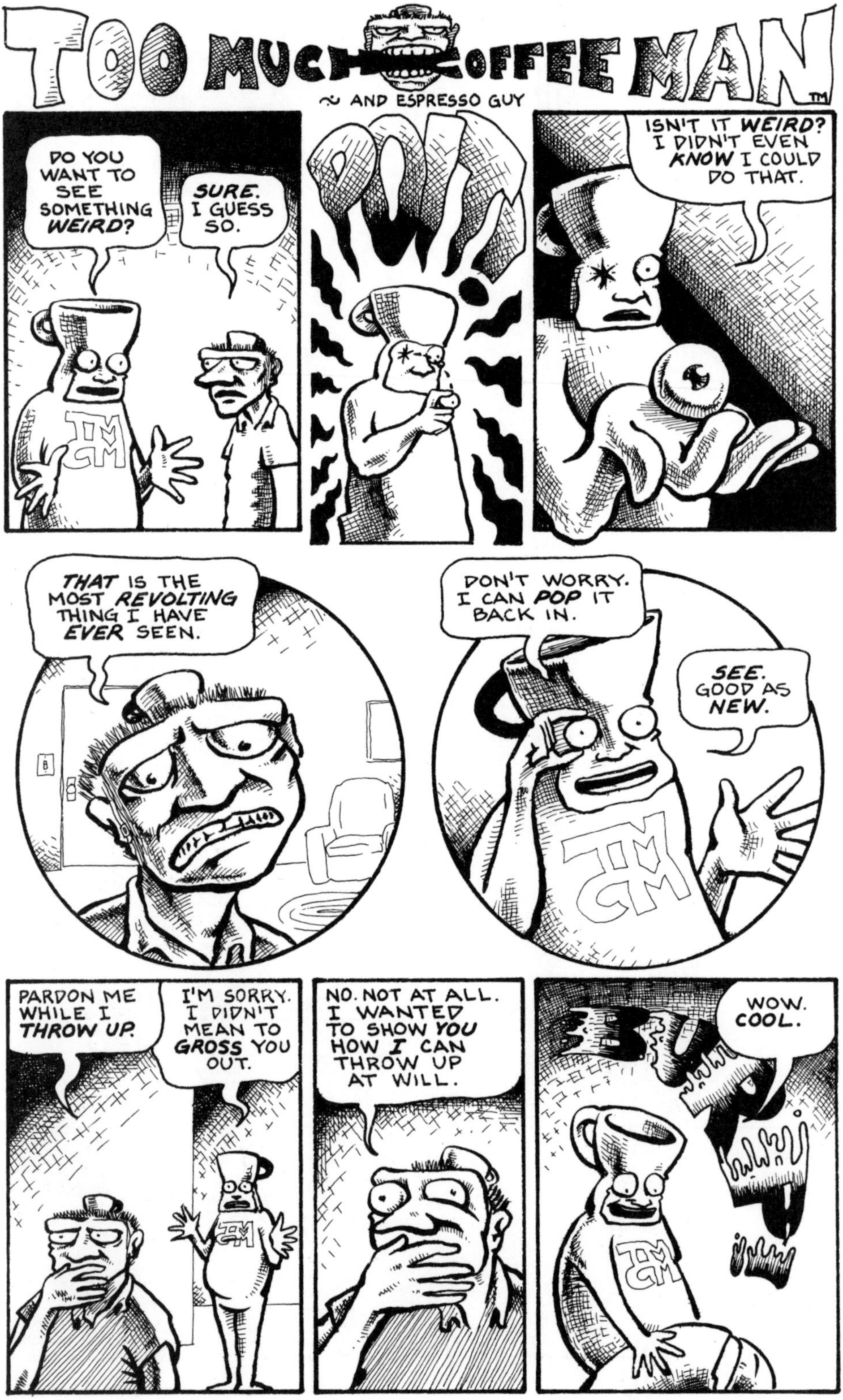
TOO MUCH COFFEE MAN
AND ESPRESSO GUY
TM
DO YOU WANT TO SEE SOMETHING WEIRD?
SURE. I GUESS SO.
ISN'T IT WEIRD? I DIDN'T EVEN KNOW I COULD DO THAT.
THAT IS THE MOST REVOLTING THING I HAVE EVER SEEN.
DON'T WORRY. I CAN POP IT BACK IN.
SEE. GOOD AS NEW.
PARDON ME WHILE I THROW UP.
I'M SORRY. I DIDN'T MEAN TO GROSS YOU OUT.
NO. NOT AT ALL. I WANTED TO SHOW YOU HOW I CAN THROW UP AT WILL.
WOW. COOL.

TOO MUCH COFFEE MAN

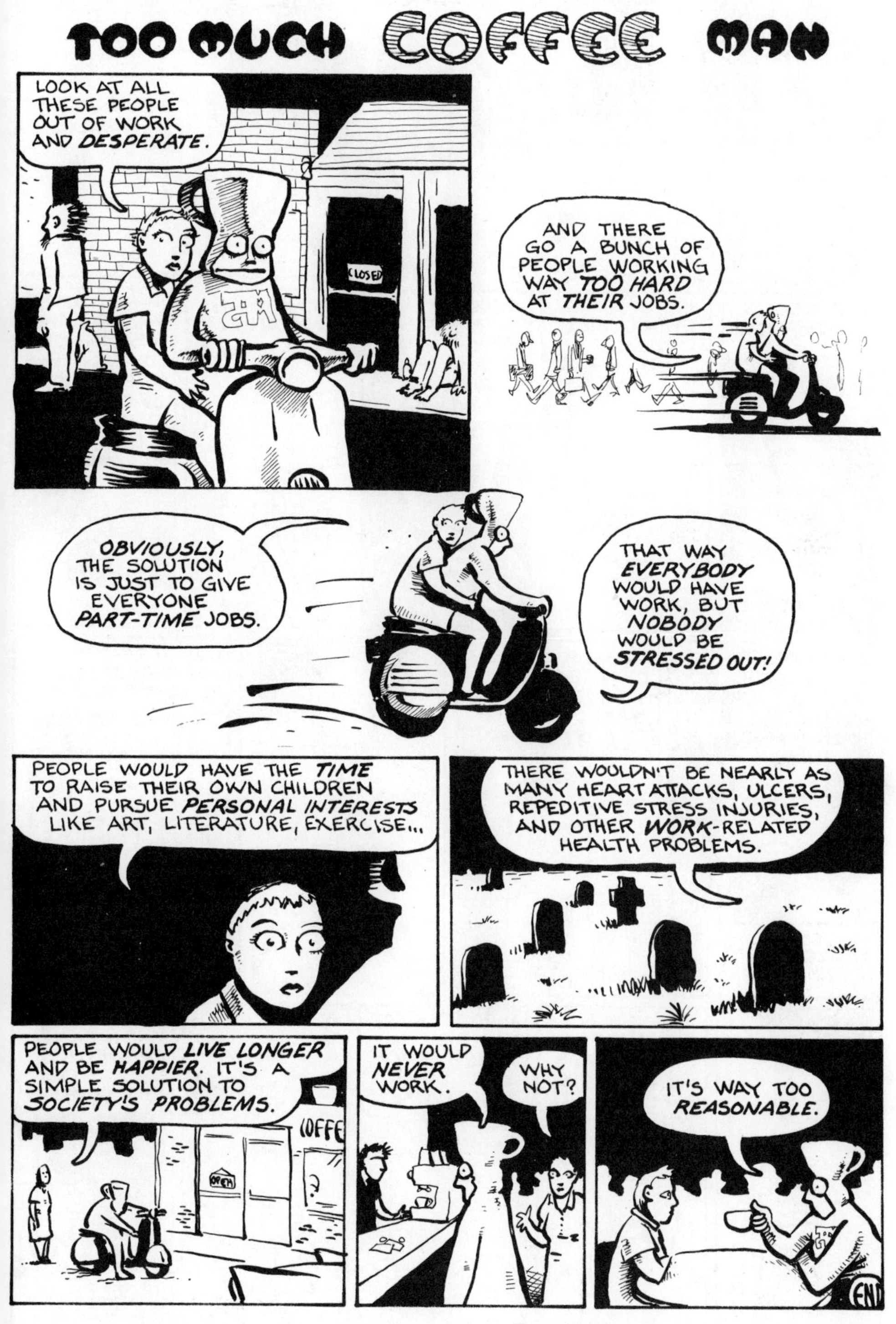

LOOK AT ALL THESE PEOPLE OUT OF WORK AND DESPERATE.
CLOSED
AND THERE GO A BUNCH OF PEOPLE WORKING WAY TOO HARD AT THEIR JOBS.
OBVIOUSLY, THE SOLUTION IS JUST TO GIVE EVERYONE PART-TIME JOBS.
THAT WAY EVERYBODY WOULD HAVE WORK, BUT NOBODY WOULD BE STRESSED OUT!
PEOPLE WOULD HAVE THE TIME TO RAISE THEIR OWN CHILDREN AND PURSUE PERSONAL INTERESTS LIKE ART, LITERATURE, EXERCISE...
THERE WOULDN'T BE NEARLY AS MANY HEART ATTACKS, ULCERS, REPEDITIVE STRESS INJURIES, AND OTHER WORK-RELATED HEALTH PROBLEMS.
PEOPLE WOULD LIVE LONGER AND BE HAPPIER. IT'S A SIMPLE SOLUTION TO SOCIETY'S PROBLEMS.
OPEN
IT WOULD NEVER WORK.
WHY NOT?
IT'S WAY TOO REASONABLE.
END

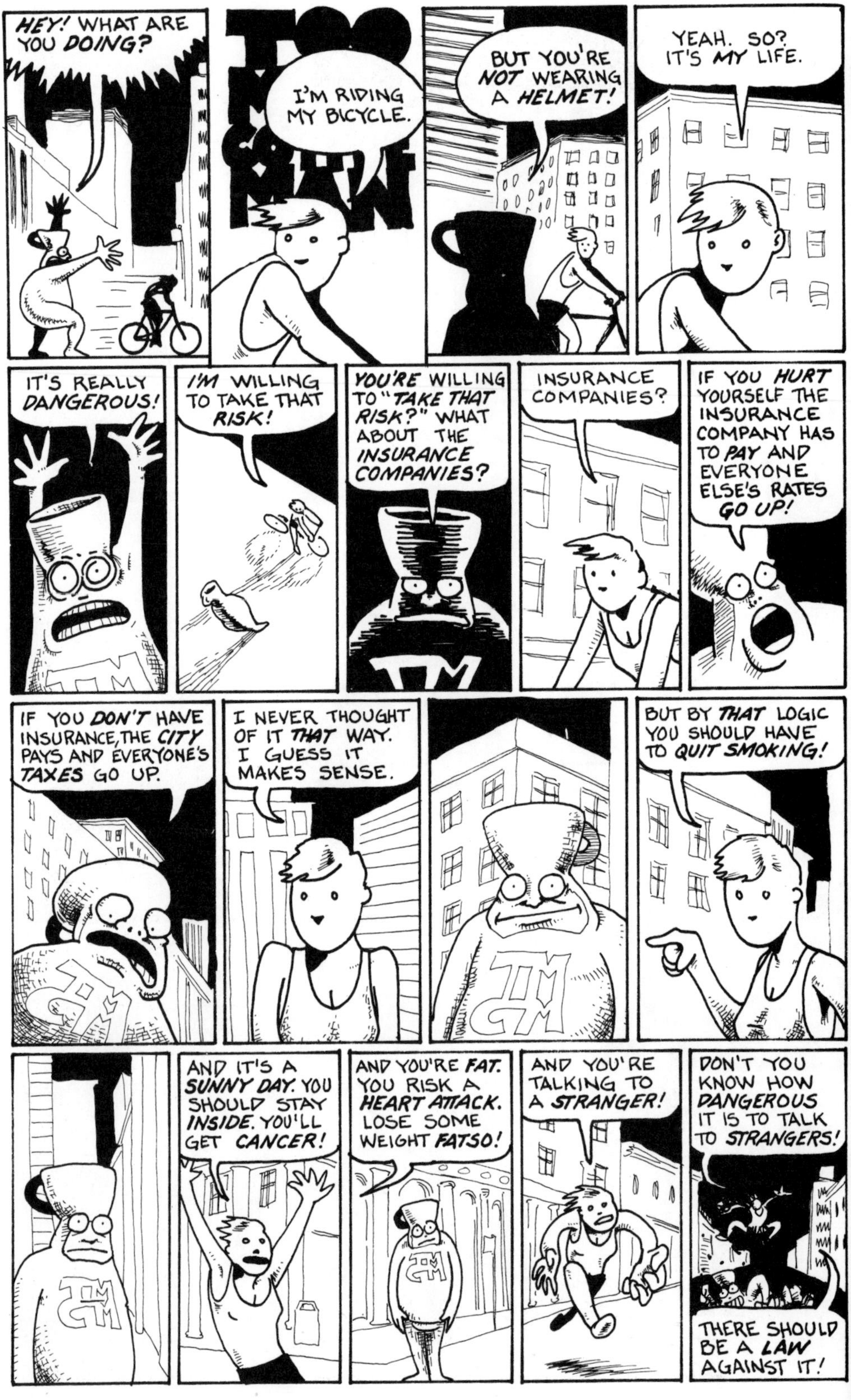
HEY! WHAT ARE YOU DOING?
I'M RIDING MY BICYCLE.
BUT YOU'RE NOT WEARING A HELMET!
YEAH. SO? IT'S MY LIFE.
IT'S REALLY DANGEROUS!
I'M WILLING TO TAKE THAT RISK!
YOU'RE WILLING TO "TAKE THAT RISK?" WHAT ABOUT THE INSURANCE COMPANIES?
INSURANCE COMPANIES?
IF YOU HURT YOURSELF THE INSURANCE COMPANY HAS TO PAY AND EVERYONE ELSE'S RATES GO UP!
IF YOU DON'T HAVE INSURANCE, THE CITY PAYS AND EVERYONE'S TAXES GO UP.
I NEVER THOUGHT OF IT THAT WAY. I GUESS IT MAKES SENSE.
BUT BY THAT LOGIC YOU SHOULD HAVE TO QUIT SMOKING!
AND IT'S A SUNNY DAY. YOU SHOULD STAY INSIDE. YOU'LL GET CANCER!
AND YOU'RE FAT. YOU RISK A HEART ATTACK. LOSE SOME WEIGHT FATSO!
AND YOU'RE TALKING TO A STRANGER!
DON'T YOU KNOW HOW DANGEROUS IT IS TO TALK TO STRANGERS!
THERE SHOULD BE A LAW AGAINST IT!

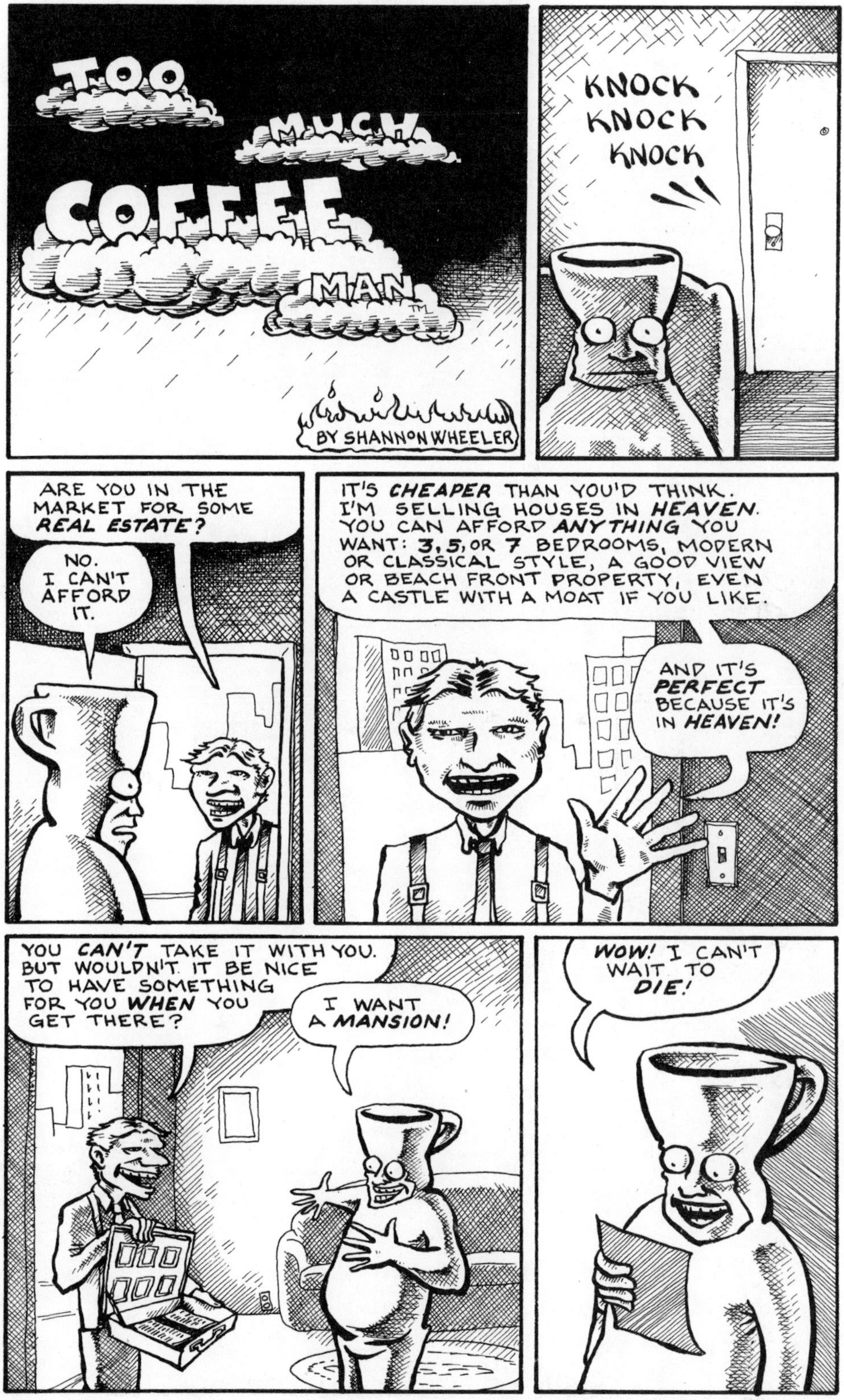
TOO MUCH COFFEE MAN™
BY SHANNON WHEELER
KNOCK KNOCK KNOCK
ARE YOU IN THE MARKET FOR SOME REAL ESTATE?
NO. I CAN'T AFFORD IT.
IT'S CHEAPER THAN YOU'D THINK. I'M SELLING HOUSES IN HEAVEN. YOU CAN AFFORD ANYTHING YOU WANT: 3, 5, OR 7 BEDROOMS, MODERN OR CLASSICAL STYLE, A GOOD VIEW OR BEACH FRONT PROPERTY, EVEN A CASTLE WITH A MOAT IF YOU LIKE.
AND IT'S PERFECT BECAUSE IT'S IN HEAVEN!
YOU CAN'T TAKE IT WITH YOU. BUT WOULDN'T IT BE NICE TO HAVE SOMETHING FOR YOU WHEN YOU GET THERE?
I WANT A MANSION!
WOW! I CAN'T WAIT TO DIE!

AFTERWORD

Earlier today I was waiting for the bus while I talked on my cell phone to my agent. The bus came, and I got on. I paid my dollar just as I was asking about the merchandising rights and percentages. Only after I hung up and sat down in the rear with the students, bums, and businessmen, did I think about the absurdity of it all. It's almost a scene for one of my comics.

Too Much Coffee Man started as a joke. I was trying to think up an iconographic character that would allow me some recognition with an audience. It was a bad visual pun. The handle on the mug on his head is the metaphorical handle for people to "grab" on to for quick and easy recognition.

My biggest burden now with **Too Much Coffee Man** is having people tell me that they love my comic because they love coffee. I wish they'd tell me that they love my comic because it's clever, or well drawn, or insightful. At least they're enjoying it, even if it is for reasons that I don't feel flatter me. That type of complaint falls in the category of "things you can't complain about." And, at least, I was able to do a cartoon about that.

In all fairness to myself, I put a lot of work into creating each and every cartoon. I agonize, sometimes all night, over a single page. I worry that it's too complicated and my thoughts are not communicated. Other times I think I've sacrificed too much for brevity's sake and the cartoon has lost its meaning.

I love drawing cartoons. It's all real. All the emotions come from my heart. I do my best to share my honest feelings, insecurities, anxieties, and observations about life. And I really can catch flies.

— Shannon Wheeler

Thanks to everyone who's been around to help me through these last 6 years of cartooning. Without them I'd have been by myself.
— Shannon Wheeler

collection editor
JAMIE S. RICH

consulting **collection editor**
LYNN ADAIR

assistant editor
BEN ABERNATHY

collection designer
COREY STEPHENS

"Too Much Coffee Man Meets His Coffee Maker" originally edited by Bob Schreck and Scott Allie.

Special thanks to Rich Powers for his tireless effort on getting this hodge-podge together for final film.

NEIL HANKERSON • executive vice president
DAVID SCROGGY • product development
ANDY KARABATSOS • vice president & controller
MARK ANDERSON • general counsel
RANDY STRADLEY • director of editorial
CINDY MARKS • director of production & design
MARK COX • art director
SEAN TIERNEY • computer graphics director
MICHAEL MARTENS • director of sales & marketing
TOD BORLESKE • director of licensing
DALE LAFOUNTAIN • director of m.i.s.
KIM HAINES • director of human resources

This book collects stories from issues one through three of **JAB** (published by Adhesive Comics), the Dark Horse comic-book **TOO MUCH COFFEE MAN SPECIAL**™, and one page comics from various sources.

Published by
Dark Horse Comics, Inc.
10956 SE Main Street
Milwaukie, OR 97222

First edition: May 1998
ISBN: 1-56971-289-1

Limited hardcover edition
ISBN: 1-56971-283-2

1 3 5 7 9 10 8 6 4 2
Printed in Canada